THE BEDFORD SERIES IN HISTORY AND CULTURE

William Lloyd Garrison and the Fight against Slavery

Selections from *The Liberator*

Related Titles in
THE BEDFORD SERIES IN HISTORY AND CULTURE
Advisory Editors: Natalie Zemon Davis, Princeton University
Ernest R. May, Harvard University

Narrative of the Life of Frederick Douglass, An American Slave, Written by Himself
Edited with an introduction by David W. Blight, *Amherst College*

Dred Scott, Slavery, and the Crisis of the Union (forthcoming)
Edited with an introduction by Paul Finkelman, *Virginia Tech*

The Confessions of Nat Turner
Edited with an introduction by Kenneth S. Greenberg, *Suffolk University*

Women's Rights and the Antislavery Movement, 1830–1865 (forthcoming)
Edited with an introduction by Kathryn Kish Sklar, *Binghamton University*

THE BEDFORD SERIES IN HISTORY AND CULTURE

William Lloyd Garrison and the Fight against Slavery

Selections from *The Liberator*

Edited with an introduction by

William E. Cain

Wellesley College

BEDFORD BOOKS   Boston ✿ New York

For Bedford Books

President and Publisher: Charles H. Christensen
Associate Publisher/General Manager: Joan E. Feinberg
History Editor: Niels Aaboe
Developmental Editor: Louise Townsend
Editorial Assistant: Richard Keaveny
Managing Editor: Elizabeth M. Schaaf
Production Editor: Heidi Hood
Copyeditor: Barbara Flanagan
Indexer: Steve Csipke
Text Design: Claire Seng-Niemoeller
Cover Design: Richard Emery Design, Inc.
Cover Art: Detail from an engraving in *William Lloyd Garrison: 1805–1879* by Francis Jackson Garrison and Wendell Phillips Garrison. Houghton, Mifflin and Company, 1894.

Library of Congress Catalog Card Number: 94-65204

For information, write: Bedford Books, 75 Arlington Street, Boston, MA 02116
(617-426-7440)

ISBN: 0-312-10386-7 (paperback)
ISBN: 0-312-12245-4 (hardcover)

Acknowledgments

Pages 32, 79, 184: Reprinted by courtesy of the Trustees of the Boston Public Library.
Page 46: Collection of the New-York Historical Society.
Page 128: Courtesy of The Schlesinger Library, Radcliffe College.
Page 130: Courtesy of Chicago Historical Society, negative ICHi–22029.
Pages 155, 185: Courtesy of the Boston Athenaeum.

Foreword

The Bedford Series in History and Culture is designed so that readers can study the past as historians do.

The historian's first task is finding the evidence. Documents, letters, memoirs, interviews, pictures, movies, novels, or poems can provide facts and clues. Then the historian questions and compares the sources. There is more to do than in a courtroom, for hearsay evidence is welcome, and the historian is usually looking for answers beyond act and motive. Different views of an event may be as important as a single verdict. How a story is told may yield as much information as what it says.

Along the way the historian seeks help from other historians and perhaps from specialists in other disciplines. Finally, it is time to write, to decide on an interpretation and how to arrange the evidence for readers.

Each book in this series contains an important historical document or group of documents, each document a witness from the past and open to interpretation in different ways. The documents are combined with some element of historical narrative—an introduction or a biographical essay, for example—that provides students with an analysis of the primary source material and important background information about the world in which it was produced.

Each book in the series focuses on a specific topic within a specific historical period. Each provides a basis for lively thought and discussion about several aspects of the topic and the historian's role. Each is short enough (and inexpensive enough) to be a reasonable one-week assignment in a college course. Whether as classroom or personal reading, each book in the series provides firsthand experience of the challenge—and fun—of discovering, recreating, and interpreting the past.

Natalie Zemon Davis
Ernest R. May

"My happiness is augmented with yours: in your sufferings I participate."

WILLIAM LLOYD GARRISON
speaking to an African American
audience (June 1831)

Preface

William Lloyd Garrison (1805–1879) was one of the earliest and most important abolitionists, and he was dedicated both to winning freedom and to securing civil rights for African Americans. As he explained in the March 7, 1835, issue of his weekly paper *The Liberator,* he believed in and hoped for "the IMMEDIATE EMANCIPATION of two millions and a half of American SLAVES" *and* "the education and equalization of the colored with the white population of this country."

But while Garrison's roles — abolitionist, pacifist, advocate of women's rights, mentor to the African American orator and antislavery leader Frederick Douglass — have been acknowledged, he is underread and unevenly understood. Garrison has been identified by one recent scholar as "ultimately responsible for the emancipation of the slaves" and designated the "Founding Father of the American civil rights movement."[1] Yet his actual work as a speaker and writer, the sheer thrust and sound of his voice, is not widely known.

This book gathers selections from Garrison's central achievement, the newspaper that he named *The Liberator* and edited from January 1831 to December 1865. The only piece not from it is his July 4, 1829, address in Boston. He gave many speeches and reproduced a number of them in *The Liberator,* but this is the most significant. It laid out the abolitionist themes that Garrison would reiterate during the next four decades.

It is only when one reviews the entire set of *The Liberator* that one can appreciate the range and amount of Garrison's contributions to it — editorials, commentaries, letters, reprints of lectures and addresses he presented at antislavery and reform meetings and conventions. *The Liber-*

---

[1] This comment is made by Louis Ruchames in *The Letters of William Lloyd Garrison,* ed. Walter M. Merrill and Louis Ruchames, 6 vols. (Cambridge: Harvard University Press, 1971–81), 2:vii. Walter M. Merrill, in *Against Wind and Tide: A Biography of William Lloyd Garrison* (Cambridge: Harvard University Press, 1963), states that Garrison "deserves primary credit for bringing the problem of slavery to the attention of the nation" (xvi).

ator also includes dozens of lengthy essays and speeches by other white abolitionists and statesmen and many more by women and blacks active in the antislavery cause. In addition, week after week, Garrison printed letters and excerpts from congressional debates, news reports, and editorials and articles from papers and journals. He also regularly reprinted attacks on himself and denunciations of antislavery and abolition in order to make vivid to readers the hostility that the campaign for black freedom and rights had aroused.

I have concentrated here on Garrison's abolitionist writings, though I have supplied examples of his writings on peace, women's rights, and the nature of reform. In a number of instances I have given excerpts. Garrison was a journalist and an agitator who declared a position, disdained consensus, attacked opponents. He was at his sharpest in short pieces and in the more inspired parts of longer ones.

In the Introduction I survey the main events of Garrison's career, the issues he raised and the controversies he kindled, and the emergence and development of abolition and antislavery, which were related but different in their emphases. (These terms are often used interchangeably, but strictly speaking *abolition* meant a commitment to ending slavery everywhere, while *antislavery* meant no further *expansion* of slavery into new states and territories.) I devote attention, too, to the *facts* of slavery itself, facts that are less well known to general readers and to students in history, literature, and American Studies courses than they should be. These are important to establish and remember so that the scope, power, and influence of the system that the abolitionists indicted, and that at last ended as a result of the Civil War, can be clearly seen.

In my Introduction I have also highlighted Garrison's commentary on and fiery critique of politics, both because it was a key element of policy for him and because it dramatizes the questions of how "change" occurs and by what means it should be fought for. Garrison believed that the American political system was corrupt and that working within it was foolhardy. Politics, for him, was not the path to true reform, but instead a sure route to moral compromise, to the bending and breaking of principles. His critics within the movement, however, replied that only *through* the political system could the goals of freedom and rights for black persons be achieved. This is, I think, the sound and sensible position, yet it was not really the one that triumphed in the 1850s and 1860s. The political arena became the place where the contest between slavery and antislavery was focused, not where it was resolved. Its resolution required a war, and it was a war that Garrison supported.

ACKNOWLEDGMENTS

I would like to emphasize first how much this volume has benefited from the excellent biographical work on Garrison that Walter M. Merrill, Russel B. Nye, Louis Ruchames, James Brewer Stewart, and John L. Thomas have done. Like all Garrison scholars, I have also made ample use of Wendell Phillips Garrison and Francis Jackson Garrison's *William Lloyd Garrison, 1805–1879: The Story of His Life Told by His Children,* published in four volumes between 1885 and 1889.

For helpful readings of the manuscript, I am indebted to Robert H. Abzug, David Blight, Jacqueline Jones, John McKivigan, Louis Masur, Donald Pease, and Eric Sundquist. I am grateful for their expert advice and good suggestions.

I also want to express my thanks to the superb staff at Bedford Books for their support of this project at its inception and their encouragement and assistance at every stage of the process. In particular I want to mention Chuck Christensen and Joan Feinberg, publishers of Bedford Books; co-series editor Ernest May; acquisitions editor Sabra Scribner; editorial assistant Richard Keaveny; development editor Louise Townsend; managing editor Elizabeth Schaaf; production associate Heidi Hood; and copyeditor Barbara Flanagan. I have worked especially closely Louise and have benefited time and again from her excellent ideas; Barbara's meticulous copyediting greatly improved the style and organization of the book as well.

The staff of Clapp Library at Wellesley College, notably Karen Jensen and Joan Stockard, aided me countless times in my research. For help with two troublesome glosses, I would like to thank my colleagues Edward Hobbs and Phil Finkelpearl. My student assistants, Amy Burns and Maureen Paulsen, also provided crucial help in tracking down hard-to-find sources. Friends and colleagues in English and in other departments at Wellesley have spurred me on by their exemplary commitment to their scholarly work.

Finally, and most important of all, I want to thank my wife, Barbara, and my daughters, Julia and Isabel. I could not have written this book without them.

William E. Cain

Contents

1831–1840: The First Decade of *The Liberator:* Arguments for Abolition

1861–1865: The Final Phase of *The Liberator:* Garrison and Lincoln

PART ONE

Introduction:
William Lloyd Garrison
and the Fight
against Slavery

We shall surely be vindicated at the court of conscience and at the tribunal of God, and the verdict of posterity will be, —The Abolitionists were in the right, and the nation was in the wrong. —William Lloyd Garrison,
No Fetters in the Bay State
(Boston, 1859)

"I COULD BRING THEM TO REASON":
GARRISON IN 1835 AND 1863

The Boston mob chased William Lloyd Garrison, the twenty-nine-year-old editor of the abolitionist newspaper *The Liberator,* from the Anti-Slavery Society office on Washington Street to Wilson's Lane, where he hid behind planks of wood in a corner of a second-floor storage loft in a carpenter's shop. It was midafternoon on Wednesday, October 21, 1835. A dozen men found him and threatened to throw him from the window. But someone said, "Don't let's kill him outright." A rope was then coiled around his waist and he was made to crawl out the window, down a ladder to the crowd, several thousand in number, that surged below. Garrison was roughed up, his clothes were torn, and he was hauled by the rope along Wilson's Lane toward State Street.

Just a month earlier, on the night of September 10, a gallows nearly nine feet high had been erected in front of Garrison's Brighton Street house. Two nooses hung from it, one for Garrison and another for his good friend, the British abolitionist George Thompson. It seemed certain on this October afternoon that Garrison would be lynched, though some mentioned later that the plan had been first to dye his hands and face in indelible black ink and then to tar and feather him. Several men intervened, however, seizing Garrison and saying, "Don't hurt him! He is an American!" (that is, not the Englishman Thompson). They hurried him to City Hall, to Mayor Theodore Lyman's office.

Lyman and the police fended off the mob, and Garrison—charged with "disturbing the peace"—was rushed by horse cab for his own safety to the county jail on Leverett Street. There he spent the night and was released the next morning. Throughout the ordeal Garrison was at peace, for it was, he reflected, "indeed a blessed privilege thus to suffer for Christ." One observer, the wealthy, Harvard-educated Wendell Phillips, decided as he surveyed the spectacle from his law office that such mobs endangered social order and civil liberty, and soon he enlisted in the abolitionist cause.[1] Another, a political foe of Garrison's named Ebenezer Bailey, when queried how Garrison had handled himself, answered: "No man could have done better. He showed perfect courage and self-possession. He was only very absurd in one thing. He kept saying, 'Oh, if they would only hear me five minutes, I am sure I could bring them to reason.' Now, you know, that that was ridiculous, for they were all ready to tear him in pieces."[2]

[1] George Lowell Austin, *The Life and Times of Wendell Phillips* (Boston: Lee and Shepard, 1888), 64–67; and James Brewer Stewart, *Wendell Phillips: Liberty's Hero* (Baton Rouge: Louisiana State University Press, 1986), 42–43.
[2] Wendell Phillips and Francis Jackson Garrison, *William Lloyd Garrison, 1805–1879: The Story of His Life Told by His Children*, 4 vols. (Boston: Houghton Mifflin, 1885–1889), 2:26, cited in the text and notes as *Life*. This is an essential source. Modern biographies of Garrison include Walter M. Merrill, *Against Wind and Tide: A Biography of William Lloyd Garrison* (Cambridge: Harvard University Press, 1963); John L. Thomas, *The Liberator: William Lloyd Garrison, a Biography* (Boston: Little, Brown, 1963); and James Brewer Stewart, *William Lloyd Garrison and the Challenge of Emancipation* (Arlington Heights, Ill.: Harlan Davidson, 1992). See also Aileen S. Kraditor, *Means and Ends in American Abolitionism: Garrison and His Critics on Strategy and Tactics, 1834–1850* (New York: Pantheon, 1969); Benjamin Quarles, *Black Abolitionists* (New York: Oxford University Press, 1969); Merton L. Dillon, *The Abolitionists: The Growth of a Dissenting Minority* (De Kalb: Northern Illinois University Press, 1974); James Brewer Stewart, *Holy Warriors: The Abolitionists and American Slavery* (New York: Hill and Wang, 1976); Ronald G. Walters, *The Antislavery Appeal: American Abolitionism after 1830* (Baltimore: Johns Hopkins University Press, 1976); and Herbert Aptheker, *Abolitionism: A Revolutionary Movement* (Boston:

This episode certainly shows Garrison's bravery. Perhaps it testifies as well to his naive confidence in the power of "reason" and to his courting of martyrdom, to his relishing of occasions for affliction that would confirm his rectitude. As he had noted in a letter reprinted in *The Liberator* (Aug. 27, 1831),[3] "the path which I am destined to tread, is full of briers and thorns." Garrison yearned for the challenge of unsympathetic, indifferent, or enraged audiences. He blended humble faith in God with arrogant self-confidence: he knew that he walked righteously in the truth and was convinced that he could efface evil from hard-hearted sinners. If they persisted in turning away from him, he would feel nonetheless that he had performed his Christian duty: he had borne witness to God and they had damned themselves.

Yet by the late 1850s and early 1860s, Garrison could see indications of the changes in American attitudes and institutions that his and other abolitionists' acts and arguments had helped to create. On May 28, 1863, nearly three decades after the mob had assaulted him, he watched one of the state's regiments of black troops, the 54th Massachusetts, parade in review in the center of Boston, led by Colonel Robert Gould Shaw, the son of Garrison's friends Mr. and Mrs. Francis G. Shaw and the childhood playmate of Garrison's sons. As the black soldiers marched down State Street singing the popular song "John Brown's Body," Garrison noticed with a start that he was in the same place on the corner of Wilson's Lane where he had been dragged by a rope in 1835. He realized, too, that he was near the site of the March 5, 1770, Boston Massacre, in which a black man named Crispus Attucks had been one of those shot by British troops. It had long been Garrison's demand that America fulfill for *all* of its people the promises of the Declaration of Independence. This was now occurring, Garrison believed, as hundreds of armed black men in the Union uniform strode through the streets of Boston on their way to fight the Confederate armies.

BEGINNING *THE LIBERATOR*

Garrison's career is filled with coincidences and conjunctions of this kind, and for him it amounted ultimately to a great success story, to vindication and triumph. Garrison was born in December 1805 in Newburyport,

---

Twayne, 1989). For a good collection of reprinted pieces from books and scholarly journals, see *Antislavery,* vol. 14 of *Articles on American Slavery,* ed. Paul Finkelman (New York: Garland, 1989).

[3] Issues of *The Liberator* are cited in this introduction by date.

Massachusetts, and he grew up poor. His father, Abijah, was a sailing master whose fortunes collapsed with the Embargo Act passed by Congress in 1807. President Thomas Jefferson had requested this embargo, prohibiting all exports, to apply pressure to France and Great Britain, which had been interfering with American shipping in their military conflicts with one another. But the result was very damaging to American commerce: New England's merchants suffered huge losses, docks were closed, and port areas became deserted. Abijah abandoned his wife and children in 1808, and the family's life became a harsh, painful one. The young Garrison sold homemade molasses candy on street corners, where he was teased and taunted by other children. He also made money for the family by delivering wood and was sent by his mother with a tin pan to collect scraps of food and leftovers from rich households in town. These experiences left scars—and also compassion for outcasts.

Separated from his family for long periods, Garrison spent troubled, unhappy years in various apprenticeships until in 1818 he found work in the office of the Newburyport *Herald,* the first in a series of newspaper jobs he held as writer and editor in Newburyport, Boston, and Bennington, Vermont. These early jobs equipped Garrison with the training— especially in how to wage partisan struggles and respond quickly and resolutely to the issues of the moment—that he would capitalize on when he became editor of *The Liberator.*

Garrison's vocation as an abolitionist began in earnest in April 1829 when the Quaker Benjamin Lundy, whom Garrison had met in Boston in March 1828, invited him to become coeditor of *The Genius of Universal Emancipation,* an antislavery paper that Lundy had started in 1821 and that was based in Baltimore. While assisting Lundy in Baltimore, Garrison boarded with free blacks and saw the horrors of slavery and the slave trade at firsthand. After serving a forty-nine-day jail sentence from April to June 1830 for libeling a slave trader, a Newburyport merchant named Francis Todd, Garrison broke with Lundy, returned to Boston, lectured in favor of immediate abolition, and on January 1, 1831, published the inaugural issue of *The Liberator,* the weekly that he would edit for thirty-five years. (See Document 2.)

Samuel Sewall, a Boston lawyer and friend, had told Garrison that the new paper's name was inflammatory and recommended that it be called *The Safety Lamp* instead. But the provocative nature of *The Liberator* as a title captivated Garrison and he stuck with it. The first issue was four pages long, four columns per page, fourteen by nine and a quarter inches. (Beginning with the March 4, 1837, issue, the paper was expanded to sixteen by twenty-three inches.) At the top of the first page in boldface capitals was printed THE LIBERATOR. In black letter type, the masthead read, in a phrase adapted from Thomas Paine, "Our Country Is the World—Our Countrymen Are Mankind." Subscriptions were two dollars per year.

Garrison was listed as editor, Garrison and Isaac Knapp (a childhood friend, printer, and newspaper publisher in Newburyport) as publishers, Stephen Foster as printer. Soon they were aided by an African American apprentice, Thomas Paul, whose hiring in February was cited by Garrison's foes as evidence of his foolish faith in the capacities of black persons. Garrison's and his co-workers' small editorial office (eighteen feet square) in Merchants Hall contained a desk, two chairs, and a table. Eventually the office included a mattress in a corner where Garrison slept. They had a press, purchased cheaply, and two composing stands with secondhand type. For the first three issues, Garrison had to borrow type, use it in the middle of the night, and then return it. The two editors worked sixteen hours per day, except on Sunday, and lived on bread, milk, and fruit.

Financial help came from Sewall, from Ellis Gray Loring, another Boston lawyer, and from Arthur Tappan, a New York merchant and reform-minded evangelical Christian. But the bulk of support—three-quarters of the subscription list—derived from the free black population in the North. By the close of the first year, there were only fifty white subscribers; after two years the number was still less than four hundred. Nearly half of the mailings were to New York, Philadelphia, and Boston, where significant numbers of blacks resided. From the start, the paper was in debt ($2,000 by the third year). It never met expenses, and its maximum number of subscribers never exceeded the 2,500–3,000 range. Garrison's annual salary as editor was $700. There were 1,820 issues of the paper in its thirty-five years of weekly publication: Garrison did not miss a single week.

In August 1831 the slave Nat Turner and a small band of followers rebelled against their white masters in Southampton County, Virginia. Before the militia stopped them, they had rallied dozens of slaves to their side and killed sixty whites. Turner was captured on October 30 and executed on November 11. Immediately, in both the North and the South, Garrison was accused of instigating Turner's revolt through his militant rhetoric in *The Liberator.* There is no evidence that Turner ever read *The Liberator* or even that any copies could be found in Southampton County. But the connection nonetheless was made between the start-up of *The Liberator* in January 1831 and the bloody slave uprising that took place eight months later. (See Document 8.)

State and federal officials declared that antislavery agitation would surely lead to further revolts and rebellions, and they called for the suppression of abolitionist mailings and papers. This sentiment against abolitionism intensified when reports began to arrive in the United States of a massive slave revolt in Jamaica in December 1831. The events in Virginia and Jamaica, the terrifying memories of the major rebellion by black slaves in Saint Domingue (the western part of Haiti) in the Caribbean in August 1791, and the recollections of earlier planned revolts in Virginia (1800), Louisiana (1811), and South Carolina (1822) heightened fears in the white population about the consequences of easing or ending slavery.[4]

It was Turner's uprising that led the governors of Virginia and Georgia to contact the mayor of Boston, Harrison Gray Otis, to protest against the paper. *The Liberator* had been in existence for ten months, yet Otis reported that he knew nothing about it: "it appeared on enquiry that no member of the city government, nor any person of my acquaintance, had ever heard of the publication. Some time afterward, it was reported to me by the city officers that they had ferreted out the paper and its editor; that his office was an obscure hole, his only visible auxiliary a negro boy, and his supporters a very few insignificant persons of all colors" (*Life* 1:244–45).

Garrison in fact craved notice and took such pride in stormy denigrations of himself and his antislavery work that he packed the paper with them. The front page of the January 15, 1831, issue included a section, "Panegyric," that reprinted three blasts against Garrison's "ravings." Soon Garrison labeled an entire section of each issue "Slavery Record," later renaming it "The Refuge of Oppression." Here he printed reams of onslaughts against abolition and recirculated proslavery arguments.

Garrison said in an editorial (Jan. 8, 1847) that the "Refuge" documented the struggle and the state of public opinion. But it was not just the "Refuge" where these attacks on Garrison and his band could be found. Nearly half of the front page of the March 26, 1852, issue, for example, was taken up by reprints of scathing denunciations of Garrison's words and deeds. He thrived on attention, especially, it seemed, when it was hostile and vicious; it proved to him that he must be right if his enemies were driven to such searing language about him.

---

[4] On Nat Turner, see Herbert Aptheker, *Nat Turner's Slave Rebellion* (New York: Humanities Press, 1966); Stephen B. Oates, *The Fires of Jubilee: Nat Turner's Fierce Rebellion* (New York: New American Library, 1975); and Henry Irving Tragle, ed., *The Southampton Slave Revolt of 1831: A Compilation of Source Material* (Amherst: University of Massachusetts Press, 1971). On slave revolts in general, see Herbert Aptheker, *American Negro Slave Revolts* (1943; reprint, New York: International, 1974); Eugene D. Genovese, *From Rebellion to Revolution: Afro-American Slave Revolts in the Making of the Modern World* (Baton Rouge: Louisiana State University Press, 1979); and Robin Blackburn, *The Overthrow of Colonial Slavery* (London: Verso, 1988).

The Liberator was Garrison's paper and no one else's. On occasion, when Garrison was ill, traveling abroad, or in the midst of a lecture tour in the States, others, such as Isaac Knapp or his friends and co-workers Edmund Quincy and C. K. Whipple, did the main labor on it and wrote the editorials. But it was Garrison who exerted "through crisis after crisis personal editorial control of the paper, which was his in the sense that few influential organs of public opinion have ever belonged to one man."[5] Garrison was "the single most visible antislavery radical," and the title he chose dramatized the mission he had set for himself: he was the liberator and his paper was the vehicle for his emancipatory message.[6]

Garrison cultivated his antislavery identity even among the members of his family. This can be seen in a September 4, 1835, letter to George W. Benson, the father of his wife, Helen:

> So completely absorbed am I in that cause [abolition], that it was undoubtedly wise in me to select as a partner one who, while her benevolent feelings were in unison with mine, was less immediately and entirely connected with it. . . . By her unwearied attentions to my wants, her sympathetic regards, her perfect equanimity of mind, and her sweet and endearing manners, she is no trifling support to abolition-ism, inasmuch as she lightens my labors, and enables me to find ex-quisite delight in the family circle, as an offset to public adversity. (*Letters* 1:493)

Helen, whom Garrison married in September 1834, was not a public woman like Angelina and Sarah Grimké, the famed antislavery advocates from South Carolina whose rights as speakers Garrison upheld when they were mobbed in the 1830s. One wonders whether he would have enjoyed close competition from her if she had given it. He determined the place of the wife he loved amid the antislavery ranks: she benefited abolition by being her husband's benevolent aide.

Garrison performed versions of his role at home. His daughter Helen Frances (Fanny Garrison Villard) recalled, "I was hardly more than an infant when my father came to my crib to give me a good-night kiss. He said: 'What a nice warm bed my darling has! The poor little slave child is not so fortunate and is torn from its mother's arms. How good my darling ought to be!' " She also remembered that, "as my hands were ex-ceptionally cold in winter, I often warmed them on my father's bald head.

---

[5] This observation is made by Walter M. Merrill, *The Letters of William Lloyd Garrison,* ed. Walter M. Merrill and Louis Ruchames, 6 vols. (Cambridge: Harvard University Press, 1971–1981), 3:1. These volumes are cited in the text and notes as *Letters.*

[6] Alan Kraut, "William Lloyd Garrison," in *Dictionary of Afro-American Slavery,* ed. Randall M. Miller and John David Smith (Westport: Greenwood, 1988), 286.

For a long time I could not understand why he said: 'You come to my incendiary head, my darling, to warm your cold hands?' "[7] "Incendiary" was the charge that the South hurled against Garrison; in his paper, they said, he was exhorting slaves to the manifold horrors of insurrection— arson, pillage, rape, and murder. Garrison ironically evoked this rendering of himself for his favorite child, displaying to her that he was steadfast despite peril and persecution and could mock his accusers.

Garrison gave this daughter his mother's and wife's name, Helen. One of his sons was William Lloyd, after himself. The other children were given the names of prominent abolitionists: Elizabeth Pease, Charles Follen, George Thompson, Wendell Phillips, and Francis Jackson. His family incarnated abolition. Mirrorlike, it included both Garrison's own children and the beloved persons whose names the children bore. Garrison's friends and associates referred to him as "Father Garrison." He headed a family of his own in two senses and thereby enjoyed a familial network that doubly made up for the family he had lacked as a boy.

It is also intriguing that some readers of *The Liberator* assumed that Garrison was black: it seemed inconceivable to them that a white person would devote his life to persons of another race. During his first trip to England in 1833, when Garrison arrived for a meeting in London with British abolitionists, his host Thomas Fowell Buxton was puzzled: "Have I the pleasure of addressing Mr. Garrison of Boston, in the United States?" Garrison identified himself, to which Buxton answered in amazement: "Why, my dear sir, I thought you were a black man. And I have consequently invited this company of ladies and gentlemen to be present to welcome Mr. Garrison, the black advocate of emancipation from the United States of America!" Garrison recalled: "That is the only compliment I have ever had paid me that I care to remember, or tell of. For Mr. Buxton had somehow or other supposed that no white man could plead for those in bondage as I had done."[8]

Usually, however, the racial references were nastier. Rumors were spread early on, for example, that Garrison intended to marry a black woman and that he was campaigning for this reason for repeal of the Massachusetts law against intermarriage. As late as May 1850, the antiabolitionist New York *Herald,* edited by James Gordon Bennett, was circulating the tall tale that Garrison was a mulatto.[9] For Bennett, one way

---

[7] Fanny Garrison Villard, *William Lloyd Garrison on Non-Resistance, Together with a Personal Sketch by His Daughter, and a Tribute by Leo Tolstoi* (New York: Nation, 1924), 5–6.

[8] Cited in Ralph Korngold, *Two Friends of Man: The Story of William Lloyd Garrison and Wendell Phillips* (Boston: Little, Brown, 1950), 70.

[9] Lindsay Swift, *William Lloyd Garrison* (Philadelphia: George W. Jacobs, 1911), 279.

to smear a white abolitionist like Garrison was to say he was black or partly black himself—the point being that no person who was really white would degrade his own race by aiding an "inferior" one. But Garrison deemed such attacks, as well as mistakes like Buxton's, as the highest flattery because they suggested the degree of his attachment to the abolitionist cause. He always declared that he was *one* with the slaves, that he more than anyone knew and shared in their sufferings. Buxton and Bennett, in their different ways, confirmed for Garrison his sense of himself and illustrated the depth of his sympathy for those held in bondage.

FROM COLONIZATION TO "IMMEDIATE" ABOLITION

Garrison launched his abolitionist career in these early and middle years of the 1830s by laying bare the false claims of an institution, the American Colonization Society, that seemed at first sight to be sympathetic to blacks. The society had been organized in Washington, D.C., in December 1816–January 1817 and included such distinguished statesmen as Henry Clay, John Randolph, James Monroe, and John Marshall among its members. Its program was to encourage manumissions and enable free blacks to emigrate from the United States, in particular to territory on the west coast of Africa, acquired in 1822, that became the nation of Liberia in 1830.

The motives for the society, however, were sullied. Some members did promote emancipation and the return of slaves to their own continent. But the overriding desire in the society was to siphon off free blacks who jeopardized Southern slavery and white supremacy. Northern supporters of the society, it should be said, tried to affirm in its charter that its aim was the "extirpation of slavery." But when it became apparent that this phrase would mean losing the backing of slaveholders, it was left out. The American Colonization Society was not antislavery and it was permeated by racism.[10]

[10] James M. Wright, *The Free Negro in Maryland, 1634–1860,* vol. 97, no. 3 of *Columbia Studies in History, Economics, and Public Law* (New York: Longman, 1921), 266. On colonization, see Penelope Campbell, *Maryland in Africa: The Maryland State Colonization Society, 1831–1857* (Urbana: University of Illinois Press, 1971); Douglas R. Egerton, " 'Its Origin Is Not a Little Curious': A New Look at the American Colonization Society," *Journal of the Early Republic* 5 (1985): 463–80; George M. Fredrickson, *The Black Image in the White Mind: The Debate on Afro-American Character and Destiny, 1817–1914* (1971; reprint, New York: Harper and Row, 1972), 1–42; and P. J. Staudenraus, *The African Colonization Movement, 1816–1865* (New York: Columbia University Press, 1961).

Colonization was impractical. As Garrison's mentor Benjamin Lundy noted, to deport and attempt to colonize the slave population's natural increase alone would exhaust "the wealth of Croesus. We might as well bail dry the old Ocean with a thimble."[11] But plans for colonization were espoused by influential people—which is why Garrison had to wrestle with it strenuously. By 1833, there were 97 local colonization societies in the North and 136 in the South. But in the period from 1820 to 1833, only 2,885 blacks were colonized. In 1832, the 200 auxiliary societies had a combined income of $43,000, and the number of emigrants shipped to Liberia was a paltry 796. At the time there were 2 million slaves in the United States and 319,000 free Negroes. The total sent to Liberia from 1820 to 1856 was 9,502, of whom 3,676 were freeborn.[12]

Garrison argued that colonization was not feasible, but above all he emphasized the moral case against it. As he wrote in a July 30, 1831, letter: "the moving and controlling incentives of the friends of African Colonization may be summed up in a single sentence: *they have an antipathy against the blacks.* They do not wish to admit them to an equality. They can tolerate them only as servants and slaves, but never as brethren and friends. They can love and benefit them four thousand miles off, but not at home" (*Letters* 1:124; see also 3:480–86, 490–94). (See Document 6.)

Though Garrison was an arch foe of colonization in the 1830s, in the 1820s he had been agreeable to the idea himself; like Lundy, Arthur and Lewis Tappan, the Kentucky antislavery lawyer James Birney, and the New York philanthropist Gerrit Smith, he speculated that colonization would eliminate the specter of racial conflict after emancipation.[13] But Garrison rejected colonization by late 1829–1830, publicly apologized for his error, and then, as was typical of him, he censured all who were committed to it. When he held a position, he held it absolutely and blasted those with whom he differed. In a 240-page anticolonization pamphlet,

---

[11] Cited in Gilbert Hobbs Barnes, *The Anti-Slavery Impulse, 1830–1844* (1933; reprint, New York: Harcourt, Brace, and World, 1964), 27. On Lundy, see Merton L. Dillon, *Benjamin Lundy and the Struggle for Negro Freedom* (Urbana: University of Illinois Press, 1966).

[12] See Philip S. Foner, ed., *The Life and Writings of Frederick Douglass*, 5 vols. (New York: International, 1950–1975), 1:30; and Dwight Lowell Dumond, *Antislavery: The Crusade for Freedom in America* (1961; reprint, New York: Norton, 1966), 129.

[13] Colonization was also the solution to the slavery problem embraced by American presidents, up to and including Abraham Lincoln until the midpoint of the Civil War. See, for example, George M. Fredrickson, " 'A Man but Not a Brother' ": Abraham Lincoln and Racial Equality" (1975), in *The Arrogance of Race: Historical Perspectives on Slavery, Racism, and Social Inequality* (Middletown: Wesleyan University Press, 1988), 54–72.

Thoughts on African Colonization, which was published on June 2, 1832, and which sold extremely well, Garrison stated: "the colonization scheme [is] inadequate in its design, injurious in its operation, and contrary to sound principle."[14] In a July 21, 1832, letter, he added: "I look upon the overthrow of the Colonization Society as the overthrow of slavery itself — they both stand or fall together" (*Letters* 1:158; see also 1:194).

Garrison realized that colonization was a dream that distracted from abolition, and in this he was seconded by key American and British allies. "I object to the Colonization Society," said the antislavery reformer Lydia Maria Child in 1833, "because it tends to put public opinion asleep, on a subject where it needs to be wide awake." As George Thompson recounted in an October 9, 1834, speech in Boston: "The scheme of colonization *pleased all.* It gratified prejudice — soothed the conscience — left slavery uncondemned and unmolested — while it professed to promote the freedom and happiness of the free colored population, and at the same time advance the interests of Africa, by preventing the slave-trade along her coast, and diffusing the blessings of the gospel amongst her benighted tribes." The English woman of letters Harriet Martineau highlighted this point as well: colonization "alienates the attention and will of the people" and prevents them from adopting "the principle of abolition," she wrote. Colonization was appealing to whites. Abolition, or, as it was usually termed, "immediate emancipation" (or more simply "immediatism"), was *not,* for it connoted emancipation (1) without compensation to slave owners for their lost "property" and (2) without any expectation or requirement that freed blacks would be transported abroad.[15]

In 1829–1830, then, Garrison rejected colonization and embraced immediatism, invoking it repeatedly in *The Liberator* as "the sheet anchor of our cause" (Feb. 14, 1840). To be sure, he was not the first immediatist. Earlier proponents included George Bourne of Virginia in *The Book and Slavery Irreconcilable* (1816), James Duncan of Kentucky in *Treatise on Slavery* (1824), and especially, as Garrison noted (*Liberator,* Aug. 15, 1845), the British Quaker Elizabeth Heyrick in her pamphlet

---

[14] William Lloyd Garrison, *Thoughts on African Colonization* (1832; reprint, New York: Arno, 1968), 2.

[15] Lydia Maria Child, *An Appeal in Favor of That Class of Americans Called Africans* (Boston: Allen and Ticknor, 1833), 133; George Thompson, *Letters and Addresses* (1837; reprint, New York: Negro University Press, 1969), 7–8; and Harriet Martineau, *Society in America,* ed. Seymour Martin Lipset (1962; reprint, New Brunswick: Transaction, 1982), 191. Child is an important, interesting figure whom Garrison greatly influenced. See *Lydia Maria Child: Selected Letters, 1817–1880,* ed. Milton Meltzer and Patricia G. Holland (Amherst: University of Massachusetts Press, 1982); and Deborah Pickman Clifford, *Crusader for Freedom: A Life of Lydia Maria Child* (Boston: Beacon Press, 1992).

Immediate, Not Gradual Emancipation (1824).[16] But Garrison was the most persistent immediatist in America, and this position was associated with his name.

As a rallying cry, however, "immediate" emancipation was ambiguous, and not everyone meant the same thing by it that Garrison did. To some, it betokened the immediate beginning of gradual emancipation, whereas to others, that slavery would end immediately but that the rights of freed blacks would be restricted, probably permanently. For Garrison, though, immediatism meant that slavery would be abolished at once *and* that over time blacks would rise to complete social and political equality. Not right away, he conceded: freed persons needed education, training, preparation for citizenship. But eventually freedom would lead to equal rights.

This is why Garrison was admonished for maligning colonization, why he was besieged by mobs, why he was hated. For most Americans, and not only Southerners, abolition evoked the disturbing prospect of millions of free black persons. The issue was not slavery but rather "the presence of a large, unassimilable mass of laborers who were believed to be ignorant, incapable of self-discipline and self-support, savage, and dangerous."[17]

Thus when Garrison enlisted under the banner of immediate emancipation, got *The Liberator* under way in January 1831, and took part in organizing the New England Anti-Slavery Society in 1832 and the American Anti-Slavery Society in 1833, he occupied an extreme minority position. Garrison looked forward and was committed to a biracial society.[18] As he said in his July 4, 1829, speech in Boston (see Document 1):

> education and freedom will elevate our colored population to a rank with the white—making them useful, intelligent and peaceable citizens.
>
> . . . A very large proportion of our colored population were born on our soil, and are therefore entitled to all the privileges of American citizens. This is their country by birth, not by adoption. Their children possess the same inherent and unalienable rights as ours, and it is a crime of the blackest dye to load them with fetters. (*Life* 1:130–31)

---

[16] David Brion Davis, "The Emergence of Immediatism in British and American Antislavery Thought," *Mississippi Valley Historical Review* 49 (September 1962): 209–30; Anne C. Loveland, "Evangelicalism and 'Immediate Emancipation' in American Antislavery Thought," *Journal of Southern History* 32 (May 1966): 172–88; and Shelton S. Smith, *In His Image, but . . . : Racism in Southern Religion, 1780–1910* (Durham: Duke University Press, 1972), 61–66.

[17] Dan Lacy, *The White Use of Blacks in America* (New York: McGraw-Hill, 1972), 37.

[18] Ronald G. Walters, "The Boundaries of Abolitionism," in *Antislavery Reconsidered: New Perspectives on the Abolitionists*, ed. Lewis Perry and Michael Fellman (Baton Rouge: Louisiana State University Press, 1979), 4.

These were stunning words to be spoken in 1829—that blacks born in America were entitled to be citizens, that their children possessed the same rights as children born of white parents, and that they could with education and freedom reach the same level as whites. Garrison's position was unnerving precisely because it was so straightforward: slavery was wrong and had to end, and once blacks were emancipated, they had to be treated as persons with "inherent and unalienable rights." This was far more than the overwhelming majority of white Americans could accept.

ABOLITION, POLITICS, AND VIOLENT MEANS

Both the New England Anti-Slavery Society and the American Anti-Slavery Society were very small at first. The New England Society was formed by Garrison and twelve others, who met on January 6, 1832, in the basement schoolroom of the African Baptist Church in Boston. The assembly that met on December 3 and 4, 1833, in Philadelphia to form the American Society numbered only sixty-two delegates, with four women and three blacks also involved in the proceedings though not serving as delegates. Yet these small groups were tightly bound by a sense of mission and love. As Samuel J. May recalled years later about the Philadelphia meeting, "every man's heart was in his hand,—as if every one felt that he was about to offer himself a living sacrifice in the cause of *freedom,* and to do it cheerfully."[19] Through the dedicated work that Garrison, the antislavery agent and lecturer Theodore Weld, Arthur and Lewis Tappan, James Birney, Gerrit Smith, and others in the two societies executed—often in the teeth of harassment, assault, and mob violence—antislavery became a dynamic reform movement in the 1830s. (See Document 12.)

The summary of abolitionist activity that the Massachusetts Anti-Slavery Society (the successor, as of 1835, to the New England Society) furnished at its May 1839 meeting was striking indeed. The numbers of converts to the cause had grown; antislavery writings were being distributed nationwide and thousands of petitions mailed to Congress—this was largely the work of Lewis Tappan and others who ran the American Anti-Slavery office in New York City; and church leaders were objecting to preaching by slaveholders and even to the membership of slaveholders in congregations. In addition was the following evidence of abolitionist activity:

[19] Samuel J. May, *Some Recollections on Our Anti-Slavery Conflict* (1869; reprint, Miami: Mnemosyne, 1969), 96.

In 1829 not an Anti-Slavery society of a genuine stamp was in existence. In 1839 there are nearly two thousand such societies swarming and multiplying in all parts of the free States. In 1829 there was but one Anti-slavery periodical in the land. In 1839 there are fourteen. In 1829 there was scarcely a newspaper of any religious or political party which was willing to disturb the "delicate" question of slavery. In 1839 there are multitudes of journals that either openly advocate the doctrine of immediate and unconditional emancipation, or permit its free discussion in their columns.[20]

By 1840 total membership in antislavery organizations had reached 200,000.[21]

Garrison, however, faced a challenge to his leadership of the national society in 1840, when Arthur and Lewis Tappan, Birney, the lawyer and antislavery journalist Henry B. Stanton, and others sought to turn the ever-growing forces of antislavery to the political arena and, furthermore, when they stated their uneasiness about allowing antislavery to attach itself to women's rights. Garrison's rivals were defeated at a meeting in New York City, but three hundred of them then split off to form the American and Foreign Anti-Slavery Society and cast their support for the Liberty Party, the first political party based on antislavery.[22]

In the same year, Garrison also participated in the World Anti-Slavery Convention in London, where he sat in protest with the women delegates, whom the leaders of the convention refused to recognize. This marked Garrison's challenge to stereotypical gender roles and his commitment to equal rights for women—though it has to be conceded that he was capable of reinvoking these stereotypes and gender-based differentiations of rights when denouncing the evils done to husbands, wives, and the family in slavery in the South.[23] The exclusion of the women at this London

---

[20] Cited in Carlos Martyn, *Wendell Phillips: The Agitator, with an Appendix Containing Three Speeches* (1890; reprint, New York: Negro University Press, 1969), 125.

[21] See Foner, *Life* 1:38; and Bruce Levine, *Half Slave and Half Free: The Roots of Civil War* (New York: Hill and Wang, 1992), 154.

[22] C. S. Griffin, *Their Brothers' Keepers: Moral Stewardship in the United States, 1800–1865* (New Brunswick: Rutgers University Press, 1960), 152–76; and Bertram Wyatt-Brown, *Lewis Tappan and the Evangelical War against Slavery* (1969; reprint, New York: Atheneum, 1971), 185–204.

[23] See Kristin Hoganson, "Garrisonian Abolitionists and the Rhetoric of Gender, 1850–1860," *American Quarterly* 45 (December 1993): 558–95. For additional studies of the role of women in abolition, see Blanche Glassman Hersh, *The Slavery of Sex: Feminist-Abolitionists in America* (Urbana: University of Illinois Press, 1978); Wendy Hamand Venet, *Neither Ballots nor Bullets: Women Abolitionists and the Civil War* (Charlottesville: University Press of Virginia, 1991); and Shirley J. Yee, *Black Women Abolitionists: A Study in Activism, 1828–1860* (Knoxville: University of Tennessee Press, 1992).

meeting led to the organization by Lucretia Mott and Elizabeth Cady Stanton of the Seneca Falls Convention, held in July 1848, the first public meeting in the United States on the subject of women's rights. As transcendentalist editor, essayist, and critic Margaret Fuller noted in the mid-1840s, it was above all the brave group of "champions of the enslaved Africans" who, "partly from a natural following out of principles, partly because many women have been prominent in that cause, makes, just now, the warmest appeal in behalf of Woman."[24] (See Documents 13, 24, and 26.)

For Garrison, it was essential to argue for rights for women and blacks—the cause of freedom had to be pushed in that direction—but it was mistaken to become involved in political parties and campaigns. Garrison perceived abolition as a religious and moral crusade, not a political struggle, and fighting for change in the political arena would mean compromise, cooperation, and coalition building. For Garrison this could come only at the expense of the purity of abolitionist doctrine, and he was not prepared to pay such a price. Hence, while he remained active and influential in the 1840s and 1850s, he did become somewhat of an actor on the fringes as the antislavery cause was adopted by the Liberty, Free Soil, and Republican parties.

Neither the Free Soil nor the Republican party favored outright abolition, a fact that angered Garrison; both stressed instead the need to curtail slavery expansion so that the institution could not spread and add to the strength of the Southern slave states. As William H. Seward, lawyer and politician from New York, stated in a May 26, 1845, letter to an antislavery convention in Cincinnati (a letter that Garrison reprinted in the July 18, 1845, *Liberator*): "Emancipation is now a political enterprise, to be effected through the consent and action of the American people."[25] It was above all a moral enterprise for Garrison. The issue for him was not how to win the consent of the governed—not if this entailed modifying one's own position. Rather, the issue was converting people, awakening them to higher laws. For Garrison the cause was the termination of slavery everywhere, not tolerating it where it already existed and combatting only its extension.

Garrison's response to political antislavery was principled but awkward and self-aggrandizing: he opposed it yet wanted to claim credit for preparing the moral ground for it, and he viewed the Liberty, Free Soil, and

---

[24] See Margaret Fuller, *The Woman and the Myth: Margaret Fuller's Life and Writings,* ed. Bell Gale Chevigny (Old Westbury, N.Y.: Feminist Press, 1976), 244.

[25] On this point, see also John M. Taylor, *William Henry Seward: Lincoln's Right Hand* (New York: HarperCollins, 1991), 61.

Republican parties as inevitable even as he scoffed at those enlisted in them.

The events of the 1840s and 1850s intensified the sectional crisis and spurred the growth of antislavery sentiment, though not in the form that Garrison had advocated. After disputes between the United States and Mexico over the annexation of Texas to the Union in 1845 and several incidents along the border, President James K. Polk asked Congress for and received a declaration of war. U.S. troops soon won major victories that led to the cessation of hostilities in February 1848 and to the acquisition of extensive lands in the Southwest through the Treaty of Guadalupe Hidalgo. The question then became whether those lands should be slave or free, with Garrison and others arguing that the purpose of the war, waged by a pro-South Democratic president, was to enlarge the domain of slavery. In Garrison's view, this war signaled once more the hold of slavery over the national government and again made clear the folly of political means. (See Document 21.)

Yet it is important to note, too, that one of the main opponents to slavery expansion was an antislavery Democratic congressman from Pennsylvania, David Wilmot, who introduced a measure in the House (the so-called Wilmot Proviso) in August 1846 that would have prohibited slavery in any territory acquired during the war. This measure was debated for years (it never received full congressional approval), and it showed the cracks in political parties caused by the battles over slavery. Garrison was correct that slavery was at bottom a moral issue, but by the 1840s it was steadily becoming an issue that, somehow, was going to be focused and decided politically, in congressional debates and laws, party conventions, and state and national elections.[26]

The Compromise of 1850 reinforced this point. Supported by the distinguished U.S. Senators Henry Clay, Stephen A. Douglas, and Daniel Webster, the Compromise was intended to resolve the sectional strife that slavery had engendered. But its chief provision, a stricter Fugitive Slave Law, enraged many citizens in the North, for it mandated that all citizens assist in the capture of runaways from slavery and set penalties of fines and imprisonment for anyone who harbored, rescued, or concealed fugitives. The transcendentalist philosopher, poet, and essayist Ralph Waldo

---

[26] On the Mexican war, see Alfred Hoyt Bill, *Rehearsal for Conflict: The War with Mexico, 1846–1848* (New York: Knopf, 1947); and Robert W. Johannsen, *To the Halls of the Montezumas: The Mexican War in the American Imagination* (New York: Oxford University Press, 1985). On the Wilmot Proviso, see Chaplain W. Morrison, *Democratic Politics and Sectionalism: The Wilmot Proviso Controversy* (Chapel Hill: University of North Carolina Press, 1967).

Emerson called the law a "filthy enactment," adding "I will not obey it, by God."[27] (See Document 22.)

The Compromise was followed in January 1854 by the Kansas-Nebraska Act, which allowed settlers in the Kansas and Nebraska territories to choose for themselves whether to allow slavery. Illinois Senator Douglas believed that his tenet of "popular sovereignty"—"let the people living in the territory decide"—would solve the sectional strife over slavery expansion. But in his eagerness for compromise, Douglas seemed to be ignoring morality altogether; the act he supported meant that slavery could expand westward and thus was not limited to the boundaries of the states where it existed. Three years later, in 1857, the Supreme Court's Dred Scott decision gave even freer rein to slavery by affirming that (1) slaves were not and could not become U.S. citizens; (2) blacks had no rights that white persons were bound to respect; and (3) Congress had no power to exclude slavery from any territory belonging to the United States.[28] (See Document 30.)

Garrison lashed these laws and the Court's decision. Yet he also found much that was encouraging, as each event led to heightened opposition and protest. At a meeting of the Massachusetts Anti-Slavery Society on January 27, 1859, looking back over the 1850s, he referred to a heartening shift "in the public feeling and sentiment of the North." (See also Document 34.) Of course, much of this shift was taking place in the formation and growth of new antislavery political groups and parties. But Garrison stressed not what had happened but who had triggered it and how. He said that the "revolution in the public mind had not been effected in consequence of any dilution of doctrine or compromise of principle on the part of the abolitionists; for never had they faltered, or lowered their standard—never were they so exacting in their demands, or so bold in speech, as now" (*Liberator*, Feb. 4, 1859). Antislavery had steadily gained in political popularity and Garrison was convinced that it would never have done so if he had compromised a jot and had gotten involved in politics himself.

The alarming developments on the national scene that enraged aboli-

---

[27] Ralph Waldo Emerson, *Emerson in His Journals*, ed. Joel Porte (Cambridge: Harvard University Press, 1982), 429. See Len Gougeon, *Virtue's Hero: Emerson, Antislavery, and Reform* (Athens: University of Georgia Press, 1990).

[28] On Douglas, popular sovereignty, and the Kansas-Nebraska Act, see David M. Potter, *The Impending Crisis, 1848–1861*, completed and edited by Don E. Fehrenbacher (New York: Harper and Row, 1976); and Robert W. Johannsen, *The Frontier, the Union, and Stephen A. Douglas* (Urbana: University of Illinois Press, 1989). On the Dred Scott decision, see Don E. Fehrenbacher, *The Dred Scott Case: Its Significance in American Law and Politics* (New York: Oxford University Press, 1978).

tionists also prompted many of them to call for and engage in violent measures that they had at first shunned. Not only did white and black abolitionists resort to law-breaking violence to free fugitive slaves—for example, the rescues of the fugitive Shadrach in Boston in February 1851 and the fugitive Jerry in Syracuse, New York, in October 1851—but some of them spoke as well of the need for slave revolt and rebellion.

Garrison was aware of the moral ambiguity of standing firm against violence in theory and yet accepting or at least condoning it in practice. In part he was driven to this position as he witnessed the tragic failure of legal measures to prevent the return to slavery of two fugitives in Boston, Thomas Sims (1851) and Anthony Burns (1854). But Garrison's response to calls for and acts of violent resistance by slaves had always been strained—though in his own mind it was based on a clear principle. At the start of his career, he criticized the militant rhetoric employed by the Boston abolitionist David Walker, whose eighty-page *Appeal to the Coloured Citizens of the World* went through three editions in 1829–1830, and he regretted Nat Turner's bloody insurrection in 1831. But he acknowledged that Walker was simply employing the same language of resistance to tyranny that the patriots of 1776 had used and, further, that Turner's vengeance resulted from the wrongs that he and other slaves had suffered. (See Documents 5 and 8.)

In the first issue of *The Liberator* (Jan. 1, 1831), Garrison included his poem "Universal Emancipation," which began:

> Though distant be the hour, yet come it must—
> Oh! hasten it, *in mercy,* righteous Heaven!
> When Afric's sons, uprising from the dust,
> Shall stand erect—their galling fetters riven;
> When from his throne Oppression shall be driven,
> An exiled monster, powerless through all time;
> When freedom—glorious freedom, shall be given
> To every race, complexion, caste, and clime,
> And nature's sable hue shall cease to be a crime!
> Wo if it come with storm, and blood, and fire,
> When midnight darkness veils the earth and sky!
> Wo to the innocent babe—the guilty sire—
> Mother and daughter—friends of kindred tie!
> *Stranger and citizen alike shall die!*
> Red-handed Slaughter his revenge shall feed,
> And Havoc yell his ominous death-cry,
> And wild Despair in vain for mercy plead—
> While Hell itself shall shrink, and sicken at the deed!

Garrison was opposed to violence, but he said repeatedly that the American Revolution itself testified to the rightness of warfare for freedom. Garrison could never quite bring himself to say that violent resistance was correct in principle, even as he approved of it in specific cases. Was violence justified or not?

Garrison raised another version of this vexing question in a review he published of Harriet Beecher Stowe's novel *Uncle Tom's Cabin* (1852), which had as its origin Stowe's indignation at the passage of the Fugitive Slave Law. (See Document 23.) If it was proper for the slave Tom to refrain from violence and suffer martyrdom at the hands of the wicked Simon Legree, then, asked Garrison, shouldn't whites be obliged to behave in the same manner? He saw a double standard: white America could not accept the idea of slaves who killed for their freedom, yet year after year America honored the patriots and soldiers who waged war for America's rights during the Revolutionary era. The more Garrison made this point, the less he seemed a true pacifist: he was seeking to adhere to nonresistance and nonviolence while conceding that there were exceptions.

As late as December 1859, about sixteen months before the outbreak of the Civil War, Garrison both criticized and sympathized with the radical abolitionist John Brown's raid in October 1859 on the federal arsenal in Harpers Ferry, Virginia, which Brown had designed as part of a plan to spur uprisings of slaves. (See Documents 32 and 33.) Garrison had met Brown in Boston in January 1857, and the two men had "discussed peace and non-resistance together, Brown quoting the Old Testament against Garrison's citations from the New" (*Life* 3:487–88). Two years later, in May 1859, after attending the New England Anti-Slavery Convention in Boston, Brown said: "These men are all talk; what is needed is action— action!" (*Life* 3:488). Yet while Garrison endorsed Christian pacifism, he declared that he knew why slaves and abolitionists would be driven to violence, why Brown—like Turner two decades earlier—therefore merited praise, and, indeed, why Brown's act should be replicated. How could Americans celebrate their revolt against British oppression in the 1770s and then deny this right to slaves?[29]

[29] On John Brown, see Oswald Garrison Villard, *John Brown, 1800–1859*, rev. ed. (1911; New York: Knopf, 1943); and Stephen B. Oates, *To Purge This Land with Blood: A Biography of John Brown* (New York: Harper and Row, 1970). On the issue of violence in antislavery and abolition, see John Demos, "The Antislavery Movement and the Problem of Violent 'Means,'" *New England Quarterly* 36 (1964): 501–26; and Jeffrey S. Rossbach, *Ambivalent Conspirators: John Brown, the Secret Six, and a Theory of Slave Violence* (Philadelphia: University of Pennsylvania Press, 1982).

For decades Garrison warned that violence and war would erupt if abolition failed to occur. Abraham Lincoln spoke of a "house divided" in a speech on June 16, 1858 at the Illinois Republican State Convention.[30] But Garrison had been making this argument since the 1830s and had amplified it during the 1840s and 1850s. The American Union could not contain freedom *and* slavery; the house must not, could not, be divided. This was Garrison's phrase, and his before it was Lincoln's. As he stated in a resolution he introduced at the May 1855 meeting in New York City of the American Anti-Slavery Society: "A Church or Government which accords the same rights and privileges to Slavery as to Liberty, is a house divided against itself, which cannot stand" (*Life* 3:420). No union could reconcile "elements which are eternally hostile. God has never made it possible for Liberty and Slavery to live together in partnership" (*Liberator*, Jan. 23, 1857; see also Jan. 30, 1857).

Garrison maintained that if Southern and Northern defenders of slavery were converted to righteousness, slavery would end peacefully. If they were not, the result would be secession, disunion, bloody rebellion. He found the prospect of war, of impending apocalypse, frightening and fascinating: if and when it happened, as it very likely would happen, it would show that he had been right. Garrison had concluded that there could be no compromise, no middle path, between freedom and slavery, and thus this man of peace repeatedly invoked the terrors of insurrection and mass slaughter. (See Documents 1 and 8.)

SLAVERY: THE HISTORICAL RECORD

When the war that Garrison foresaw finally came in April 1861, it proved immensely damaging. Its overall cost was $20 billion—five times the total expenditure of the government from the 1780s to 1861. Far worse were the numbers of wounded and dead. Between 700,000 and 800,000 men served in the Confederate armies, about 2.3 million in the Union armies. The number of casualties was 1 million, in a country whose population was 31 million. The death toll was 618,000: 360,000 from the North, 258,000 from the South. This exceeds the number of deaths in all of America's other wars combined.[31]

---

[30] Abraham Lincoln, *Speeches and Writings*, 2 vols. (New York: Library of America, 1989), 1:426. A good biography is Benjamin P. Thomas, *Abraham Lincoln* (New York: Knopf, 1952).

[31] See Maris A. Vinovskis, "Have Social Historians Lost the Civil War? Some Preliminary Demographic Speculations," in *Toward a Social History of the Civil War: Exploratory Essays*, ed. Maris A. Vinovskis (New York: Cambridge University Press, 1990), 5–9; and T. Harry

Having begun with twenty blacks conveyed for sale to the Jamestown, Virginia, settlement by a Dutch merchant in August 1619, slavery had so embedded itself in America that its abolition required terrible bloodshed. The moral appeal that Garrison favored and practiced was forceful, forthright, and ultimately inadequate, as Garrison's own ambivalent words on the subject of violent means suggest. The inevitability of war was also the tormented insight that Lincoln expressed in his second inaugural address on March 4, 1865—that slavery "was, somehow, the cause of the war" and that the lives sacrificed in battle were the price that God had decreed the nation must pay for it.[32] Garrison too had warned of divine retribution as he reminded audiences and readers that the new land of liberty had been conceived (and had grown prosperous) in the midst of slavery. This was why the South campaigned for it with such determination and why the North had tolerated it.

How had this state of affairs arisen? Why had slavery not ended with the Revolution? What was the evolving nature of this institution that the abolitionists set themselves against?

When revolution simmered in the 1760s and early 1770s, slavery was legal in every one of the thirteen colonies. In 1763 there were, for example, 5,200 black slaves in Massachusetts, employed as seamen, farmhands, lumberjacks, craftsmen, and domestic servants.[33] And it had been the New England colonies, not those in the South, that had been at the forefront of the Atlantic slave trade.[34] As historian Jack P. Greene has shown, in the early 1770s "slavery was an expanding institution in all of Britain's continental American colonies except Nova Scotia, New Hampshire, and Canada."[35] Slavery had indeed benefited the North, making a "vital contribution" to the economy of settlements and colonies—so much so that slave trading itself was considered as "honorable" as other types of commerce.[36]

Williams, *Selected Essays* (Baton Rouge: Louisiana State University Press, 1983), 32–33. For slightly different numbers, see James M. McPherson, *Ordeal by Fire: The Civil War and Reconstruction* (New York: Knopf, 1982), 149, 181, 488. A seminal study of the entire period is W. E. B. Du Bois, *Black Reconstruction* (1935; reprint, New York: Atheneum, 1975).

[32] Lincoln, *Speeches* 2:686.

[33] John White and Ralph Willett, *Slavery in the American South* (London: Longman, 1973), 5.

[34] Jay Coughtry, *The Notorious Triangle: Rhode Island and the African Slave Trade* (Philadelphia: Temple University Press, 1981).

[35] Jack P. Greene, "The Constitution of 1787 and the Question of Southern Distinctiveness," in *The South's Role in the Creation of the Bill of Rights,* ed. Robert J. Haws (Jackson: University Press of Mississippi, 1991), 21.

[36] Edgar J. McManus, *Black Bondage in the North* (Syracuse: Syracuse University Press, 1973), 17–18.

But while the Founding Fathers lived in the midst of slavery, they did not expect that slavery would endure and expand as it did later. It seemed to many of them that the Revolution would make a difference and that slavery should, and somehow would, fade as the decades passed.

This did occur in the North, where black and white resistance and state abolition societies, inspired by the ideals of the Revolution, dealt slavery a fatal blow, at the same time as antislavery dovetailed with the system's ebbing profitability there. In 1787 the Northwest Ordinance prohibited slavery in the Ohio Valley. Slavery was abolished by the constitutions of Vermont (1777), Ohio (1802), Illinois (1818), and Indiana (1816); by judicial decision and by the state bill of rights in Massachusetts (1783); by gradual abolition acts in Pennsylvania (1780), Rhode Island (1784), Connecticut (1784, 1797), New York (1799, 1817), and New Jersey (1804, 1820); and by constitutional interpretation in New Hampshire (1792).[37]

There were encouraging trends on the national scene as well. In 1794, U.S. law prohibited "American ships or foreign ships clearing American ports from carrying on the slave trade between foreign ports"; and in 1808 the Atlantic slave trade (the importation of slaves) was abolished as a provision in the Constitution (art. I, sec. 9) had allowed.[38]

While ending the slave trade was significant, however, this was "the aspect of slavery most easily dispensed with, for it did not touch the heart of the system at all, and there were strong economic arguments against a large influx of new slaves."[39] Many might detest the overseas slave trade yet not agree that slavery should cease where it was central to the economy. Maintaining fewer slaves kept their value high, and eliminating overseas trade induced the development of a well-paying trade—"Negro speculation"—within and between states. As Lydia Maria Child observed in 1833, "the breeding of negro cattle for the foreign markets (of Louisiana, Georgia, Alabama, Arkansas, and Missouri) is a very lucrative branch of business."[40]

---

[37] Leon F. Litwack, *North of Slavery: The Negro in the Free States, 1790–1860* (1961; reprint, Chicago: University of Chicago Press, 1971), 3; and 1860 census (U.S. Government Printing Office, 1864), xiv.

[38] William O. Douglas, *Mr. Lincoln and the Negroes* (New York: Atheneum, 1963), 19. It should be noted that the slave trade in Rhode Island reached its height *after* the Revolution and that the merchants in this state "did everything they could to save it," fighting abolition, agitating Congress, breaking laws. See Coughtry, *Triangle*, 17–18.

[39] James H. Broussard, *The Southern Federalists, 1800–1816* (Baton Rouge: Louisiana State University Press, 1978), 314.

[40] Child, *Appeal*, 30. See also Michael Tadman, *Speculators and Slaves: Masters, Traders, and Slaves in the Old South* (Madison: University of Wisconsin Press, 1989). Fortunes were

Thomas Jefferson and other Southern patriots like George Mason and Richard Henry Lee had condemned such slave trading for profit and inveighed against the evils of slavery. But whatever their hopes for abolition in the long run, they could not readily envision slavery's actual demise, given its importance to the economy; they themselves engaged in the practices they castigated and "by general agreement" excluded slavery "from national politics."[41] In addition, neither they nor anyone else could imagine how the two races could live together free without falling into miscegenation and hurtling the South into race war.[42] A number of the early abolitionists were Southerners (among them the Grimké sisters and James Birney), but on the whole antislavery sentiment in the South declined as Southern agriculture expanded and crop production grew, as planters took advantage of the cotton gin (invented by Eli Whitney in 1793) to increase yield, and as Southern plantations fed the textile industries of Great Britain and New England.[43]

The Revolution did spur a number of owners to manumit (free) their slaves, and the number of voluntary manumissions rose in the immediate aftermath of the Revolution. The Manumission Act of 1782 in Virginia, for example, led to freedom for 10,000 slaves during the next ten years. In 1805, however, a change in the law "allowed owners to free slaves only if Negroes then left the state"—which was a return to an earlier law of 1691 that had permitted freedom for slaves only if they were transported from the colony within six months. Freed slaves meant a free black population, and this alarmed nearly everybody: no state or territory wanted free blacks. Manumissions lapsed; slavery thrived.[44]

Slaves were precious property. The value of slave property in 1790 was about $140 million—twice the entire Revolutionary War debt. Within

---

made from the slave trade. During the period from the 1810s to the 1840s, a man named Isaac Franklin became wealthy from slave trading and investing his profits in land. He presided over the finest estate in Tennessee, named "Fairvue," and had extensive holdings in Louisiana and Texas. It was not until the mid-1830s that Franklin retired from trafficking in the slave trade: it was not fit for the best gentlemen except when required for good order and discipline or economic necessity. At his death, Franklin owned 600 slaves. See Wendell Holmes Stephenson, *Isaac Franklin: Slave Trader and Planter of the Old South* (Baton Rouge: Louisiana State University Press, 1938), 11, 22, 93.

[41] Jean V. Matthews, *Toward a New Society: American Thought and Culture, 1800–1830* (Boston: Twayne, 1991), 83.

[42] William J. Cooper, Jr., *Liberty and Slavery: Southern Politics to 1860* (New York: Knopf, 1983), 33–36.

[43] Foner, *Life,* 1:29–30.

[44] Thaddeus W. Tate, *The Negro in Eighteenth-Century Williamsburg* (Charlottesville: University of Virginia Press, 1972), 122–26. See also Jackson T. Main, "The One Hundred," *William and Mary Quarterly* 11 (July 1954): 354–84.

two years of the invention of the cotton gin, the price of slaves had doubled. A field hand priced at $500 in 1794 cost three times that amount by 1825. During the antebellum period, the cotton that slaves raised was the nation's most important commercial crop and major export, amounting to 50–60 percent of America's total exports. Slave labor was crucial, too, for rice, sugar, corn, and tobacco. The more slavery was practiced, the more necessary it was reckoned on economic grounds; and the larger the slave population, the more imperative that blacks be defined and re-strained by slavery.

During the period from 1780 to 1810, almost as many Africans were shipped to the United States as in the entire 160 years from 1620 to 1780. The slave population expanded by 33 percent between 1800 and 1810 and by another 29 percent between 1810 and 1820. Despite the Atlantic slave trade's termination in 1808, the slave population in the United States soared, its number boosted by illegal trading (approximately 1,000 per year brought in illegally) and slave breeding and interstate slave trading. Between 1808 and 1860, the slave population tripled; and the profit from investment in slaves averaged an impressive 10 percent during the 1840s and 1850s. Slaves were "capital assets" that brought a return equal to or exceeding other kinds of investments; and by the 1850s, slave owners in the East were shipping and selling 25,000 slaves to the West each year.[45]

Between 1770 and 1860, then, slavery simultaneously diminished and grew, dying out in the North and West and enlarging in the South and consequently in the body politic. Four million slaves lived in the South when the Civil War began, compared with 500,000 at the outset of the Revolution in 1775. By the decade of the 1850s, slavery was "flourishing as never before" in the South.[46]

The statistics highlighted thus far demonstrate the magnitude of slav-ery in the United States, and antislavery agitators like Garrison repeatedly

[45] Roger L. Ransom and Richard Sutch, "Who Pays for Slavery?" in *The Wealth of Races: The Present Value of Benefits from Past Injustices,* ed. Richard F. America (Westport, Conn.: Greenwood, 1990), 31. For other statistics cited here, see Steven Mintz, ed., *African-American Voices: The Life Cycle of Slavery* (St. James, N.Y.: Brandywine, 1993); David Northrup, *The Atlantic Slave Trade* (Lexington, Mass.: D. C. Heath, 1994); and Richard H. Sewell, *A House Divided: Sectionalism and Civil War, 1848–1865* (Baltimore: Johns Hopkins University Press, 1988), 6. It is estimated that 10 million Africans survived the transatlantic journey (the "middle passage") to slavery. Most were sent to Brazil and the West Indies; only 4 to 6 percent of the total were delivered to the American colonies. But 66 percent of the slaves in the New World were in the American South by 1860, the result of a high birthrate and relatively stable (if precarious) family relationships.

[46] C. Vann Woodward, *The Future of the Past* (New York: Oxford University Press, 1989), 181.

called attention to them. But they sought, too, to give slavery a human face by showing the price paid by persons held in bondage. There were not only innumerable articles in *The Liberator* and other antislavery newspapers, but also books, pamphlets, and slave narratives that depicted the inhumanity of slavery—its murders, tortures, and everyday brutalities, its separation of families, sexual outrages, denial of literacy, and restrictions on religious practices. Graphic antislavery works included Theodore Weld's *American Slavery as It Is: Testimony of a Thousand Witnesses* (1839), the black abolitionist Frederick Douglass's *Narrative* (1845) and *My Bondage and My Freedom* (1855), and Massachusetts Senator Charles Sumner's antislavery orations "The Crime against Kansas" (1856) and "The Barbarism of Slavery" (1860), first delivered in the U.S. Senate and widely distributed in pamphlet form.

Most important of all was Stowe's *Uncle Tom's Cabin,* which appeared first in a serialized version in the abolitionist journal *The National Era* from June 1851 to April 1852 and then was published as a book. (Garrison reprinted chapter 7 of the novel—recounting the slave Eliza's escape and crossing of the Ohio River on chunks of ice—in the April 2, 1852, issue of *The Liberator.*) The 5,000 copies of the first edition of the novel sold out in forty-eight hours, and for the next two years the presses never caught up with the demand; 300,000 copies sold in 1852 alone. Total sales in the United States reached 1 million in the next seven years and were about the same in England. White antislavery men and women like Weld, Sumner, and Stowe and black abolitionists like Douglass strove to make Northerners see slavery as it affected black *persons* and thereby made the grim statistics compellingly alive.

In reply, Southern slaveholders, statesmen, clergy, professors, and men of letters produced an enormous body of passionate, detailed, and perversely complicated proslavery literature. Their position was a hard one to defend, for while slaves were members of a different race (and much of the pro-slavery argument hinged on that fact), they were nonetheless in an important sense fellow Americans. As Garrison had stressed as early as his July 4, 1829, speech in Boston, this was their country, too, for they were "born on our soil" (see Document 1). By 1840, 96 percent of the slaves in the United States were native-born; by 1860, the figure reached nearly 100 percent. These were black *Americans* who were being held in bondage. But despite being a native population— and, in this respect, a more truly American population than were many whites—slaves could not own property, assemble with other slaves (except in church), testify in court against whites, or be taught to read and write. In 1860 only 10 percent of all black persons in the South could read.[47]

Still, in countless speeches, essays, monographs, and two mammoth multiauthor collections, *Pro-Slavery Arguments as Maintained by the Most Distinguished Writers of the Southern States* (1852) and *Cotton Is King, and Pro-Slavery Arguments* (1860), many skillful, well-educated Southerners sought to prove the rightness of slavery. Religion, the social and natural sciences, literature, economics, philosophy, political theory—every discipline of knowledge and branch of culture was drawn on and deployed to confirm the rewards of the institution and the necessity for locating black people (an "inferior," "dependent" race) within it.

Slaveholders and their Northern allies could not conceive of the South deprived of slaves, for slavery was not only a labor system but a means of policing black persons. As historian Allan Nevins has pointed out, the slave states in the Union and, later, the Confederacy could have won much support in Europe and in the North if their leaders had announced that slavery would henceforth be understood as a "transitional system" and that plans thus would be devised for "abolishing the internal slave trade, legalizing slave marriages, and providing education for slave children."[48] But they said nothing of the sort. Article I, section 9(4) of the Constitution of the Confederate States of America (1861) read: "no bill of attainder, *ex post facto* law, or law denying or impairing the right of property in negro slaves shall be passed"; and Article IV, sections 1, 2, and 3 amply reinforced it.[49]

The proslavery argument, ratified in the Confederate Constitution, was

---

[47] Sally G. McMillen, *Southern Women: Black and White in the Old South* (Arlington Heights, Ill.: Harlan Davidson, 1992), 80; and Mark E. Neely, Jr., *The Last Best Hope of Earth: Abraham Lincoln and the Promise of America* (Cambridge: Harvard University Press, 1993), 107. On the proslavery argument, see Drew Gilpin Faust, ed., *The Ideology of Slavery: Proslavery Thought in the Antebellum South, 1830–1860* (Baton Rouge: Louisiana State University Press, 1981); and Larry E. Tise, *Proslavery: A History of the Defense of Slavery in America, 1701–1840* (Athens: University of Georgia Press, 1987).

Important studies of slavery include Kenneth M. Stampp, *The Peculiar Institution: Slavery in the Antebellum South* (New York: Knopf, 1956); Eugene D. Genovese, *Roll, Jordan, Roll: The World the Slaves Made* (New York: Pantheon, 1974); Herbert G. Gutman, *The Black Family in Slavery and Freedom, 1750–1925* (New York: Pantheon, 1976); Jacqueline Jones, *Labor of Love, Labor of Sorrow: Black Women, Work, and the Family from Slavery to the Present* (New York: Basic, 1985); Elizabeth Fox-Genovese, *Within the Plantation Household: Black and White Women of the Old South* (Chapel Hill: University of North Carolina Press, 1988); and Peter Kolchin, *American Slavery, 1619–1877* (New York: Hill and Wang, 1993). See also Henry Louis Gates, Jr., and Charles T. Davis, eds., *The Slave's Narrative: Texts and Contexts* (New York: Oxford University Press, 1984).

[48] Allan Nevins, *The Statesmanship of the Civil War* (New York: Macmillan, 1953), 53.

[49] *The Messages and Papers of Jefferson Davis and the Confederacy, 1861–1865*, ed. James D. Richardson, 2 vols. (New York: Chelsea House, 1983), 1:43, 50–51.

keyed to "property" rights yet was at bottom tautological: the presence of slaves—black slaves—required perpetual slavery. The South could not endure the elimination of slaves because, central as the economic rationale for slavery was, it could not abide several million free black people living among whites. The majority of white Northerners understood this concern; though opposed to slavery—which threatened job prospects and wages for white workers—they did not want to live in the midst of a large black population either. Slavery was a powerful economic engine for the American economy *and* a form of racial control, and this is why abolition was doubly hard to argue for.

MORALITY VERSUS POLITICS: STRATEGIES FOR ABOLITION

The national scale and impact of slavery and its profound presence in the body politic likely make Garrison's detachment from politics all the more ironic. For him, slavery was a blatant form of injustice, but it was not one that should lead to political activity nor was it the only cause that mattered. Garrison took an antipolitical stance and he endorsed other reforms besides abolition, and these positions ignited opposition to him within the broad, increasingly politicized antislavery movement. He seemed to many to be imperiling the cause he championed, undercutting it when it was accruing strength nationally. As Lewis Tappan explained, Garrison's "new views in reference to Women's rights, Human Government, Nonresistance, the emancipation of Mind, etc. led him to subordinate the Anti-slavery cause, properly so called, to these doctrines." The antislavery journalist Gamaliel Bailey concurred in 1837: Garrison had created discord among abolitionists by churning up subjects, such as women's rights, that "contraven[ed] the sole object of their union." Another Garrison critic, Elizur Wright, was likewise upset about the "vexatious question" of women's rights—this he regarded in 1840 as "pack-saddling our cause with an innovation upon received customs."[50]

---

[50] For Tappan, see Annie H. Abel and Frank J. Klingsberg, eds., *A Side-Light on Anglo-American Relations, 1839–1858, Furnished by the Correspondence of Lewis Tappan and Others with the British and Foreign Anti-Slavery Society* (Lancaster, Pa.: Association for the Study of Negro Life and History, 1927), 314. For Bailey, see Stanley Harrold, *Gamaliel Bailey and Antislavery Union* (Kent: Kent State University Press, 1986), 22; and for Wright, see Lawrence B. Goodheart, *Abolitionist, Actuary, Atheist: Elizur Wright and the Reform Impulse* (Kent: Kent State University Press, 1990), 107. See also Lawrence Friedman, *Gregarious Saints: Self and Community in American Abolitionism, 1830–1870* (New York: Cambridge University Press, 1982), 87–91; and Valarie H. Ziegler, *The Advocates of Peace in Antebellum America* (Bloomington: Indiana University Press, 1992), 48–115.

Theodore Weld and the antislavery poet John Greenleaf Whittier said the same. They concluded that talk of winning rights for women would entail abandonment of the slave.[51] For Garrison, however, antislavery dramatized not only the cruel mistreatment of blacks but also the denial of rights to women—who were told they should not debase themselves by engaging in public work—and the corruption of religious and political institutions. Abolition and other reforms, such as women's rights, were indissolubly linked, in Garrison's view. As he observed in an April 25, 1834, letter to his future wife, Helen, "men are profane—impure—vicious—rebellious. The leprosy of corruption covers society, and the cancer of selfishness is preying upon its vitals" (*Letters* 1:331). Twenty-five years later, on the eve of the Civil War, Garrison remained convinced that the fight against slavery had disclosed other evils and related causes: "The scope of Anti-Slavery is boundless. . . . There is nothing which pertains to the intellect, heart, soul, or interests of man that is not wrapped up in this movement" (*Liberator*, Feb. 11, 1859). As Lydia Maria Child said, in Garrison's mind all evils were connected and all truths were united: it was impossible for him "to present a single ray of light without producing a rainbow."[52]

Garrison's accent on women's rights generated less opposition than did his mistrust of politics, however. To his critics within the abolitionist movement, he must have seemed strange indeed, as he exempted himself from politics (where concrete antislavery progress was being made) and yet pushed for women's rights (which upset and divided and weakened antislavery groups). Garrison contended that abolitionists should not vote, for voting would imply cooperation with a slavery-sustaining government. He presented his case in a June 28, 1839, article in *The Liberator* by quoting words that Elizur Wright had formerly voiced: " 'Abolitionists have but one work: it is *not to put any body in office, or out of it,* but TO SET RIGHT THOSE WHO MAKE OFFICERS. It is not an action *upon Church or State,* but UPON THE MATERIALS OF BOTH' " (*Letters* 2:473). (See Document 15.)

Garrison judged that abolitionists should alter "the moral vision of the people" (*Letters* 2:481). But his foes within antislavery thought that this

---

[51] For Weld, see Gilbert H. Barnes and Dwight L. Dumond, eds., *Letters of Theodore Dwight Weld, Angelina Grimké Weld, and Sarah Grimké, 1822–1844,* 2 vols. (1934; reprint, Gloucester, Mass.: Peter Smith, 1965), 1:425–27; and Whittier, *Letters,* ed. John B. Pickard, 3 vols. (Cambridge: Harvard University Press, 1975), 1:249–51. For biographies of Weld, see Benjamin P. Thomas, *Theodore Weld: Crusader for Freedom* (New Brunswick: Rutgers University Press, 1950); and Robert H. Abzug, *Passionate Liberator: Theodore Dwight Weld and the Dilemma of Reform* (New York: Oxford University Press, 1980).

[52] Child, "William Lloyd Garrison," *Atlantic Monthly* (Aug. 1879): 236.

was bad counsel that deprived abolition of a weapon. Yes, they replied, change the public's moral vision, but make use of the ballot and political convention and campaign to do so.

Lewis Tappan, James Birney, and others active in the Liberty, Free Soil, and Republican parties judged that their natural destination was politics: center antislavery in a political organization, rally support for it, destabilize the major parties, and amend the laws of the land. To Garrison this approach was sinful, and in this respect he was an extreme, and rather peculiar, example of the revival and reform spirit kindled by the Second Great Awakening of the 1820s and 1830s. Many took this movement, whose leaders included the charismatic preacher Charles Grandison Finney, to mean that reborn, renewed Christian men and women should work for social change, obtaining and authenticating their salvation through it. For Garrison, too, this Christian message and vision required reform, but not at the price of participating in institutions that were wicked.

Garrison's views intensified as he came under the influence of the religious perfectionist and leader John Humphrey Noyes, whom Garrison had met in spring 1837. Noyes emphasized that human governments were sinful and that the established churches and religious institutions—the majority of which defended or were indifferent to slavery—were ungodly and corrupt as well. In a March 22, 1837, letter to Garrison, Noyes wrote: "Every person who is, in the usual sense of the expression, a citizen of the United States, i.e., a voter, politician, etc., is at once a slave and a slaveholder—in other words, a subject and a ruler in a slaveholding government" (*Life* 2:146). He added: "I counsel you, and the people that are with you, if you love the post of honor—the forefront of the hottest battle of righteousness—to set your face toward *perfect* holiness" (*Life* 2:148).

This advice confirmed Garrison's commitment to reforms of all kinds and, furthermore, to the use of Christian principles in argument and moral suasion. (See Document 14.) He would in effect be permanently at odds with America's institutions, though his instruments would be spiritual only, and he would endure hardship as did the early Christians. His causes would constitute his life, and his life would be sanctified. As Garrison averred in an August 1840 letter to Joseph Pease, a Quaker abolitionist in England: "Christianity sanctions the use of nothing but moral and religious means and measures for the suppression of any system of iniquity—in other words, it forbids the doing of evil that good may come, however vast the good to be achieved, or small the evil to be resorted to for its accomplishment" (*Life* 2:391; see also 3:34–35).

However "small the evil": Garrison's ethics were noble but narrow, mandating that he not allow any difference of opinion to go unremarked and unrebuked. Slaveholders were craven, yet so were abolitionists whose ideas about how to end slavery differed from Garrison's own. Such differences, he was certain, would damage the antislavery movement by injecting the taint of compromise into it—and they would also undermine Garrison's sense of himself, his trust in his own right judgment. Dupes, vandals, swindlers, apostates: these were the terms that Garrison cast at his foes within abolitionism.

Garrison's basic objection to an "abolition political party," then, was that it could never be tied to the true Christian values that he embodied and fostered. "It relies upon a majority" (*Liberator,* Mar. 11, 1842), he said, and majorities, and the factions that strive to control them, were frequently in error, guilty of deceit and moral compromise for the sake of political expediency. To side with the majority meant merging with evil, and Garrison predicted that the bartering of truth would happen in the Liberty party and, later, in similar parties as each sought to widen its appeal and make deals: "selfishness must necessarily be the controlling element of every political organization, struggling for supremacy where the loaves and fishes of office are to be obtained, with great power and patronage" (*Liberator,* Mar. 6, 1846). Why, Garrison asked, couldn't men and women recognize that "political action is not moral action—any more than a box on the ear is an argument" (*Liberator,* Mar. 13, 1846)?

Garrison recognized the immensity of slavery as a fact of American life, yet he had no program for abolitionists to follow to rid the nation of it, only a moral code they should espouse. But for him this was not a flaw; it was the foundation for everything: "Change the religious sentiment of the North on the subject of slavery and the political action of the North will instantly co-operate with it" (*Liberator,* Nov. 11, 1842). Garrison had a message for voters, and it was that they should not vote until they and their fellow citizens were spiritually revivified. In a May 9, 1844, address at the meeting of the American Anti-Slavery Society, he advised the society to "persuade northern voters, that the strongest political influence which they can wield for the overthrow of slavery, is, to cease sustaining the existing compact, by withdrawing from the polls, and calmly waiting for the time when a righteous government shall supercede [*sic*] the institutions of tyranny" (*Liberator,* May 24, 1844).

In the 1840s and 1850s Garrison's creed was "disunion," and he reaffirmed it in nearly every issue of *The Liberator:* "There must be no union with slaveholders, religiously or politically" (*Liberator,* Feb. 8, 1850; *Letters* 4:4). In both the September 9 and 16, 1853, issues of *The Liberator* he professed: "it is the truth—and the truth alone—which shall make this people free. Fettered by no sect or party, we will proclaim it, as God shall give us strength." From one point of view this was brave but futile counsel. Is truth all that is needed for reform, and not concrete steps that would change laws? What happens when people defy truth and persist in evildoing? But Garrison bristled at the notion that truth might be limited as an antislavery weapon. And he stressed that in fact his policy (if that is what it could be called) made practical sense. Disunion, he said often, had "virtually" occurred already, given the stark contrast between the free and slave states. Let this contrast be made explicit through disunion, and slavery would be doomed. The South, Garrison stated, would be unable to sustain its system without the national government to protect it from slave revolts. Nor could the South ever hope to regain fugitive slaves if it were separated from the free states and ruled by a different government. (See Documents 18, 27, and 30.)

Garrison was an extreme radical, a reformer in a nation he rejected. At the May 10, 1854, anniversary of the American Anti-Slavery Society meeting in the Broadway Universalist Church, Garrison trumpeted that he "had no Constitution, no Union, no country, no Bible, no God, aside from THE SLAVE" (*Liberator,* May 19, 1854). He did revere the Declaration of Independence ("all men are created equal," endowed with "certain unalienable rights") and cited it often along with the Bible. But he assailed the Constitution, which he believed was a heinous document that betrayed the Declaration and Bible alike; it was a bargain by whites with the devil at the expense of the "colored population" held in slavery.

The Founders had not referred to slavery as such in the Constitution, Garrison conceded, but they gave it guarantees that all of them acknowledged (*Life* 3:108–9). These included, above all, the "three-fifths clause," which inflated Southern representation in Congress by providing that three-fifths of all slaves would be added to the number of free persons in determining the population of a state. There were also a provision for mustering the militia to "suppress insurrections," a protection for twenty years of the foreign slave trade, and a requirement for the return of fugitive slaves. The best that one could say, Garrison noted, was that the Founders had tried, absurdly, "to make Slavery and Freedom mingle and cohere" (*Life* 3:141). But the truth was clear: the Constitution was "A SLAVEHOLDING COMPACT; it not only tolerates slavery on the soil, but sanctions, guards, and strengthens it" (*Liberator,* Apr. 24, 1846). (See also Document 10.)

The proslavery nature of the Constitution was validated for Garrison by the publication of James Madison's papers in the mid-1840s, which included accounts of the constitutional debates: "They demonstrate that the

William Lloyd Garrison *(center)* with his fellow abolitionists Wendell Phillips *(left)* and George Thompson *(right)* in 1851.

slave population were sacrificed on the altar of political expediency—with some tinges of conscience, it is true, but nevertheless sacrificed—on the maxim that the end sanctifies the means, and that it is right to do evil that good may come" *(Liberator,* Sept. 13, 1844). Garrison's colleague Wendell Phillips similarly maintained that the makers of the Constitution had intended to protect slavery, and he ridiculed anyone who said otherwise. Only a very bold person could propose "that the American people did not *believe* that slavery was alluded to in these so-called pro-slavery clauses! We hardly know of a more daring flight of genius in the whole range of modern fiction than this."[53]

Initially the important black abolitionist, orator, and writer Frederick Douglass—a former slave himself—held this position, too. But he jettisoned it when he feared that the slaves would be forsaken, without any prospect that the government would someday come to their aid. If one repudiated the Constitution, flouted the Union, and refused to vote, then what kind of concern was one actually showing for the enslaved?[54]

While Douglass judged America riddled with sin but redeemable, Garri-

[53] Wendell Phillips, *Review of Lysander Spooner's Essay on the Unconstitutionality of Slavery* (Boston, 1847), 32. See also Phillips on the Madison Papers, *Liberator,* Jan. 3, 1845, and Garrison on Spooner, *Liberator,* Aug. 22, 1845.
[54] Foner, *Life,* 2:155–56, 350–52, 467–80.

son's ally Phillips pronounced it corrupt, repellent. "I seek to be in this country like an alien, like a traveler" were his words to characterize his status in America. For which Charles Sumner reprimanded Phillips in a February 4, 1845, letter: "Take your place among citizens, & use all the weapons of a citizen in this just warfare." However loftily high-minded a Garrisonian like Phillips wished to sound, he nonetheless lived, Sumner stressed, in a nation governed by a Constitution: "What new home will you seek? Where, in the uttermost parts of the sea, shall you find a spot which is not desecrated by the bad passions of men, embodied in acts & forms of Government?"[55]

Douglass and Sumner argued cogently for *engaging* the Union, and most antislavery persons agreed with them in interpreting the Constitution positively, as a text that authorized political action against the South's hold over the government. The Massachusetts historian and jurist Richard Hildreth stated in 1854 that the clauses pertaining to slavery did not sanction it: "They contain no indorsement of the slave laws of the states; no recognition of slavery as a state institution; no express recognition even of the bare fact of the existence of slavery, and much less of its existence as an institution entitled to the favorable regard and protecting care of the Federal government."[56]

Even earlier, in 1837, in an important public letter to Henry Clay on the annexation of Texas to the United States, the esteemed Unitarian minister William Ellery Channing insisted that the Founders had quietly resolved to halt the spread of slavery: "It is worthy of remark, how anxious the framers of that instrument were to exclude from it the word 'slavery.' They were not willing that this feature of our social system should be betrayed in the construction of our free government." In *Emancipation,* published in 1840, Channing went further: slavery is "directly hostile to the fundamental principle on which all our institutions rest. No nation can admit an element at war with its vital central law without losing something of its stability. The idea of human rights is the grand distinction of our country. Our chief boast as a people is found in the fact that the toils,

---

[55] For Phillips, see Lillie Buffum Chace Wyman and Arthur Crawford Wyman, *Elizabeth Buffum Chace, 1806–1899,* 2 vols. (Boston: W. B. Clarke, 1914), 1:83; for Sumner, see Irving Bartlett, *Wendell and Ann Phillips: The Community of Reform, 1840–1880* (New York: Norton, 1979), 151. For further discussion of slavery and the Constitution, see William M. Wiecek, *The Sources of Antislavery Constitutionalism in America, 1760–1848* (Ithaca: Cornell University Press, 1977); and Paul Finkelman, *An Imperfect Union: Slavery, Federalism, and Comity* (Chapel Hill: University of North Carolina Press, 1981).

[56] Richard Hildreth, *Despotism in America: An Inquiry into the Nature, Results and Legal Basis of the Slaveholding System in the United States* (1854; reprint, New York: Kelley, 1970), 239–40.

sacrifices, heroic deeds of our fathers had for their end the establishment of these."[57]

As the writings by Sumner, Douglass, Hildreth, and Channing show, there was much resistance to the idea that the Constitution was proslavery. Yet in one sense Garrison's analysis of it was accurate: the South believed that the Constitution protected slavery, and once it inferred that this protection was gone, it would not remain in the Union. Garrison believed that there could be no permanent union with slaveholders, though the Constitution had presumed that there could be (*Life* 3:369, 455). At the May 25, 1853, New England Anti-Slavery Convention, Garrison declared: "To undertake to rescue the Constitution from the charge of pro-slavery, and make it coherently and logically anti-slavery, in the face of all the facts attending its adoption and administration, [is] as difficult as to blot the sun from the heavens at mid-day. . . . Did not Washington, and Jefferson, and Patrick Henry, and John Marshall, and their contemporaries, understand the Constitution?" (*Liberator*, June 3, 1853; see also *Liberator*, Oct. 23, 1857).

Garrison argued that antislavery interpretations of the Constitution revealed more about the desires of the present than about the realities of the past, and to an extent he was correct. Was it really true to say, as did Charles Sumner in a July 11, 1860, speech in New York City, that "at the beginning of our history, Slavery was *universally* admitted to be an evil" and that when the Constitution was written "*all* looked to the glad day" of abolition "as almost at hand"?[58] But it was a crucial moral and political fact that slavery was not named in the text of the Constitution itself, one that led Sumner and others to claim that the tools for change that the Constitution made possible, from laws to elections, could be deployed against slavery.

Because Garrison stressed that the Constitution was proslavery, he was oddly appealing to the same slaveholding South that hated his rabid abolitionism. John A. Campbell, a lawyer in Alabama and later a Supreme Court justice, remarked in a November 20, 1847, letter to John C. Calhoun, South Carolina statesman and political philosopher: "Garrison and Phillips say that the Constitution of the U.S. is a pro-slavery con-

---

[57] William Ellery Channing, *Works* (Boston: American Unitarian Association, 1888), 780, 849. Channing was a much-admired Unitarian minister and scholar, and his commentaries on the slavery question were influential. See Andrew Delbanco, *William Ellery Channing: An Essay on the Liberal Spirit in America* (Cambridge: Harvard University Press, 1981).

[58] Charles Sumner, *Works*, 15 vols. (Boston: Lee and Shepard, 1880), 5:201–2. On the antislavery career and contributions of this important Republican senator, see David B. Donald, *Charles Sumner and the Coming of the Civil War* (New York: Knopf, 1960).

tract—containing powerful and stringent securities for the slaveholder. Phillips has written quite an able pamphlet [*The Constitution: A Pro-Slavery Document,* 1844] to prove this—a pamphlet we might circulate to great advantage excluding a few paragraphs." The Georgia lawyer and statesman Robert Toombs touched on this point in a February 27, 1850, speech in Congress: the Garrisonians' "line of policy is the fairest, most just, most honest and defensible of all the enemies of our institutions," for they admitted "some, at least, of the constitutional obligations to protect slavery."[59]

Garrison replied that the resemblance was false. He loathed the Constitution because slavery was evil; the South honored it because its spokesmen assumed that slavery was a positive good that the Union must keep secure (*Liberator,* July 18, 1851; Mar. 12, 1852). But Garrison was united with Campbell and Toombs in perceiving an essential strife between slavery and freedom, the South and the Union as a whole, and in claiming that no compromise or midway reform was possible.

Garrison's most shocking staging of defiance against the Constitution, and the most potent instance of his antipolitical, moral perfectionist strategy, unfolded at the July 4, 1854, outdoor meeting of the Massachusetts Anti-Slavery Society in Framingham, Massachusetts. He always possessed a great sense of theater and was keenly aware of how he could effectively publicize his fortitude and scorn of his enemies. With full awareness of the irony, Garrison held this meeting on the Fourth of July, the day on which America celebrated its independence and proclaimed its ideal of equality for all. And it occurred shortly after both the return of the fugitive Anthony Burns to Richmond, Virginia, where he was manacled and jailed, and the passage of the Kansas-Nebraska Act, which opened the western territories for slavery.

The platform for the Framingham meeting was draped in black crepe. Behind the rostrum were hung the insignia of Virginia, which was decorated with ribbons of triumph, and, next to it, the seal of the Commonwealth of Massachusetts, inscribed with the words "Redeem Massachusetts" and decked in "the crepe of servitude." Two flags flew above the rostrum, with the names "Kansas" and "Nebraska." In the background was the American flag, upside down and bordered in black. After his introductory comments to the several thousand in attendance (one of whom was Henry David Thoreau, who lectured at this same meeting on

---

[59] For Campbell, see J. Franklin Jameson, ed., *Correspondence of John C. Calhoun,* Annual Report of the American Historical Association, 1899 (Washington, D.C., 1900), 1143; for Toombs, see Ulrich B. Phillips, *The Life of Robert Toombs* (New York: Macmillan, 1913), 76.

"slavery in Massachusetts"), Garrison read from Scripture and then closed his Bible and lit a candle.

He told the audience that he would "now proceed to perform an action which would be testimony of his own soul, to all present, of the estimation in which he held the proslavery laws and deeds of the nation." Garrison burned copies of the Fugitive Slave Law and the documents that ordered Burns back to Virginia, in each instance asking the audience to answer "Amen" in line with the formula in Deuteronomy (27:15–26). Finally he burned a copy of the Constitution, alleging as he held it high that it was "a covenant with death, an agreement with hell. . . . So perish all compromises with tyranny," to which the audience uttered "Amen" as Garrison ground the ashes under his heel.

The seizure of fugitive slaves on Northern soil, the controversy about (and fierce fighting in) the Kansas and Nebraska territories in the mid-1850s, the election of the pro-South Democratic candidate for president, James Buchanan, in 1856, the Dred Scott decision in 1857, and John Brown's raid on the arsenal in Harpers Ferry in 1859 accelerated the growing crisis over slavery that Garrison in his own way dramatized here. It climaxed in November 1860, when Abraham Lincoln defeated Stephen Douglas and two other minor candidates in the presidential election; he received only 39 percent of the popular vote and not a single electoral vote in the Southern slave states. His victory and the rise of the antislavery Republican party signaled to the South that slavery would not survive in the Union. South Carolina seceded from the Union on December 20, 1860, and six more states soon did the same. On April 12, 1861, a little more than a month after Lincoln's inauguration, Confederate forces attacked and captured Fort Sumter in Charleston, South Carolina, harbor. Four more states seceded to join the Confederacy, and by July full-scale battles were under way in Virginia.

Garrison was a pacifist and nonresister, but in July 1861 he declared his support for the Northern cause and in December he provided *The Liberator* with a new motto: "Proclaim Liberty Throughout All the Land, to All the Inhabitants of the Land." It was indeed liberty for slaves that he demanded, not solely the triumph of the North's armies. In an editorial published in the midst of the war, Garrison wrote of his burning of the Constitution that "no act of ours do we regard with more conscientious approval or higher satisfaction, none do we submit more confidently to the tribunal of Heaven and the moral verdict of mankind." If the North ended the war without abolishing slavery, he said he would set fire to the Constitution again (*Liberator,* Apr. 24, 1863).

GARRISON'S PUNITIVE STYLE: THE LANGUAGE OF ABOLITION

Past and present critics have cited the burning of the Constitution to prove that Garrison was fanatical about his own virtue and self-glorifying in his displays of it. But perhaps the more frequent critique of and complaint about him is that he employed an obnoxious, insulting form of language — that he spoke and wrote in dogmatic, divisive, unbearable ways.

Garrison said what he meant. For example: the Constitution "is an evil instrument, to be regarded with abhorrence by all good men. The Union, erected as it is on the prostrated bodies of three millions of people, deserves to be held in eternal execration, and dashed to pieces like a potter's vessel" (*Liberator,* Nov. 10, 1848). But it was Garrison's indictment of individuals that incensed his contemporaries. Of slaveholders, he concluded: "we do not acknowledge them to be within the pale of Christianity, of republicanism, of humanity." Yet Garrison asserted that such language was simply a controlled reflection of truth: "this we say dispassionately, and not for the sake of using strong language" (*Life* 3:33; see also 3:50).

Garrison targeted prominent persons. He described the acclaimed historian George Bancroft, who had backed the Democrat James Polk for president, as "an ambitious, unprincipled time-serving demagogue, who would sell his country as Judas sold his Lord" (*Liberator,* June 14, 1844). In a March 16, 1849, letter to Kentucky Senator Henry Clay, reprinted in *The Liberator,* Garrison pummeled Clay for compromising with slavery and serving the South's interests: "Truly, you are a pitiable object; the sands of your life are nearly run out; years are pressing heavily upon you; yet no sign of repentance do you give for the countless wrongs and outrages you have inflicted, on an unoffending, weak and helpless race. You have been an awful curse to them, to your country, to the world. You have long stood at the head of as cruel a conspiracy against God and man as was ever contrived" (*Life* 3:609). Garrison also showered abuse on Daniel Webster, the renowned lawyer, statesman, and Massachusetts senator who had supported the Compromise of 1850: he was "lick spittle of the slaveholding oligarchy" (*Liberator,* July 26, 1850). (See also Document 22.)

Garrison had decided that the sin of slavery mandated direct terms, and when he started *The Liberator* he seemed to trust that once uninformed Americans were verbally jarred from their complacency, they would cease propping up a slaveholding Union: "The people, at large, are astonishingly ignorant of the horrors of slavery. Let information be circulated among them as prodigally as the light of heaven, and they cannot long act and reason as they now do" (*Liberator,* July 30, 1831). "The language of reform," he said, "is always severe—unavoidably severe, and simply because crime has grown monstrous, and endurance has passed its bounds. . . . *If I have exceeded the bounds of moderation, the monstrous turpitude of the times has transported me"* (*Letters* 1:229–30, 439; 3:412, 457). When America failed to heed his voice, Garrison did not moderate it but, if anything, held forth with still greater ferocity. (See Document 18.)

Garrison chose Jesus as his model—the wrathful Jesus who expelled moneychangers from the temple and flailed the Pharisees. (See Document 12.) As he remarked in rebuttal to an antagonist, "with gospel simplicity and plainness, I charge you with being a deceitful and bigoted man. This will sound harshly in your ear—but the Lord judge between us" (*Liberator,* Oct. 27, 1837). Garrison felt that his language was simple and pure: it was language that Christ himself would use, and the problem or fault thus lay not with the speaker but with hearers who were sinful. "My testimonies must be delivered in plain, unequivocal language," he stated, "let who will be offended; so shall reformation advance, and my own soul obtain perfect satisfaction" (*Liberator,* Apr. 26, 1839).

This language was fused with Garrison's conception of what it meant to be a reformer. As he declared to William Ladd, the founder in 1828 of the American Peace Society:

> You do not understand the philosophy of reform. If you would make progress, you must create opposition; if you would promote peace on earth, array the father against the son, and the mother against the daughter; if you would save your reputation, lose it. It is a gospel paradox, but nevertheless true—the more peaceable a man becomes, after the pattern of Christ, the more he is inclined to make a disturbance, to be aggressive, to "turn the world upside down." (*Liberator,* Nov. 23, 1838)

Garrison was not alone in brandishing extreme language. In an 1835 message to the state legislature, Governor George McDuffie of South Carolina charged that abolitionists were "felons" and "enemies of the human race" who should be dispatched to "death without benefit of clergy" for interfering with slavery—an institution that, rather than being a "political evil," was *"the cornerstone of our republican edifice"* (cited in *Life* 2:62). James Henry Hammond, slaveholder and statesman from South Carolina, decreed in an August 19, 1835, open letter to M. M. Noah, editor of the New York *Evening Star:*

The Northern fanatics must not expect to find in us the unrepresented colonial subjects of an arrogant monarchy. . . . We do not believe that all or perhaps a majority of the Northern people favour the views of these Incendiaries but what does it boot us if they do not so long as they give them an asylum from which to hurl their murderous missiles. These men must be silenced in but one way—*Terror—Death.* The non-slaveholding states must pass laws denying protection to them & yielding them up to demand to those whose laws and whose rights they have violated.[60]

The Alabama jurist Joseph W. Lesesne likewise complained in a September 12, 1847, letter to John Calhoun:

Their [the abolitionists'] conduct has been most atrocious. No language is strong enough to denounce it. The shameless impudence with which they have trampled the Constitution under their feet, and their mean and despicable contrivances to deprive us of our Slave property ought to be held up to the scorn of the whole Union. Not half has been said on the subject that ought to be.[61]

Garrison professed that his language was made righteous by truths that the barbarous language of the slaveholders profaned. As early as June 1830, in a letter to the editor of the Newburyport *Herald,* he observed: "Why so vehement? so unyielding? so severe? Because the times and the cause demand vehemence. An immense iceberg, larger and more impenetrable than any which floats in the arctic ocean, is to be dissolved, and a little *extra heat* is not only pardonable, but absolutely necessary" (*Life* 1:188, 335–36). A quarter-century afterward, he drove home his intention again in an indictment of sinful slaveholders: "My aim is to stain the character and render infamous the conduct of the slaveholder, throughout the civilized world. I am for his immediate exclusion from the professedly Christian church, and from every honorable position in the State" (*Liberator,* Nov. 16, 1855; *Letters* 4:361).

Such language prompted William Ellery Channing, Richard Hildreth, Charles Sumner, Arthur and Lewis Tappan, James Birney, and many others to accuse Garrison of setting back emancipation and fomenting slave insurrections. The legal scholar Francis Wayland of Brown University, in response to Garrison's early editorials, warned him: "The tendency of your paper is to produce rebellion. Its attitude to slave-owners is menacing and vindictive. The tendency of your remarks is to preju-

[60] Hammond, cited in Elizabeth Merritt, *James Henry Hammond, 1807–1864,* in *Johns Hopkins University Studies* 41 (1923), 32.

[61] Lesesne in Jameson, *Correspondence,* 1133.

dice their minds against a cool discussion of the subject." In a discourse on the slavery question, delivered in 1839 in Hartford, Connecticut, the Congregational clergyman and theologian Horace Bushnell, while not naming Garrison, no doubt had him in mind when he recommended that abolitionist societies disband, for their belligerent language only served to alienate the South: "noise and combination is not always power."[62]

A friend and admirer of Garrison's, the transcendentalist educator and philosopher A. Bronson Alcott, recorded in his February 14, 1850, journal entry that Garrison "persists, and must, in precipitating every man he meets headforemost into the pit of his indignation, and sets his conscience forthwith to fork the poor victim into the flames raging in his own veins, impaling his prey there most unmercifully, as he were doing Satan's behest in the Lord's name." To the proslavery sympathizer Charles Hodge, in *The Bible Argument on Slavery* (1860), "the idea of inducing the Southern slaveholder to emancipate his slaves by denunciation, is about as rational as to expect the sovereigns of Europe to grant free institutions, by calling them tyrants and robbers."[63]

It is true that Garrison's language can seem overblown, exaggerated, and repetitive. As a speaker and writer, he was sometimes insufferable, particularly when he directed his fire toward his former associates. The tragic dimension of the abolitionist community centered in Garrison's family and friends is the list of friends whom he rejected, including Gerrit Smith, Garrison's *Liberator* partner Isaac Knapp, the black abolitionist Frederick Douglass, and Nathaniel P. Rogers, editor of the *Herald of Freedom,* published in Concord, New Hampshire. Even Wendell Phillips was judged an apostate. He and Garrison were close comrades for decades but they grew estranged in the 1860s over differences about Lincoln's wartime policies, as Phillips savaged the president and clamored for extreme antislavery measures while Garrison, though somewhat critical of Lincoln too, counseled patience and sympathy for the president's complex political and military situation. Branded a traitor to the community he had dwelled within, Phillips was permitted to return to the fold only toward the end of Garrison's life.

Garrison said he was not an excommunicator: these men had withdrawn from genuine abolitionism and had suffered isolation as a result of

[62] Wayland, cited in Russel B. Nye, *William Lloyd Garrison and the Humanitarian Reformers* (Boston: Little, Brown, 1955), 51; and Horace Bushnell, "A Discourse on the Slavery Question," delivered in the North Church, Hartford, Jan. 10, 1839 (Hartford, 1839), 29.

[63] Alcott, *Journals*, ed. Odell Shepard (Boston: Little, Brown, 1938), 225; and Hodge, in E. N. Elliott, ed., *Cotton Is King and Pro-Slavery Arguments* (Augusta, Ga.: Pritchard, Abbott, and Loomis, 1860), 843.

what they had done (*Liberator,* Aug. 12, 1842; May 26, 1843). They had brought pain upon themselves by leaving the community; they had lost faith; they were at fault. As Garrison observed in a September 13, 1837, letter to the evangelical reformer Lewis Tappan, *"true-hearted abolitionists never will quarrel with each other.* . . . Let the blame rest on the heads of those who have virtually abandoned our cause, if they ever belonged to it" (*Letters* 2:300).

From Garrison's perspective, he was not violating any code of fair play when he condemned slaveholders, nor was he being cruel when he assailed Douglass and Phillips: sinners and traitors to the cause got what they deserved. As Garrison saw it, he was a vehicle for truth and named the deeds that others had wrongly done but were unable to face in themselves. Except for the error of supporting colonization, to which he confessed early in his career, Garrison seems never to have admitted that he made mistakes in policy or in verbal tactics himself. He believed he was right, and consistently so.

But it was more than his self-conception that Garrison could not allow to be shaken. He needed friendship and praised its rewards, yet he did not wish to be personally indebted to others. In sacrificing and casting out friends, Garrison seems at times to have been fearfully determined not to be dependent on anyone. He was fortunate in the number of patrons, mentors, and friends he enjoyed, but connected to his closeness to them was his dread of being exposed to their will and power over him.

But would Garrison have been more successful had he been more accommodating in his tone of voice? Did he slow the progress of the cause he represented because of his harsh language toward slaveholders and acerbic behavior toward antislavery allies? Perhaps he should have been less abusive and more willing to compromise, yet there is no proof that Garrison slowed down reforms by slave owners of their system: he "did not retard emancipation. . . . There was nothing to retard."[64] It was not the *kind* of discussion of slavery that Garrison fostered, but any discussion at all, that proslavery forces were concerned about. As Harriet Martineau said in *Society in America* (1837), the South "requires nothing short of a dead silence upon the subject of human rights."[65] Replying to the accusation that he had "retarded" antislavery, Garrison exclaimed: "What an idiotic absurdity it is to say that earnest, persistent, uncompromising moral opposition to a system of boundless immorality is the way to

---

[64] Dumond, *Antislavery,* 173. See also Michael C. C. Adams, *Fighting for Defeat: Union Military Failure in the East, 1861–1865* (1978; reprint, Lincoln: University of Nebraska Press, 1992), 4.

[65] Martineau, *Society,* 201.

strengthen it; and that the way to abolish such a system is to say nothing about it!" (*Liberator,* Apr. 23, 1858).

The following resolution was passed at a Southern mass meeting in 1836: "Freedom of speech and press does not imply a moral right to freely discuss the subject of slavery . . . a question too nearly allied to the vital interests of the slave-holding states to admit of public disputation." A writer for the Raleigh, North Carolina, *Star* stated: "The institutions of the South relative to slavery are unalterable, firm, fixed and decided. Her stand has been taken. Cool, deliberate reflection justifies her position. IT WILL BE OCCUPIED TO THE LAST EXTREMITY" (Feb. 2, 1837). Senator Calhoun in 1837 objected to abolition petitions in Congress by noting that "all usurpations should be resisted in the beginning; and those who would not do so were prepared to be slaves themselves."[66]

Calhoun introduced resolutions, the so-called Gag Rules, which the Senate rejected but which the House of Representatives passed, that forbade the reading of antislavery petitions in Congress, sent there in great numbers by the American Anti-Slavery Society. Former President John Quincy Adams, who had become a member of the House in 1831, argued in reply that Calhoun was denying the rights to practice free speech and to petition the government, and the Gag Rules were repealed in 1844. But to Calhoun there simply could be *no* discussion of slavery: it lay outside the boundaries of free speech. Once statesmen, writers, anyone, started to debate it and set abolition looming, he warned, then the liberties of whites in the South would deteriorate and collapse. The persons in bondage would be white as well as black.

Many powerful Northerners concurred with Calhoun in demanding that slavery be left alone, and this point needs to be remembered in evaluating Garrison's notorious, slashing verbal tactics. In May 1835 a prominent New York merchant told Garrison's comrade Samuel J. May: "We cannot afford, sir, to let you and your associates succeed in your endeavor to overthrow slavery. . . . We mean, sir, to put you Abolitionists down, — by fair means if we can, by foul means if we must." In the words of the Ohio lawyer, legislator, and Free Soil leader Albert Gallatin Riddle: "The spirit of freedom and justice that finally extirpated slavery at the South had

---

[66] Southern mass meeting, cited in Nye, *Garrison,* 100; Raleigh *Star,* cited in Guion Griffis Johnson, *Ante-Bellum North Carolina* (Chapel Hill: University of North Carolina Press, 1937), 564; and Calhoun, in *Union and Liberty: The Political Philosophy of John C. Calhoun,* ed. Ross M. Lence (Indianapolis: Liberty, 1992), 464–65. On Calhoun, see Irving H. Bartlett, *John C. Calhoun: A Biography* (New York: Norton, 1993).

first to make a conquest of the North, every foot of which in 1835 was pro-slavery."[67]

It was not Garrison's language that forestalled abolition, but, instead, the challenge of abolition itself to the racial order in the South and the North and to "capitalist complicity in slavery" and "profitable economic ties between slave masters and allied merchants and manufacturers."[68] (See Document 9.) Textile merchants in Massachusetts, for example, did not want the slavery question agitated; they depended on the cotton crop and were enjoying their prosperity. The Unitarian clergyman and author Edward Everett Hale recalled that in Boston from 1820 to 1840, "there was plenty of money, and the rich men of Boston really meant that here should be a model and ideal city. The country was prosperous; they were prosperous, and they looked forward to a noble future."[69] When Garrison started his Boston-based newspaper, he thus was attacking both the institution of slavery and the conditions of life that benefited privileged classes in his own city.

Similarly, in New York, merchants made money from slavery, selling equipment and luxury items to the owners of large, lucrative plantations. Abram J. Dittenhoefer, born in Charleston, South Carolina, but a lawyer, foe of slavery, and supporter of the Republican party, said that New York City in the 1840s and 1850s "was virtually an annex of the South, the New York merchants having extensive and very profitable business relations with the merchants south of the Mason and Dixon line."[70] In the 1830s a legislative committee in Alabama estimated that one-third of the price of cotton went to New York merchants; and in the 1850s, it was reported that merchants received 40 cents of every dollar paid for Southern cotton. Other reports showed that during the 1840s and 1850s, the South annually purchased tens of millions of dollars of merchandise from New York firms; one account tabbed the figure for total business from the five major cotton states at $200 million per year.[71]

New York City in the 1850s, stated the clergyman and editor Lyman Abbott, was "anti-agitation" on slavery: "King Cotton ruled the market

[67] May, *Recollections*, 128; and Riddle, *Recollections of War Times: Reminiscences of Men and Events in Washington, 1860–1865* (New York: Putnam's, 1895), 38.

[68] Louis S. Gerteis, *Morality and Utility in American Antislavery Reform* (Chapel Hill: University of North Carolina Press, 1987), xi.

[69] Edward Everett Hale, *A New England Boyhood* (New York: Cassell, 1893), xiii.

[70] Morris U. Schappes, ed., *A Documentary History of the Jews in the United States, 1654–1875* (New York: Citadel, 1950), 395.

[71] Philip S. Foner, *Business and Slavery: The New York Merchants and the Irrepressible Conflict* (Chapel Hill: University of North Carolina Press, 1941), 7.

place, the press, the schools, the churches." William Howard Russell, correspondent for the London *Times,* remarked in July 1861: "The South believed New York was with them. . . . I remember hearing it said by Southerners in Washington, that it was very likely New York would go out of the Union!"[72]

Bankers, merchants, and many others, including the proprietors of Northern resorts, benefited from the business and patronage of Southerners. Garrison's language thus was harsh and uncompromising because it was clear to him that the North's complicity in upholding slavery was unmistakable and, furthermore, that it was deepening year by year as profits from slavery increased. By 1821 cotton was the leading American export, 35 percent of the total; by 1850, cotton amounted to 60 percent of total exports. This indicates the extent of its role in Northern manufacturing, banking, shipping, and trade. From 1830 to 1860, the world's cotton consumption increased 5 percent annually. In 1826, the output of cloth from the mills in Massachusetts was 23 million yards; by 1860, it exceeded 400 million yards. For many in the North, there was *no* proper way to criticize slavery; to them, the less said about slavery, the better for everybody reaping dividends from it.[73]

In a powerful sermon, "Our Blameworthiness," on January 4, 1861, the influential New York City clergyman Henry Ward Beecher observed: "We clothe ourselves with the cotton which the slave tills. Is he scorched? is he lashed? does he water the crop with his sweat and tears? It is you and I that wear the shirt and consume the luxury. Our looms and our factories are largely built on the slave's bones."[74]

Garrison had been making this argument for decades, and more caustically. To him, "call[ing] things by their right names" was "to use neither hard nor improper language," however much these names unnerved businessmen and riled racists. Slavery was a sin that language could not even express: "The whole scope of the English language is inadequate to describe the horrors and impieties of slavery, and the transcendent wickedness of those who sustain this bloody system." Slavery *paid,*

---

[72] Abbott, *Silhouettes of My Contemporaries* (New York: Doubleday, Page, 1921), 296; and Russell, *My Diary, North and South,* ed. Eugene H. Berwanger (1863; reprint, New York: Knopf, 1988), 222.

[73] Holman Hamilton, *Prologue to Conflict: The Crisis and Compromise of 1850* (1964; reprint, New York: Norton, 1966), 5; Harold D. Woodman, *King Cotton and His Retainers: Financing and Marketing the Cotton Crop of the South, 1800–1925* (Lexington: University of Kentucky Press, 1968), 152–53; Thomas H. O'Connor, *Lords of the Loom: The Cotton Whigs and the Coming of the Civil War* (New York: Scribner's, 1968), 47; Levine, *Half Slave,* 21; and Alexander Keyssar, *Out of Work: The First Century of Unemployment in Massachusetts* (New York: Cambridge University Press, 1986), 22–23.

[74] Henry Ward Beecher, *Patriotic Addresses* (Boston: Pilgrim, 1887), 257.

Garrison emphasized, and it exploited persons different in skin color from whites. Critics of the abolitionists' harsh language "do not regard the negro race as equal to the Anglo-Saxon; hence it is impossible for them to resent a wrong or an outrage done to a black man as they would to a white."[75] As Garrison's associate Oliver Johnson said, the obstacle was that "slaves were black": if "the slaves had been made white, all excuses for slavery would have been overthrown, and the whole people would have risen up as one man to demand its instant abolition. . . . Mr. Garrison's primary fault was his belief in the absolute humanity of the negro."[76]

GARRISON, DOUGLASS, AND RACIAL PREJUDICE

Garrison is not always given credit for his defense of equal rights and blows against prejudice. His broken friendship with Frederick Douglass has triggered charges that he was insincere and hypocritical, not the enemy of bigotry that his egalitarian rhetoric suggested he was. One scholar has said that Garrison's attacks on Douglass were perhaps his "least defensible act" and has added that he, like white abolitionists generally, reneged on commitments to equality.[77] But Garrison's quarrel with Douglass had less to do with race than with Douglass's unwillingness to remain loyal to Garrison's opinions—something that always stunned Garrison, whether the person was black or white. Their relationship was troubled and Garrison was imperfect in his dealings with blacks. But in the antebellum period, Garrison was far ahead of most whites and more enlightened than the majority of abolitionists.

Douglass had escaped from slavery in Maryland in September 1838 and had soon become an avid reader of *The Liberator*—"my meat and my drink." When reading it, he said,

> my soul was set all on fire. Its sympathy for my brethren in bonds—its scathing denunciations of slaveholders—its faithful exposures of slavery—and its powerful attacks upon the upholders of the institution—sent a thrill of joy through my soul, such as I had never felt before![78]

[75]William Lloyd Garrison, *Selections from the Writings and Speeches* (Boston: Wallcut, 1852), 121, 122, 132.

[76]Oliver Johnson, *W. L. Garrison and His Times* (1881; reprint, Miami: Mnemosyne, 1969), 36–37.

[77]Louis Filler, *The Crusade against Slavery, 1830–1860* (New York: Harper and Row, 1960), 206.

[78]Douglass, *The Narrative and Selected Writings*, ed. Michael Meyer (New York: Modern Library, 1984), 119.

The young Frederick Douglass escaped from slavery in 1838 and became an agent and speaker for
the American Anti-Slavery Society.

Douglass met Garrison and heard him speak at the annual meeting of
the Bristol Anti-Slavery Society, held in New Bedford, Massachusetts, on
August 9, 1841. On the next day, Douglass joined Garrison and forty
others on a steamboat trip to Nantucket, where another antislavery
meeting was to take place. During the trip itself, Douglass was heartened
by the protest that Garrison mounted against segregation aboard the
vessel. At the Nantucket meeting, Douglass spoke for the first time in
public, with Garrison following him. (See Document 16.)

It was at this same meeting that Douglass was invited to become an
antislavery lecturer for the Massachusetts Anti-Slavery Society.[79] During
the next four years, Douglass was a speaker for the society, often
traveling with Wendell Phillips; and both Phillips and Garrison wrote
prefatory remarks for Douglass's *Narrative,* first printed in May 1845 by
the Anti-Slavery Society in Boston. The *Narrative* described in vivid detail

[79] Benjamin Quarles, *Frederick Douglass* (1948; reprint, New York: Atheneum, 1969),
12–14.

Douglass's childhood and life as a young man in slavery, his work for various masters, his determined efforts to educate himself, and, finally, his escape to the North and the profound inspiration he drew from reading Garrison's paper. In 1846 he and Garrison lectured together in Great Britain, solidifying contacts between American and British abolitionists, and the two of them spoke on an antislavery tour the following August in New York, Pennsylvania, and Ohio. (See Document 20.)

The first sign of Garrison's worries about Douglass occurred when Douglass announced plans to start his own newspaper, which he had formulated during his long residence in England, Ireland, and Scotland from 1845 to 1847. In a July 23, 1847, editorial, Garrison summarized the difficulties that Douglass would face and the damage he would cause the movement if he introduced yet another antislavery paper into an already crowded field where financial backing and readership were limited. Yet Garrison nonetheless urged support of *The North Star* (*Liberator*, Jan. 5, 1849), as Douglass's paper was called, and printed extracts from it in *The Liberator*.

Garrison also wished Douglass well when *The North Star* became *Frederick Douglass's Paper* in 1851. But by then he was emphasizing his disagreement with Douglass's new, antislavery interpretation of the Constitution (*Liberator*, July 4, 1851). And to hammer home his point, he published a letter from Reverend Samuel May (a cousin of Samuel J. May) that slammed Douglass's alliance "with slaveholders and slave-traders as voluntary supporters of one Constitution and Government." It was not the rival paper as much as the shift in Douglass's thinking about the Constitution that thrust him and Garrison apart. The final break came at the meeting of the American Anti-Slavery Society in May 1851, when Douglass repudiated Garrison's proslavery interpretation of the Constitution.[80]

Now Garrison's anger and unfairness really surfaced. In a September 23, 1853, editorial, "Frederick Douglass and His Paper," Garrison said that, contrary to reports, he was not offended by Douglass's paper or his interpretation of the Constitution. Rather, the problem lay in Douglass's attitude: "he is an altered man in his temper and spirit; the success of his paper he makes paramount to principle; and the curse of worldly ambition is evidently the secret of his alienation" (see also Nov. 18, 1853, and, especially, "The Mask Entirely Removed," Dec. 16, 1853). But in truth the issues of policy and personality were linked. To Garrison, obsessed with loyalty, Douglass's paper and reversal on the Constitution resulted

---

[80] Thomas, *Liberator*, 476; and William S. McFeely, *Frederick Douglass* (New York: Norton, 1991), 168–69. McFeely's book is the standard biography, but David W. Blight, *Frederick Douglass' Civil War* (Baton Rouge: Louisiana State University Press, 1989), should also be consulted.

from ambition. He believed that Douglass was preocuppied with advancing his own career.

When Douglass's *Narrative* was expanded and published as *My Bondage and My Freedom* in 1855, Garrison's preface was omitted. And in this second book Douglass detailed the shabby treatment he had received from white abolitionists and the prohibitions that his white friends had imposed on him:

> During the first three or four months, my speeches were almost exclusively made up of narrations of my own personal experience as a slave. "Let us have the facts," said the people. So also said Friend George Foster, who always wished to pin me down to my simple narrative. "Give us the facts," said Collins, "we will take care of the philosophy." Just here arose some embarrassment. It was impossible for me to repeat the same old story month after month, and to keep up my interest in it. It was new to the people, it is true, but it was an old story to me; and to go through with it night after night, was a task altogether too mechanical for my nature. "Tell your story, Frederick," would whisper my then revered friend, William Lloyd Garrison, as I stepped upon the platform. I could not always obey, for I was now reading and thinking.[81]

Douglass felt that his white colleagues in Garrison's group imprisoned him: he was to parrot "the facts" and not presume to move beyond them. Douglass's irony is restrained but piercing—"my *then* revered friend, William Lloyd Garrison"; and it intimates his yearning for liberation—"I could not always obey." The whispering Garrison whom Douglass depicts dimly apprehended the coercive nature of his advice, and he shied from making public the nature of the control he exercised over the black man. He could not grant Douglass autonomy, a voice of his own, for this would mean accepting the idea of disagreement. When the moral issues were so clear, it seemed to him, how could there be any disagreement about them?

Such conduct toward Douglass hardly shows Garrison in an attractive light, but not exactly because he failed to take a black person seriously. Race did not count, disagreement did. Garrison's conception of himself as the intrepid pioneer of abolition, the man valiant enough to withstand mobs, the epitome of good conscience whose truths others could not accept—all of this roused Garrison to be indignant, rigid, and narrow-minded in the face of *any* resistance.

[81] Frederick Douglass, *My Bondage and My Freedom* (1855; reprint, New York: Dover, 1969), 361.

Racism permeated the North: Garrison knew this and, to his credit, repeatedly criticized it. The "stigma of color and slavery vastly increased the distance between Negroes and white people," and it dragged down efforts at integration.[82] In 1830 the free black population in the North was about 125,000; most were unskilled or semiskilled workers living in or near major cities. By 1860 the number was 250,000, and they were subjected to discrimination in every aspect of their lives. Blacks were mistreated and segregated in courts, schools, churches, public transportation, housing, prisons, hospitals, cemeteries. Ohio (1804), Indiana (1831), Illinois (1813), Iowa (1839), and Michigan (1827) passed laws designed to curb black immigration. And New Jersey (1807), Connecticut (1818), and Pennsylvania (1838) stripped political rights from blacks. By 1860, only Massachusetts, Maine, New Hampshire, Vermont, and Rhode Island allowed blacks the same right to vote as whites, and these states accounted for a mere 6 percent of the North's free black population.[83]

In his study of the United States, based on a May 1831–February 1832 visit, the French aristocrat and public official Alexis de Tocqueville concluded that "slavery recedes, but the prejudice to which it has been given birth is immovable," for it was sealed by tradition and skin color. Once Northern blacks achieved legal freedom, they suffered insult, injury, and intolerance. The black abolitionist and orator Samuel Ringgold Ward described Northern injustice toward blacks as "a cherished, defended keystone, a cornerstone of American faith." Harriet Jacobs, who had been held in slavery in North Carolina, reported in *Incidents in the Life of a Slave Girl* (1861) that during her time as a servant in New York, she was "eyed with a defiant look, as if my presence were a contamination."[84]

The former slave Austin Steward reviewed in the mid-1850s the bias that black persons had experienced in the North and the Midwest: "In all parts of this nominally free Republic [blacks] are looked down upon by the white population as being little above the brute creation; or, as belonging to some separate class of degraded beings, too deficient in intellect to provide for their own wants, and must therefore depend on the superior

---

[82] Filler, *Crusade*, 144.

[83] William H. and Jane H. Pease, *They Who Would Be Free: Blacks' Search for Freedom, 1830–1861* (New York: Atheneum, 1974), 27; Eric Foner, *Reconstruction: America's Unfinished Revolution, 1863–1877* (New York: Harper and Row, 1988), 25–26; and Donald G. Nieman, *Promises to Keep: African-Americans and the Constitutional Order, 1776 to the Present* (New York: Oxford University Press, 1991), 28.

[84] Alexis de Tocqueville, *Democracy in America*, 2 vols. (1835, 1840; reprint, New York: Knopf, 1945), 1:373–74; Ward, cited in Charles H. Nichols, *Many Thousands Gone: The Ex-Slaves' Account of Their Bondage and Freedom* (1963; reprint, Bloomington: Indiana University Press, 1969), 145; and Jacobs, *Incidents in the Life of a Slave Girl*, ed. Jean Fagan Yellin (1861; reprint, Cambridge: Harvard University Press, 1987), 176.

ability of their oppressors, to take care of them." Another former slave, James L. Smith, recalled in his postwar autobiography (1881) that while he traveled through Connecticut the people acted "as though they had never seen a colored man before; they would shake hands with me and then look at their hands to see if I had left any black on them."[85]

Sometimes blacks were so embittered that they called for emigration to Africa, the Caribbean, or Central America. In a letter that Garrison published in *The Liberator* in May 1852, the black editor and writer Martin Delany judged that the situation in Massachusetts and the nation was hopeless: "The majority of white men cannot see why colored men cannot be satisfied with their condition in Massachusetts—what they desire more than the *granted* right of citizenship. Blind selfishness on the one hand, and deep prejudice on the other, will not permit them to understand that we desire the *exercise* and *enjoyment* of these rights, as well as the *name* of their possession."[86] Garrison could no more accept blacks' plans for emigration than he could whites' schemes for black colonization. But he understood the impulse, for he was acutely aware of the many restrictions that Northern blacks encountered.

Garrison and the abolitionists he led aimed to end slavery *and* caste. Whatever their belief in racial, ethnic, regional, and national differences, they affirmed the equality of all persons, and they did so in the midst of popular and scientific anti-Negro opinion.[87]

The Garrisonians led in efforts to alleviate the restrictions of racial caste, as the Declaration of Sentiments that Garrison wrote at the founding of the American Anti-Slavery Society bore witness: "All persons of color who possess the qualifications which are demanded of others, ought to be admitted forthwith to the enjoyment of the same privileges, and the exercise of the same prerogatives, as others. . . . The paths of preferment, of wealth, and of intelligence, should be opened as widely to them as to persons of a white complexion. . . . The colored population of the

[85] Austin Steward, *Twenty-Two Years a Slave and Forty Years a Freeman* (1856; reprint, New York: Negro University Press, 1968), 174–75; and James L. Smith, in Arna Bontemps, ed. *Five Black Lives: The Autobiographies of Venture Smith, James Mars, William Grimes, the Rev. G. W. Offley, and James L. Smith* (1971; reprint, Middletown: Wesleyan University Press, 1987), 187. See also Henry Louis Gates, Jr., ed., *The Classic Slave Narratives* (New York: New American Library, 1987).

[86] Martin Delany, in Carter Woodson, ed., *The Mind of the Negro as Reflected in Letters Written during the Crisis, 1800–1860* (Washington, D.C.: Association for the Study of Negro Life and History, 1926), 293. On Delany, see Victor Ullman, *Martin R. Delany: The Beginnings of Black Nationalism* (Boston: Beacon Press, 1971); and Floyd John Miller, *The Search for a Black Nationality: Black Emigration and Colonization, 1787–1863* (Urbana: University of Illinois Press, 1975).

[87] James M. McPherson, *The Struggle for Equality: Abolitionists and the Negro in the Civil War and Reconstruction* (1964; reprint, Princeton: Princeton University Press, 1972), 147; and Friedman, *Saints*, 160–95.

United States" should be accorded "all the rights and privileges which belong to them as men and as Americans" (*Liberator,* Dec. 14, 1833). (See Document 11.) This amplified the position—"the immediate enfranchisement of our slave population"—that Garrison had heralded in the first issue of *The Liberator* when he took his stand as a defender of "the great cause of human rights" and that he reiterated throughout his career.[88] To him the truth about blacks was obvious: "Why, their country is ours. They were born here. They are bone of our bone, and blood of our blood" (*Liberator,* Feb. 20, 1852).

Garrisonians backed their words with actions. As historian Leon F. Litwack has demonstrated, they "supported Negro attempts to secure equal political and legal rights with whites and to break down the segregation barrier in public places." Black and white abolitionists also achieved "remarkable success in Massachusetts" in securing "the repeal of the ban on interracial marriages, the abandonment of 'Jim Crow'[89] seating in railroad cars, and the organization of integrated lyceums, as well as the integration of Boston's public schools."[90]

Garrison hence was highly unusual in condemning slavery *and* contesting inequality, and blacks appreciated this fact. When Massachusetts in 1855 ended segregation by race in its school system, black leaders in Boston held a celebratory dinner at which Garrison and Wendell Phillips were the only white speakers. Such intimacy and respect between whites and blacks startled the Northern white majority—not just those who were indifferent to slavery but also those who, while disliking slavery, hated blacks. These persons were keen for abolition as long as segregation or colonization accompanied it, and it was this cruel paradox that, in the pages of *The Liberator,* Garrison unmasked and censured.

Garrison was enlightened and generous in his dealings with black persons; he offered love, inspiration, and support to them. Or at least he did until they disagreed and argued with him. Garrison then took deep personal offense and simply would not allow his confidence in his own virtue to be questioned or challenged. He could be arrogant and dogmatic—as Frederick Douglass painfully discovered. The strength and limitation of Garrison's personality was his firm belief that he embodied

---

[88] Waldo E. Martin, Jr., *The Mind of Frederick Douglass* (Chapel Hill: University of North Carolina Press, 1984), 23; and Ray Allen Billington, "James Forten: Forgotten Abolitionist" (1949), in *Blacks in the Abolitionist Movement,* ed. John H. Bracey, Jr., August Meier, and Elliott Rudwick (Belmont, Calif.: Wadsworth, 1971), 4.

[89] Jim Crow was a character in a popular song of the 1830s, and the name became a derogatory term to refer to black people and later signified discriminatory laws and practices.

[90] Leon F. Litwack, "The Abolitionist Dilemma: The Antislavery Movement and the Northern Negro," *New England Quarterly* 34 (Mar. 1961): 72.

moral principle. This gave him the courage to fight for abolition amid danger and hostility, even as it also led him to cease his relationships with friends and allies who said that their principles were different.

ENDINGS: GARRISON IN 1865 AND AFTER

Lincoln's Emancipation Proclamation of January 1, 1863—issued in preliminary form on September 22, 1862—declared the slaves free in all states in rebellion against the Union and allowed blacks to enlist in the Union army. Garrison wished for a stronger statement—Lincoln's did not affect slaves in the loyal border states—but concluded that it nevertheless sounded the death knell for slavery. The war was now tied to abolition, and black men would be fighting against the Confederate slave power and on behalf of the U.S. government that formerly had acquiesced in their bondage. (See Documents 36 and 37.)

In two years' time, after appalling carnage, the war was finally moving to its close. Charleston, South Carolina, fell to the Union forces on February 18, 1865, and on March 9 Garrison addressed an enthusiastic crowd in the Music Hall in Boston. He spoke while standing on a Confederate flag draped over the steps of the auction block of the Charleston slave mart, which had been sent North with other testimonies to the barbarism of slavery. Hundreds of persons waved and cheered, and Garrison felt exhilarated by the applause he received (*Letters* 4:262–63).

Several weeks later, in early April, Secretary of War Edwin M. Stanton invited Garrison and George Thompson to be present as the government's guests at a flag-raising ceremony at Fort Sumter, to be held on April 14. The chartered steamer, filled with statesmen, politicians, and reporters, left New York on April 8. When the ship reached Charleston harbor, it was saluted with booming cannon and bravos and songs from the crowds of freed persons on shore.

On April 13 Garrison and others visited Mitchelville, a self-governing settlement of 3,000 freed persons located near Hilton Head. Black men and women welcomed him with hymns in a celebration at a church. Garrison read Moses' song from Exodus 15 ("I will sing to the Lord, for he has triumphed gloriously") and then recounted the history of antislavery from its exacting early days in the 1830s, when he had launched *The Liberator* and a mob had attacked him, to Lincoln's Emancipation Proclamation.

The next day, Garrison attended the stirring ceremony at Fort Sumter. The tattered flag—the same one that had been removed in 1861 when the fort fell—was raised just as the news arrived of Confederate General Robert E. Lee's surrender to Union General Ulysses S. Grant. Accompanied by his son George, to whom Secretary of War Stanton had given a furlough for the occasion, Garrison heard former commander of the fort Major General Robert Anderson and Henry Ward Beecher speak.[91] Beecher affirmed that *"one nation, under one government, without slavery* has been ordained, and shall stand," and he closed with a tribute to Lincoln:

> We offer to the President of these United States our solemn congratulations that God has sustained his life and health under the unparalleled burdens and sufferings of four bloody years, and permitted him to behold this auspicious consummation of that national unity for which he has waited with so much patience and fortitude, and for which he has labored with such disinterested wisdom.[92]

Later on the evening of the 14th, Garrison delivered a speech himself, as did George Thompson, at a celebratory banquet in the Charleston Hotel.

On the morning of April 15, Garrison cried as he heard the band of the 127th Regiment playing "John Brown's Body" as it marched through the Charleston streets. He stood at the tomb of John C. Calhoun, in the small cemetery near the eighteenth-century St. Philip's Church, laid his hand on the large, plain slab of marble, which contained only the name CALHOUN, and rendered this judgment: "Down into a deeper grave than this slavery has gone, and for it there is no resurrection." Thousands of ecstatic freed men and women greeted him in the city square at eleven o'clock. He was carried round the square on the shoulders of the crowd and presented by the superintendent of public instruction to hundreds of black schoolchildren. When the children heard his name, they cheered and threw their caps in the air.

Garrison was escorted to a huge building known as Zion's Church, and before an audience of several thousand former slaves and one thousand guests, he received bouquets of flowers from two girls for all he had done on behalf of the slaves. Their father, an ex-slave named Samuel Dickerson, said to Garrison: "We welcome and look upon you as our savior. We thank you for what you have done for us." He added: "Now Sir, through your labors and those of your noble coadjutors, they are mine, and no man can take them from me. Accept these flowers as the token of our

---

[91] Edmund L. Drago, ed., *Broke by the War: Letters of a Slave Trader* (Columbia: University of South Carolina Press, 1991), 4.

[92] Beecher, *Patriotic Addresses*, 679, 696.

gratitude and love, and take them with you to your home, and keep them as a simple offering from those for whom you have done so much" (*Liberator,* May 5, 1865).

Garrison replied: "It was not on account of your complexion or race, as a people, that I espoused your cause, but because you were the children of a common Father, created in the same divine image, having the same inalienable rights, and as much entitled to liberty as the proudest slaveholder that ever walked the earth." He continued: "I have faithfully tried, in the face of the fiercest opposition and under the most depressing circumstances, to make your cause my cause; my wife and children your wives and children, subjected to the same outrage and degradation; myself on the same auction block, to be sold to the highest bidder. Thank God, this day you are free!" (*Life* 4:144–46; *Letters* 5:269–70).

The whole assembly rang with hurrahs for Garrison, for Henry Wilson (Republican senator from Massachusetts and a staunch foe of slavery), and above all for President Lincoln, "their great friend and benefactor." Judge William D. Kelley, Republican congressman from Pennsylvania, asked all of those present to thank God for strengthening and guiding Garrison and Lincoln. When the speeches and services were done, Garrison was led back to his hotel in a procession that numbered two thousand, in yet another counterpoint to that afternoon in October 1835 when the Boston mob had assaulted him. This was a magnificent day of vindication, of triumph. No one yet knew that President Lincoln, shot the night before by John Wilkes Booth, had died that same morning.

The Liberator reported Lincoln's death in its April 21 issue, the columns of the paper marked with thick black lines of mourning. The news of Garrison's grand appearances at Zion Church and Citadel Square, reprinted from the Charleston *Courier,* was not published until May 5.

Garrison grieved at Lincoln's death yet held tightly to the belief that the war had been successful: the Confederacy had been defeated and slavery destroyed. In May, opposing both Phillips and Douglass, Garrison urged that the American Anti-Slavery Society be disbanded. The society had been established in order to abolish slavery, and now this job had been done; the nation as a whole, he said, was with the abolitionists. For Phillips and Douglass, however, the society had to remain in existence to conduct the campaign for equal rights for the emancipated slaves. When the issue whether to disband came up for a vote and Garrison lost by a wide margin, he resigned as president and left the society, which lasted until April 1870, to the control of others. "I never should have accepted that post if it had been a popular one," he wrote. "I took it because it was unpopular; because we, as a body, were everywhere denounced, proscribed, outlawed. To-day, it is popular to be President of the American Anti-Slavery Society. Hence, my connection with it terminates here and now" (*Life* 4:160–61). Garrison closed down *The Liberator* at the end of December 1865 and withdrew from the Massachusetts Anti-Slavery Society in January 1866. (See Document 41.)

Garrison stayed active, however, from the end of the war until his death in 1879. He wrote and lectured in favor of the postwar amendments to the Constitution that ended slavery, made blacks citizens, and gave them the right to vote; he supported the unsuccessful effort in the U.S. Senate to impeach President Andrew Johnson in 1867–68 for blocking Reconstruction measures; he traveled to England and France in 1867 and to England again in 1877; from 1868 to 1875, he was a contributor to an influential weekly paper, the New York *Independent,* which had become anti-slavery and pro-Republican under the editorship of Henry Ward Beecher and Theodore Tilton; he supported a host of causes, including free trade, civil service reform, and woman suffrage; and he attacked the mistreatment of Chinese immigrants and Native Americans.

But Garrison's main activity in the postwar years was performing the role of abolitionist hero, the person who had initiated the struggle when doing so was most lonely and arduous. Always conscious of their firm integrity, Garrison and those affiliated with him had represented themselves before and during the war as akin to Christ and his disciples, reviled in their own day but surely to be justified by history. After the war, they cherished this vision all the more, and they spoke and wrote frequently about its glories.

As early as a September 28, 1849, editorial, Garrison himself had asserted that "the experience of the faithful abolitionists has been like that of the early disciples of Christ, in almost every particular." (See also *Liberator,* Oct. 11, 1850; Jan. 13, 1854; Dec. 18, 1863.) "We are opposed as Jesus was," he later stated, "because of the blindness and selfishness of men" (*Liberator,* Dec. 12, 1856). In his speech on the twenty-fifth anniversary of the formation of the Massachusetts Anti-Slavery Society, Garrison reflected that its first meeting had included twelve persons — an appropriately "apostolic number" (*Liberator,* Jan. 9, 1857).

Plenty of kindred homages to the noble, virtuous, Christ-like Garrison appeared in *The Liberator* and they multiplied as victory drew near. At the January 26, 1865, meeting of the Massachusetts Anti-Slavery Society, Garrison described his journey as a self-made reformer, single-minded in his selfless devotion: "A young man thirty-six years ago, without influence, without friends, solitary and alone, seeing the slave in his fetters, and recognizing his claim to immediate freedom, I warmly espoused his cause" (*Liberator,* Feb. 17, 1865). At this same meeting A. Bronson Alcott referred to Garrison as "the nation's teacher," the true "President of the United States," and depicted Garrison and antislavery in biblical terms of prophetic duty (*Liberator,* Feb. 17, 1865). There was also a lavish commendation by Lydia Maria Child, which Garrison slotted as the lead article on the front page of the March 24, 1865, *Liberator,* and a worshipful editorial by Edmund Quincy (Dec. 1, 1865).

These tributes were elaborated and fleshed out in the histories and memoirs that co-workers and friends composed. Among them were Samuel J. May's *Some Recollections on Our Anti-Slavery Conflict* (1869), Oliver Johnson's *W. L. Garrison and His Times* (1881), and, above all, Parker Pillsbury's *Acts of the Anti-Slavery Apostles* (1884), in which the author certified that Garrison's life was "pure and spotless as the white plumage of angels, his whole character and conduct unsullied by the slightest breath of reproach."[93]

Beautiful as these tributes were, they were self-servingly tied to slanted readings of the historical record. In an August 18, 1875, letter, for example, Garrison criticized John Brown's use of violence and disputed Brown's contention that slavery would never be abolished through moral preaching alone. "Why," retorted Garrison, "it was solely by the use of such [spiritual] weapons that the slave system was shaken to its foundation, the whole country convulsed as by an all-pervading earthquake, the traffickers in human flesh driven to madness, Church & State vanquished in the field of conflict, a mighty and irresistible change wrought in public sentiment, the underground railroad established, the rebellion of the South an inevitable consequence, and the final abolition of slavery the glorious result" (*Letters* 6:386). Garrison here referred to the South's rebellion but not to the Civil War itself; for him the line ran straight from his branch of the abolitionist movement to the death of slavery. Political abolition and antislavery, the emergence of the Republican party, the election of Lincoln, the battlefields—these he passed over.

As historian Lawrence J. Friedman has said, Garrison "constantly attempted to make each member" of his group "feel loved, respected, and even indispensable," and all of them recalled his leadership with warmth, affection, and extravagant praise.[94] Wendell Phillips did so with special fervor in 1876 in his "remarks" at the funeral service for Garrison's wife, Helen: "Some of us can recollect, only twenty years ago, the large and

---

[93] Parker Pillsbury, *Acts of the Anti-Slavery Apostles* (Boston: Cupples, Upham, 1884), 21.

[94] Friedman, *Saints,* 49.

loving group that lived and worked together; the joy of companionship, sympathy with each other—almost our only joy—for the outlook was very dark, and our toil seemed almost vain. The world's dislike of what we aimed at, the social frown, obliged us to be all the world to each other; and yet it was a full life. The life was worth living; the labor was its own reward; we lacked nothing."[95]

At the funeral service for Garrison himself in 1879, Reverend Samuel May traced the image yet again: "It is pleasant now to know that that name which, within the memory of most of us, was everywhere cast out as evil, loaded with bitter reproach, spoken with fear and hate, and regarded as synonymous with all that was dangerous and destructive, is now . . . everywhere honored; is now well-neigh [sic] universally regarded with enthusiastic admiration."[96] The man beleaguered by angry crowds had overcome infamy, said May, and with his followers he had procured renown by making ready the way for the redemptive, emancipatory acts that President Lincoln carried out.

Yet the lofty commendations bestowed upon Garrison did express a certain real truth. Garrison was one of American's great radicals, an exemplary moral agent who committed himself to a cause that at first seemed impossible. He was unfair and inflexible, but brave and inspiring too. Beloved by many, scorned by others, Garrison dedicated himself to working for slaves and free black men and women through *The Liberator,* the paper that embodied his moral mission, and his impassioned words are a permanent part of the history of American social protest.

---

[95] Wendell Phillips, in William Lloyd Garrison, *Helen Eliza Garrison: A Memorial* (Cambridge, Mass.: Riverside, 1876), 39.

[96] Samuel May, in *Tributes to William Lloyd Garrison at the Funeral Services, May 28, 1879* (Boston: Houghton, Osgood, 1879), 11.

PART TWO

The Documents

1

Address to the American Colonization Society

July 4, 1829

Garrison delivered this hour-long address at four o'clock in the afternoon on July 4 in the Park Street Church in Boston. He had been invited to speak by supporters of the American Colonization Society, founded in December 1816–January 1817 to promote the emigration of blacks.

On this occasion Garrison spoke favorably about the colony of Liberia, established in 1822, but said little on behalf of the aims of the society itself. Soon he would reject colonization, arguing that it was impractical, immoral, and racist.

Garrison's general theme in this address was "Dangers to the Nation," and, as his biographer John L. Thomas has noted, it "contained the germ of almost every argument Garrison ever used." Garrison emphasized the shame and hypocrisy of slavery in a country based on freedom and equality; the corruption of the government; the national responsibility for slavery that fell upon the North as well as on the South; the need to educate the black population; the failure of Christian churches and societies to work for abolition; the difficulty of immediate emancipation; and the dangers to the country if slavery was allowed to continue.

It is natural that the return of a day which established the liberties of a brave people should be hailed by them with more than ordinary joy; and it is their duty as Christians and patriots to celebrate it with signal tokens of thanksgiving.

Fifty-three years ago, the Fourth of July was a proud day for our country. It clearly and accurately defined the rights of man; it made no vulgar alterations in the established usages of society; it presented a revelation adapted to the common sense of mankind; it vindicated the omnipotence of public opinion over the machinery of kingly government; it shook, as with the voice of a great earthquake, thrones which were seemingly propped up with Atlantean pillars; it gave an impulse to the heart of the world, which yet thrills to its extremities. . . .

Wendell Phillips and Francis Jackson Garrison, *William Lloyd Garrison, 1805–1879: The Story of His Life Told by His Children,* 4 vols. (Boston: Houghton Mifflin, 1885–89), 1:127–37.

I speak not as a partisan or an opponent of any man or measures, when I say, that our politics are rotten to the core. *We* boast of our freedom, who go shackled to the polls, year after year, by tens, and hundreds, and thousands! *We* talk of free agency, who are the veriest machines—the merest automata—in the hands of unprincipled jugglers! *We* prate of integrity, and virtue, and independence, who sell our birthright for office, and who, nine times in ten, do not get Esau's bargain[1]—no, not even a mess of pottage![2] Is it republicanism to say, that the majority can do no wrong? Then I am not a republican. Is it aristocracy to say, that the people sometimes shamefully abuse their high trust? Then I am an aristocrat. It is not the appreciation, but the abuse of liberty, to withdraw altogether from the polls, or to visit them merely as a matter of form, without carefully investigating the merits of candidates. The republic does not bear a charmed life: our prescriptions administered through the medium of the ballot-box—the mouth of the political body—may kill or cure, according to the nature of the disease and our wisdom in applying the remedy. It is possible that a people may bear the title of freemen who execute the work of slaves. To the dullest observers of the signs of the times, it must be apparent that we are rapidly approximating to this condition. . . .

But there is another evil, which, if we had to contend against nothing else, should make us quake for the issue. It is a gangrene preying upon our vitals—an earthquake rumbling under our feet—a mine accumulating materials for a national catastrophe. It should make this a day of fasting and prayer, not of boisterous merriment and idle pageantry—a day of great lamentation, not of congratulatory joy. It should spike every cannon, and haul down every banner. Our garb should be sackcloth—our heads bowed in the dust—our supplications, for the pardon and assistance of Heaven. . . .

I stand up here in a more solemn court, to assist in a far greater cause; not to impeach the character of one man, but of a whole people; not to recover the sum of a hundred thousand dollars, but to obtain the liberation of two millions of wretched, degraded beings, who are pining in hopeless bondage—over whose sufferings scarcely an eye weeps, or a heart melts, or a tongue pleads either to God or man. I regret that a better advocate had not been found, to enchain your attention and to warm your blood. Whatever fallacy, however, may appear in the argument, there is no flaw in the indictment; what the speaker lacks, the cause will supply.

Sirs, I am not come to tell you that slavery is a curse, debasing in its effect, cruel in its operation, fatal in its continuance. The day and the

---

[1]Genesis 25:29–34 tells how Esau foolishly sold his birthright to his twin brother, Jacob, for the price of a meal.
    [2] Genesis 25:30.

occasion require no such revelation. I do not claim the discovery as my own, that "all men are born equal," and that among their inalienable rights are "life, liberty, and the pursuit of happiness." Were I addressing any other than a free and Christian assembly, the enforcement of this truth might be pertinent. Neither do I intend to analyze the horrors of slavery for your inspection, nor to freeze your blood with authentic recitals of savage cruelty. Nor will time allow me to explore even a furlong of that immense wilderness of suffering which remains unsubdued in our land. I take it for granted that the existence of these evils is acknowledged, if not rightly understood. My object is to define and enforce our duty, as Christians and Philanthropists.

On a subject so exhaustless, it will be impossible, in the moiety of an address, to unfold all the facts which are necessary to its full development. In view of it, my heart swells up like a living fountain, which time cannot exhaust, for it is perpetual. Let this be considered as the preface of a noble work, which your inventive sympathies must elaborate and complete.

I assume as distinct and defensible propositions,

I. That the slaves of this country, whether we consider their moral, intellectual or social conditions, are preeminently entitled to the prayers, and sympathies, and charities, of the American people; and their claims for redress are as strong as those of any Americans could be in a similar condition.

II. That, as the free States—by which I mean non-slave-holding States—are constitutionally involved in the guilt of slavery, by adhering to a national compact that sanctions it; and in the danger, by liability to be called upon for aid in case of insurrection; they have the right to remonstrate against its continuance, and it is their duty to assist in its overthrow.

III. That no justificative plea for the perpetuity of slavery can be found in the condition of its victims; and no barrier against our righteous interference, in the laws which authorize the buying, selling and possessing of slaves, nor in the hazard of a collision with slaveholders.

IV. That education and freedom will elevate our colored population to a rank with the white—making them useful, intelligent and peaceable citizens.

In the first place, it will be readily admitted, that it is the duty of every nation primarily to administer relief to its own necessities, to cure its own maladies, to instruct its own children, and to watch over its own interests. He is "worse than an infidel" who neglects his own household, and squanders his earnings upon strangers; and the policy of that nation is unwise which seeks to proselyte other portions of the globe at the expense of its safety and happiness. Let me not be misunderstood. My benevolence is neither contracted nor selfish. I pity that man whose heart is not larger than a whole continent. I despise the littleness of that patriotism which blusters only for its own rights, and, stretched to its utmost dimensions, scarcely covers its native territory; which adopts as its creed the right to act independently, even to the verge of licentiousness, without restraint, and to tyrannize wherever it can with impunity. This sort of patriotism is common. I suspect the reality, and deny the productiveness, of that piety which confines its operations to a particular spot—if that spot be less than the whole earth; nor scoops out, in every direction, new channels for the waters of life. Christian charity, while it "begins at home," goes abroad in search of misery. It is as copious as the sun in heaven. It does not, like the Nile, make a partial inundation, and then withdraw; but it perpetually overflows, and fertilizes every barren spot. It is restricted only by the exact number of God's suffering creatures. But I mean to say, that, while we are aiding and instructing foreigners, we ought not to forget our own degraded countrymen; that neither duty nor honesty requires us to defraud ourselves that we may enrich others.

The condition of the slaves, in a religious point of view, is deplorable, entitling them to a higher consideration, on our part, than any other race; higher than the Turks or Chinese, for they have the privileges of instruction; higher than the Pagans, for they are not dwellers in a gospel land; higher than our red men of the forest, for we do not bind them with gyves,[3] nor treat them as chattels.

And here let me ask, What has Christianity done, by direct effort, for our slave population? Comparatively nothing. She has explored the isles of the ocean for objects of commiseration; but, amazing stupidity! she can gaze without emotion on a multitude of miserable beings at home, large enough to constitute a nation of freemen, whom tyranny has heathenized by law. In her public services they are seldom remembered, and in her private donations they are forgotten. From one end of the country to the other, her charitable societies form golden links of benevolence, and scatter their contributions like raindrops over a parched heath; but they bring no sustenance to the perishing slave. The blood of souls is upon her garments, yet she heeds not the stain. The clankings of the prisoner's chains strike upon her ear, but they cannot penetrate her heart.

I have said that the claims of the slaves for redress are as strong as those of any Americans could be, in a similar condition. Does any man deny the position? The proof, then, is found in the fact, that a very large proportion of our colored population were born on our soil, and are therefore entitled to all the privileges of American citizens. This is their country by birth, not by adoption. Their children possess the same

---

[3] Gyves are shackles or chains.

inherent and unalienable rights as ours, and it is a crime of the blackest dye to load them with fetters.

Every Fourth of July, our Declaration of Independence is produced, with a sublime indignation, to set forth the tyranny of the mother country, and to challenge the admiration of the world. But what a pitiful detail of grievances does this document present, in comparison with the wrongs which our slaves endure! In the one case, it is hardly the plucking of a hair from the head; in the other, it is the crushing of a live body on the wheel—the stings of the wasp contrasted with the tortures of the Inquisition.[4] Before God, I must say, that such a glaring contradiction as exists between our creed and practice the annals of six thousand years cannot parallel. In view of it, I am ashamed of my country. I am sick of our unmeaning declamation in praise of liberty and equality; of our hypocritical cant about the unalienable rights of man. I could not, for my right hand, stand up before a European assembly, and exult that I am an American citizen, and denounce the usurpations of a kingly government as wicked and unjust; or, should I make the attempt, the recollection of my country's barbarity and despotism would blister my lips, and cover my cheeks with burning blushes of shame. . . .

I come to my second proposition:—the right of the free States to remonstrate against the continuance, and to assist in the overthrow of slavery.

This, I am aware, is a delicate subject, surrounded with many formidable difficulties. But if delay only adds to its intricacy, wherefore shun an immediate investigation? I know that we, of the North, affectedly believe that we have no local interest in the removal of this great evil; that the slave States can take care of themselves, and that any proffered assistance, on our part, would be rejected as impertinent, dictatorial or meddlesome; and that we have no right to lift up even a note of remonstrance. But I believe that these opinions are crude, preposterous, dishonorable, unjust. Sirs, this is a business in which, as members of one great family, we have a common interest; but we take no responsibility, either individually or collectively. Our hearts are cold—our blood stagnates in our veins. We act, in relation to the slaves, as if they were something lower than the brutes that perish.

On this question, I ask no support from the injunction of Holy Writ,[5] which says:—"therefore all things whatsoever ye would that men should do to you, do ye even so to them: for this is the law and the prophets." I

---

[4] The Inquisition was the tribunal for the prosecution of heresy established by the medieval Roman Catholic Church. The later Spanish Inquisition, begun in the late fifteenth century, was characterized by extreme cruelty.

[5] The scriptural reference is Matthew 7:12.

throw aside the common dictates of humanity. I assert the right of the free States to demand a gradual abolition of slavery, because, by its continuance, they participate in the guilt thereof, and are threatened with ultimate destruction; because they are bound to watch over the interests of the whole country, without reference to territorial divisions; because their white population is nearly double that of the slave States, and the voice of this overwhelming majority should be potential; because they are now deprived of their just influence in the councils of the nation; because it is absurd and anti-republican to suffer property to be represented as men,[6] and *vice versa.* Because it gives the South an unjust ascendancy over other portions of territory, and a power which may be perverted on every occasion. . . .

Now I say that, on the broad system of equal rights, this monstrous inequality should no longer be tolerated. If it cannot be speedily put down—not by force, but by fair persuasion; if we are always to remain shackled by unjust Constitutional provisions, when the emergency that imposed them has long since passed away; if we must share in the guilt and danger of destroying the bodies and souls of men, *as the price of our Union;* if the slave States will haughtily spurn our assistance, and refuse to consult the general welfare; then the fault is not ours if a separation eventually take place. . . .

It may be objected, that the laws of the slave States form insurmountable barriers to any interference on our part.

Answer. I grant that we have not the right, and I trust not the disposition, to use coercive measures. But do these laws hinder our prayers, or obstruct the flow of our sympathies? Cannot our charities alleviate the condition of the slave, and perhaps break his fetters? Can we not operate upon public sentiment, (the lever that can move the moral world,) by way of remonstrance, advice, or entreaty? Is Christianity so powerful that she can tame the red men of our forests, and abolish the Burman caste,[7] and overthrow the gods of Paganism, and liberate lands over which the darkness of Superstition has lain for ages; and yet so weak, in her own dwelling-place, that she can make no impression upon her civil code? Can she contend successfully with cannibals, and yet be conquered by her own children?

Suppose that, by a miracle, the slaves should suddenly become white.

---

[6] The three-fifths clause of the Constitution (art. I, sect. 2) provided that three-fifths of all slaves would be added to the number of free persons in a state for the purpose of determining representation and taxation.

[7] *Burman* may refer to Burma, the country in southeast Asia. But perhaps Garrison meant *Brahman,* the highest, most exclusive priestly class or caste among the Hindus.

Would you shut your eyes upon their sufferings, and calmly talk of Constitutional limitations? No; your voice would peal in the ears of the taskmasters like deep thunder; you would carry the Constitution by force, if it could not be taken by treaty; patriotic assemblies would congregate at the corners of every street; the old Cradle of Liberty would rock to a deeper tone than ever echoed therein at British aggression; the pulpit would acquire new and unusual eloquence from our holy religion. The argument, that these white slaves are degraded, would not then obtain. You would say, it is enough that they are white, and in bondage, and they ought immediately to be set free. You would multiply your schools of instruction, and your temples of worship, and rely on them for security. . . .

But the plea is prevalent, that any interference by the free States, however benevolent or cautious it might be, would only irritate and inflame the jealousies of the South, and retard the cause of emancipation. If any man believes that slavery can be abolished without a struggle with the worst passions of human nature, quietly, harmoniously, he cherishes a delusion. It can never be done, unless the age of miracles return. No; we must expect a collision, full of sharp asperities and bitterness. We shall have to contend with the insolence, and pride, and selfishness, of many a heartless being. But these can be easily conquered by meekness, and perseverance, and prayer.

Sirs, the prejudices of the North are stronger than those of the South; — they bristle, like so many bayonets, around the slaves; — they forge and rivet the chains of the nation. Conquer them, and the victory is won. The enemies of emancipation take courage from our criminal timidity. They have justly stigmatized us, even on the floor of Congress, with the most contemptuous epithets. We are (they say) their "white slaves," afraid of our own shadows, who have been driven back to the wall again and again; who stand trembling under their whips; who turn pale, retreat, and surrender, at a talismanic threat to dissolve the Union. . . .

It is often despondingly said, that the evil of slavery is beyond our control. Dreadful conclusion, that puts the seal of death upon our country's existence! If we cannot conquer the monster in his infancy, while his cartilages are tender and his limbs powerless, how shall we escape his wrath when he goes forth a gigantic cannibal, seeking whom he may devour? If we cannot safely unloose two millions of slaves now, how shall we bind upwards of TWENTY MILLIONS at the close of the present century? But there is no cause for despair. We have seen how readily, and with what ease, that horrid gorgon, Intemperance, has been checked in his ravages. Let us take courage. Moral influence, when in vigorous exercise, is irresistible. It has an immortal essence. It can no more be trod out of existence by the iron foot of time, or by the ponderous march of iniquity, than matter can be annihilated. It may disappear for a time; but it lives in some shape or other, in some place or other, and will rise with renovated strength. Let us, then, be up and doing. In the simple and stirring language of the stout-hearted Lundy,[8] "all the friends of the cause must go to work, keep to work, hold on, and never give up."

If it be still objected, that it would be dangerous to liberate the present race of blacks;

I answer—the emancipation of all the slaves of this generation is most assuredly out of the question. The fabric, which now towers above the Alps, must be taken away brick by brick, and foot by foot, till it is reduced so low that it may be overturned without burying the nation in its ruins. Years may elapse before the completion of the achievement; generations of blacks may go down to the grave, manacled and lacerated, without a hope for their children; the philanthropists who are now pleading in behalf of the oppressed, may not live to witness the dawn which will precede the glorious day of universal emancipation; but the work will go on—laborers in the cause will multiply—new resources will be discovered—the victory will be obtained, worth the desperate struggle of a thousand years. Or, if defeat follow, woe to the safety of this people! The nation will be shaken as if by a mighty earthquake. A cry of horror, a cry of revenge, will go up to heaven in the darkness of midnight, and re-echo from every cloud. Blood will flow like water—the blood of guilty men, and of innocent women and children. Then will be heard lamentations and weeping, such as will blot out the remembrance of the horrors of St. Domingo.[9] The terrible judgments of an incensed God will complete the catastrophe of republican America.

And since so much is to be done for our country; since so many prejudices are to be dispelled, obstacles vanquished, interests secured, blessings obtained; since the cause of emancipation must progress heavily, and meet with much unhallowed opposition, —why delay the work? There must be a beginning, and now is a propitious time—perhaps the last opportunity that will be granted us by a long-suffering God. No temporizing, lukewarm measures will avail aught. We must put our shoulders to the

---

[8] Benjamin Lundy (1789–1839), antislavery agitator, lecturer, and editor of *The Genius of Universal Emancipation* (1821–35). He invited Garrison to assist him with this publication in 1829 and was Garrison's mentor.

[9] The French colony of Saint Domingue (the western part of Haiti), where a major slave rebellion erupted in the 1790s. Abolitionists often cited "the horrors of St. Domingo" to warn of the fate that would befall the South if slavery was not abolished: the slaves would revolt with terrible violence against their masters. Slaveholders, on the other hand, invoked these same "horrors" of murder, torture, rape, race war, and massive destruction to warn of the dangers to whites if abolition ever did occur.

wheel, and heave with our united strength. Let us not look coldly on and see our Southern brethren contending single-handed against an all-powerful foe—faint, weary, borne down to the earth. We are all alike guilty. Slavery is strictly a national sin. New-England money has been expended in buying human flesh; New-England ships have been freighted with sable victims; New-England men have assisted in forging the fetters of those who groan in bondage.

I call upon the ambassadors of Christ everywhere to make known this proclamation: "Thus saith the Lord God of the Africans, Let this people go, that they may serve me." I ask them to "proclaim liberty to the captives, and the opening of the prison to them that are bound"—to light up a flame of philanthropy that shall burn till all Africa be redeemed from the night of moral death, and the song of deliverance be heard throughout her borders.

I call upon the churches of the living God to lead in this great enterprise. If the soul be immortal, priceless, save it from remediless woe. Let them combine their energies, and systematize their plans, for the rescue of suffering humanity. Let them pour out their supplications to heaven in behalf of the slave. Prayer is omnipotent: its breath can melt adamantine rocks—its touch can break the stoutest chains. Let anti-slavery charity-boxes stand uppermost among those for missionary, tract and educational purposes. On this subject, Christians have been asleep; let them shake off their slumbers, and arm for the holy contest.

I call upon our New-England women to form charitable associations to relieve the degraded of their sex. As yet, an appeal to their sympathies was never made in vain. They outstrip us in every benevolent race. Females are doing much for the cause at the South; let their example be imitated, and their exertions surpassed, at the North.

I call upon our citizens to assist in establishing auxiliary colonization societies in every State, county and town. I implore their direct and liberal patronage to the parent society.

I call upon the great body of newspaper editors to keep this subject constantly before their readers; to sound the trumpet of alarm, and to plead eloquently for the rights of man. They must give the tone to public sentiment. One press may ignite twenty; a city may warm a State; a State may impart a generous heat to a whole country.

I call upon the American people to enfranchise a spot over which they hold complete sovereignty; to cleanse that worse than Augean stable,[10]

---

[10] The mythological Greek king Augeas did not clean his oxen's stables for thirty years; they were finally cleaned by Hercules, who diverted a river through them. To clean the Augean stable means to clear away corruption.

the District of Columbia, from its foul impurities. I ask them to sustain Congress in any future efforts to colonize the colored population of the States. I conjure them to select those as Representatives who are not too ignorant to know, too blind to see, nor too timid to perform their duty.

I will say, finally, that I despair of the republic while slavery exists therein. If I look up to God for success, no smile of mercy or forgiveness dispels the gloom of futurity; if to our own resources, they are daily diminishing; if to all history, our destruction is not only possible, but almost certain. Why should we slumber at this momentous crisis? If our hearts were dead to every throb of humanity; if it were lawful to oppress, where power is ample; still, if we had any regard for our safety and happiness, we should strive to crush the Vampire which is feeding upon our life-blood. All the selfishness of our nature cries aloud for a better security. Our own vices are too strong for us, and keep us in perpetual alarm; how, in addition to these, shall we be able to contend successfully with millions of armed and desperate men, as we must eventually, if slavery do not cease?

1831–1840: THE FIRST DECADE
OF *THE LIBERATOR*:
ARGUMENTS FOR ABOLITION

2
"To the Public"
January 1, 1831

This is the editorial in the first issue of The Liberator.

On Garrison's dedication to and suffering for the cause, see August 27, 1831, and October 6, 1832 (both reprinted in Letters *1:125, 162). For further defenses of himself, see "Tour of the Editor," October 6, 1832, and "Candor and Sagacity," September 10, 1836.*

The Liberator, Jan. 1, 1831, 1. All subsequent documents are from *The Liberator* unless otherwise noted.

In the month of August, I issued proposals for publishing "THE LIBERATOR" in Washington city; but the enterprise, though hailed in different sections of the country, was palsied by public indifference. Since that time, the removal of the Genius of Universal Emancipation[1] to the Seat of Government has rendered less imperious the establishment of a similar periodical in that quarter.

During my recent tour for the purpose of exciting the minds of the people by a series of discourses on the subject of slavery, every place that I visited gave fresh evidence of the fact, that a greater revolution in public sentiment was to be effected in the free states—*and particularly in New-England*—than at the south. I found contempt more bitter, opposition more active, detraction more relentless, prejudice more stubborn, and apathy more frozen, than among slave owners themselves. Of course, there were individual exceptions to the contrary. This state of things afflicted, but did not dishearten me. I determined, at every hazard, to lift up the standard of emancipation in the eyes of the nation, *within sight of Bunker Hill*[2] *and in the birth place of liberty.* That standard is now unfurled; and long may it float, unhurt by the spoliations of time or the missiles of a desperate foe—yea, till every chain be broken, and every bondman set free! Let southern oppressors tremble—let their secret abettors tremble—let their northern apologists tremble—let all the enemies of the persecuted blacks tremble.

I deem the publication of my original Prospectus unnecessary, as it has obtained a wide circulation. The principles therein inculcated will be steadily pursued in this paper, excepting that I shall not array myself as the political partisan of any man. In defending the great cause of human rights, I wish to derive the assistance of all religions and of all parties.

Assenting to the "self-evident truth" maintained in the American Declaration of Independence, "that all men are created equal, and endowed by their Creator with certain inalienable rights—among which are life, liberty and the pursuit of happiness," I shall strenuously contend for the immediate enfranchisement of our slave population. In Park-street Church, on the Fourth of July, 1829, in an address on slavery, I unreflectingly assented to the popular but pernicious doctrine of *gradual* abolition. I seize this opportunity to make a full and unequivocal recantation, and thus

---

[1] Benjamin Lundy's paper, *The Genius of Universal Emancipation,* with which Garrison had been associated and which had been based in Baltimore.

[2] Site of an important early battle (in fact, however, the battle took place on Breed's Hill) in the American Revolution, fought in Boston on June 17, 1775. The cornerstone for the Bunker Hill Monument was laid in a ceremony on June 17, 1825, and the completion of it celebrated on June 17, 1843.

publicly to ask pardon of my God, of my country, and of my brethren the poor slaves, for having uttered a sentiment so full of timidity, injustice and absurdity. A similar recantation, from my pen, was published in the Genius of Universal Emancipation at Baltimore, in September, 1829. My conscience is now satisfied.

I am aware, that many object to the severity of my language; but is there not cause for severity? I *will be* as harsh as truth, and as uncompromising as justice. On this subject, I do not wish to think, or speak, or write, with moderation. No! no! Tell a man whose house is on fire, to give a moderate alarm; tell him to moderately rescue his wife from the hands of the ravisher; tell the mother to gradually extricate her babe from the fire into which it has fallen;—but urge me not to use moderation in a cause like the present. I am in earnest—I will not equivocate—I will not excuse—I will not retreat a single inch—AND I WILL BE HEARD. The apathy of the people is enough to make every statue leap from its pedestal, and to hasten the resurrection of the dead.

It is pretended, that I am retarding the cause of emancipation by the coarseness of my invective, and the precipitancy of my measures. *The charge is not true.* On this question my influence,—humble as it is,—is felt at this moment to a considerable extent, and shall be felt in coming years—not perniciously, but beneficially—not as a curse, but as a blessing; and posterity will bear testimony that I was right. I desire to thank God, that he enables me to disregard "the fear of man which bringeth a snare," and to speak his truth in its simplicity and power. And here I close with this fresh dedication:

> Oppression! I have seen thee, face to face,
> And met thy cruel eye and cloudy brow;
> But thy soul-withering glance I fear not now—
> For dread to prouder feelings doth give place
> Of deep abhorrence! Scorning the disgrace
> Of slavish knees that at thy footstool bow,
> I also kneel—but with far other vow
> Do hail thee and thy hord of hirelings base:—
> I swear, while life-blood warms my throbbing veins,
> Still to oppose and thwart, with heart and hand,
> Thy brutalising sway—till Afric's chains
> Are burst, and Freedom rules the rescued land,—
> Trampling Oppression and his iron rod:
> *Such is the vow I take*—SO HELP ME GOD!

William Lloyd Garrison

Boston, January 1, 1831

3
"Working Men"
January 1, 1831

Garrison was interested in many reform movements, but not in those that involved workers and labor struggles. For him, freedom and equality included a strong emphasis on self-reliance and personal responsibility. Garrison was willing to rend asunder the Union for slaves, but not for the rights of workers, whom he did not believe were subjugated to and oppressed by their employers.

See also "The Working Classes," January 29, 1831, and "Working Classes," February 5, 1831.

An attempt has been made—it is still making—we regret to say, with considerable success—to inflame the minds of our working classes against the more opulent, and to persuade men that they are contemned and oppressed by a wealthy aristocracy. That public grievances exist, is unquestionably true; but they are not confined to any one class of society. Every profession is interested in their removal—the rich as well as the poor. It is in the highest degree criminal, therefore, to exasperate our mechanics to deeds of violence, or to array them under a party banner; for it is not true, that, at any time, they have been the objects of reproach. Labor is not dishonorable. The industrious artisan, in a government like ours, will always be held in better estimation than the wealthy idler.

Our limits will not allow us to enlarge on this subject: we may return to it another time. We are the friends of reform; but that is not reform, which, in curing one evil, threatens to inflict a thousand others.

Jan. 1, 1831, 3.

4

"Truisms"

January 8, 1831

Here Garrison mocks key tenets of the proslavery argument.
See also "Prison Anecdote," February 5, 1831.

---

1. All men are born equal, and entitled to protection, excepting those whose skins are black and hair woolly; or, to prevent mistake, excepting Africans, and their descendants.

2. If white men are ignorant and depraved, they ought freely to receive the benefits of education; but if black men are in this condition, common sense dictates that they should be held in bondage, and never instructed.

3. He who steals a sheep, or buys one of a thief, deserves severe punishment. He who steals a negro, or buys him of a kidnapper, is blameless. Why? Because a sheep can be eaten, and a negro cannot; because *he* has a *black* fleece, and *it* a *white* one; (1) because the law asserts that this distinction is just — and law, we all know, is founded in equity; and because pure benevolence actuates in the one case, and downright villany [*sic*] in the other.

4. The color of the skin determines whether a man has a soul or not. If white, he has an immortal essence; if black, he is altogether beastly. Mulattoes, however, derive no benefit from this rule.

5. The blacks ought to be held in fetters, because they are too stupid to take care of themselves; at least, we are not so stupid as to suffer them to make the experiment.

6. To kidnap children on the coast of Africa is a horrid crime, deservedly punishable with death; but he who steals them, in this country, as soon as they are born, performs not merely an innocent but a praiseworthy act.

7. In Africa, a man who buys or sells another, is a monster of hell. In America, he is an heir of heaven.

8. A man has a right to heap unbounded execration upon the foreign slave trade, and the abettors thereof; but if he utter a sentiment derogatory to the domestic traffic, or to those who assist in the transporta-

---

Jan. 8, 1831, 5.

tion of victims, he is to be imprisoned for publishing a libel, and sentenced to pay a fine of not less than one thousand dollars.

9. He who calls American slaveholders *tyrants,* is a fool, a fanatic, or a madman; but if he apologise for monarchical governments, or an hereditary aristocracy, set him down as a tory, and a traitor to his country.

10. There is not the least danger of a rebellion among the slaves; and even if they should revolt *en masse,* what could they do? Their united physical force would be utterly contemptible.

11. None but fanatics or idiots desire immediate abolition. If the slaves were liberated at once, our throats would be cut, and our houses pillaged and burnt!

12. Our slaves must be educated for freedom. Our slaves must never learn the alphabet, because knowledge would teach them to throw off their yoke.

13. People at the north have no right to alleviate physical suffering, or illumine spiritual darkness, at the south; but they have a right to assist the Greeks, or the Hindoos, or any foreign nation.

14. Were the slaves, goaded to desperation, to rise against their masters, the free states are constitutionally bound to cut their throats! "The receiver is as bad as the thief." The free states receive and consume the productions of slave labor! The District of Columbia is national property: slavery exists in that District! Yet the free states are not involved in the guilt of slavery!

15. A white man, who kills a tyrant, is a hero, and deserves a monument. If a slave kill his master, he is a murderer, and deserves to be burnt.

16. The slaves are kept in bondage *for their own good.* Liberty is a curse to the free people of color—their condition is worse than that of the slaves! Yet it would be very wicked to bind them with fetters for *their* good!

17. The slaves are contented and happy. If sometimes they are so ungrateful or deluded as to abscond, it is pure philanthropy that induces their masters to offer a handsome reward for their detection.

18. Blacks have no intellect. The laws, at the south, which forbid their instruction, were not enacted because it was supposed these brutes had brains, or for the sake of compliment, but are owing simply to an itch for superfluous legislation.

19. Slaves are held as property. It is the acme of humanity and justice, therefore, in the laws, to recognise them also as moral agents, and punish them in the most aggravated manner, if they perpetrate a crime; though they cannot read, and have neither seen nor known the laws!

20. It is foolish and cruel for an individual to denounce slavery; because the more he disturbs the security of the masters, the more vindictive will be their conduct toward the slaves. For the same reason, we ought to prefer the products of slave labor to those of free; as the more wealthy masters become, the better they will be enabled to feed and clothe their menials.

21. To deny that a man is a christian or republican, who holds slaves and dooms their children to bondage, is most uncharitable and inconsistent.

22. To say that a clerical slavite is bound to follow his own precepts, or to obey the seventh and tenth commandments, is preposterous.

23. To doubt the religious vitality of a church, which is composed of slaveholders, is the worst species of infidelity.

24. The Africans are our slaves—not because we like to oppress, or to make money unjustly—but because Noah's curse[1] must be fulfilled, and the scriptures obeyed.

[1]According to Genesis 9:20–27, Ham saw his father, Noah, lying naked, and for this Noah later cursed Ham's son, saying that he would be a slave to his brothers. This Old Testament passage was often cited in proslavery arguments to show that slavery had scriptural sanction.

5

"Walker's Appeal"

January 8, 1831

David Walker's controversial 76-page pamphlet David Walker's Appeal to the Colored Citizens of the World *was published in 1829 and reprinted later in 1829 and again in 1830.*

Walker (1785–1830), a black artisan active in the Methodist church in Boston, aided fugitive slaves and in 1827 became an agent and writer for Freedom's Journal, *a New York weekly owned and edited by blacks. In his fiery* Appeal—*Garrison published parts of it in* The Liberator—*Walker attacked colonization schemes, assailed white racism, and forcefully urged blacks to end their submissive relation to their oppressors and find strength in unity among themselves.*

Jan. 8, 1831, 6.

Believing, as we do, that men should never do evil that good may come; that a good end does not justify wicked means in the accomplishment of it; and that we ought to suffer, as did our Lord and his apostles, un-resistingly—knowing that vengeance belongs to God, and he will certainly repay it where it is due;—believing all this, and that the Almighty will deliver the oppressed in a way which they know not, we deprecate the spirit and tendency of this Appeal. Nevertheless, it is not for the American people, as a nation, to denounce it as bloody or monstrous. Mr. Walker but pays them in their own coin, but follows their own creed, but adopts their own language. *We* do not preach rebellion—no, but submission and peace. Our enemies may accuse us of striving to stir up the slaves to revenge but their accusations are false, and made only to excite the prejudices of the whites, and to destroy our influence. We say, that the possibility of a bloody insurrection at the south fills us with dismay; and we avow, too, as plainly, that if any people were ever justified in throwing off the yoke of their tyrants, the slaves are that people. It is not we, but our guilty countrymen, who put arguments into the mouths, and swords into the hands of the slaves. Every sentence that they write—every word that they speak—every resistance that they make, against foreign oppression, is a call upon their slaves to destroy them. Every Fourth of July celebra-tion must embitter and inflame the minds of the slaves. And the late dinners, and illuminations, and orations, and shoutings, at the south, over the downfall of the French tyrant, Charles the Tenth,[1] furnish so many reasons to the slaves why they should obtain their own rights by violence.

Some editors have affected to doubt whether the deceased Walker wrote this pamphlet.—On this point, skepticism need not stumble: the Appeal bears the strongest internal evidence of having emanated from his own mind. No white man could have written in language so natural and enthusiastic.

---

[1] Charles X (1757–1836) reigned as king of France from 1824 to 1830. In July 1830 he sought to ensure his power through a series of rigid controls on freedom of the press and suffrage; insurrection broke out, and he was forced to abdicate in the July Revolution of 1830.

6

"Removal to Texas"

January 22, 1831

Most of the colonization schemes that Garrison denounced involved sending blacks to Africa or the Caribbean, but as this editorial shows, other sites were considered as well.

For an example of Garrison's attack on colonization, see the reprint of his speech delivered July 13, 1833, in Exeter Hall, London, in The Liberator, *November 9, 1833.*

Formerly, the purchase of Texas by our Government, for the purpose of bestowing it as a gift upon our colored population, was a favorite opinion of ours; but we have settled down into the belief, that the object is neither practicable nor expedient. In the first place, it is not probable that Congress would make the purchase; nor, secondly, is it likely that the mass of our colored people would remove without some compulsory process; nor, thirdly, would it be safe or convenient to organise them as a distinct nation among us, —an *imperium in imperio*.[1] The fact is, it is time to repudiate all colonization schemes, as visionary and unprofitable; all those, we mean, which have for their design the entire separation of the blacks from the whites. We must take our free colored and slave inhabitants as we find them—recognise them as countrymen who have extraordinary claims upon our charities—give them the advantages of education—respect them as members of one great family, who may be made useful in society, and honorable in reputation. This is our view of the subject.

[1] A power or government within a power or government.

Jan. 22, 1831, 13.

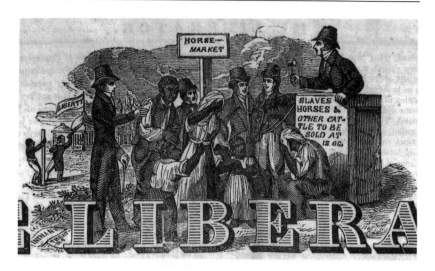

The masthead used for *The Liberator* from 1831 to 1850

7

"We Present Our Patrons . . ."
April 23, 1831

We present our patrons, to-day, a new head for the Liberator. It is illustrative of a slave auction—the scene is appropriately located at the seat of the National Government. Sales of slaves are very common at a horse market. On the right side of the vignette, stands the auctioneer with his hammer lifted up for a bid; at the side and in front of him are some southern speculators, with the family to be sold—a man and his wife, (whose attitudes express their grief,) and their two children, who are clinging to their mother. On the left side are seen in the distance, the Capitol of the United States with the American flag (on which is conspicuous the word LIBERTY) floating on the breeze; a purchaser examining a negro, as a butcher would an ox; and a whipping-post, to which a slave is chained, who is receiving a severe flagellation. Down in the dust, our

Apr. 23, 1831, 65, 67.

Indian Treaties are seen. In view of these things, who will not exultingly exclaim, "Hail Columbia! happy land!" Is it not delightful to know, that the Fourth of July is at hand, when we may laud ourselves and our country above all nations, and indignantly point the finger of scorn at foreign oppression? O consistency! thou art a precious jewel!

8

"The Insurrection"

September 3, 1831

The slave Nat Turner (1800–1831) and a small band of followers rebelled against their white masters in Southampton County, Virginia, in August 1831. Before the militia stopped them, they had rallied dozens of slaves to their side and killed sixty whites. Turner was captured on October 30 and executed on November 11. The text of Turner's November 1–3 interview with Thomas Gray, his court-appointed attorney, was published as his Confessions *and is the key source for details of his life and the revolt that he led.*

In both the North and the South, Garrison was accused of instigating Turner's revolt through his militant rhetoric in The Liberator. *There is no evidence that Turner ever read* The Liberator *or even that any copies could be found in Southampton County. But the connection nonetheless was made between the start-up of* The Liberator *in January 1831 and the bloody slave uprising that took place eight months later. State and federal officials, such as Governor John Floyd (1783–1837) of Virginia and U.S. Senator Robert Y. Hayne (1791–1839) of South Carolina, declared that antislavery agitation would surely lead to further revolts and rebellions, and they called for the suppression of abolitionist mailings and papers.*

The sentiment against abolitionism intensified when reports began to arrive in the United States of a massive slave revolt in Jamaica in December 1831. The events in Virginia and Jamaica, the memories of Saint Domingue (see Document 1), and the recollections of earlier planned revolts in Virginia (1800), Louisiana (1811), and South Carolina (1822)

heightened fears in the white population about the consequences of easing or
ending slavery.
   See also "Blood! Blood! Blood! Another Insurrection!" September 24,
1831.

What we have so long predicted, — at the peril of being stigmatized as an
alarmist and declaimer, — has commenced its fulfilment. The first step of
the earthquake, which is ultimately to shake down the fabric of oppression,
leaving not one stone upon another, has been made. The first drops of
blood, which are but the prelude to a deluge from the gathering clouds,
have fallen. The first flash of the lightning, which is to smite and consume,
has been felt. The first wailings of a bereavement, which is to clothe the
earth in sackcloth, have broken upon our ears.

   In the first number of the Liberator, we alluded to the hour of
vengeance in the following lines:

> Wo if it come with storm, and blood, and fire,
>   When midnight darkness veils the earth and sky!
> *Wo to the innocent babe* — the guilty sire —
>   *Mother and daughter* — friends of kindred tie!
>   *Stranger and citizen alike shall die!*
> Red-handed Slaughter his revenge shall feed,
>   And Havoc yell his ominous death-cry,
>   And wild Despair in vain for mercy plead —
> While hell itself shall shrink and sicken at the deed!

   Read the account of the insurrection in Virginia, and say whether our
prophecy be not fulfilled. What was poetry — imagination — in January, is
now a bloody reality. "Wo to the innocent babe — to mother and daughter!" Is it not true? Turn again to the record of slaughter! Whole families
have been cut off — not a mother, not a daughter, not a babe left. Dreadful
retaliation! "The dead bodies of white and black lying just as they were
slain, unburied" — the oppressor and the oppressed equal at last in
death — what a spectacle!

   True, the rebellion is quelled. Those of the slaves who were not killed
in combat, have been secured, and the prison is crowded with victims
destined for the gallows!

> Yet laugh not in your carnival of crime
> Too proudly, ye oppressors!

You have seen, it is to be feared, but the beginning of sorrows. All the
blood which has been shed will be required at your hands. At your hands

alone? No—but at the hands of the people of New-England and of all the free states. The crime of oppression is national. The south is only the agent in this guilty traffic. But, remember! the same causes are at work which must inevitably produce the same effects; and when the contest shall have again begun, it must be again a war of extermination. In the present instance, no quarters have been asked or given.

But we have killed and routed them now—we can do it again and again—we are invincible! A dastardly triumph, well becoming a nation of oppressors. Detestable complacency, that can think, without emotion, of the extermination of the blacks! We have the power to kill *all*—let us, therefore, continue to apply the whip and forge new fetters!

In his fury against the revolters, who will remember their wrongs? What will it avail them, though the catalogue of their sufferings, dripping with warm blood fresh from their lacerated bodies, be held up to extenuate their conduct? It is enough that the victims were black—that circumstance makes them less precious than the dogs which have been slain in our streets! They were black—brutes, pretending to be men—legions of curses upon their memories! They were black—God made them to serve us!

Ye patriotic hypocrites! ye panegyrists of Frenchmen, Greeks, and Poles! ye fustian[1] declaimers for liberty! ye valiant sticklers for equal rights among yourselves! ye haters of aristocracy! ye assailants of monarchies! ye republican nullifiers! ye treasonable disunionists! be dumb! Cast no reproach upon the conduct of the slaves, but let your lips and cheeks wear the blisters of condemnation!

Ye accuse the pacific friends of emancipation of instigating the slaves to revolt. Take back the charge as a foul slander. The slaves need no incentives at our hands. They will find them in their stripes—in their emaciated bodies—in their ceaseless toil—in their ignorant minds—in every field, in every valley, on every hill-top and mountain, wherever you and your fathers have fought for liberty—in your speeches, your conversations, your celebrations, your pamphlets, your newspapers—voices in the air, sounds from across the ocean, invitations to resistance above, below, around them! What more do they need? Surrounded by such influences, and smarting under their newly made wounds, is it wonderful that they should rise to contend—as other "heroes" have contended— for their lost rights? It is *not* wonderful.

In all that we have written, is there aught to justify the excesses of the slaves? No. Nevertheless, they deserve no more censure than the Greeks in destroying the Turks, or the Poles in exterminating the Russians, or our

---

[1]Inflated, bombastic, as of speech.

fathers in slaughtering the British. Dreadful, indeed, is the standard erected by worldly patriotism!

For ourselves, we are horror-struck at the late tidings. We have exerted our utmost efforts to avert the calamity. We have warned our countrymen of the danger of persisting in their unrighteous conduct. We have preached to the slaves the pacific precepts of Jesus Christ. We have appealed to christians, philanthropists and patriots, for their assistance to accomplish the great work of national redemption through the agency of moral power—of public opinion—of individual duty. How have we been received? We have been threatened, proscribed, vilified and imprisoned— a laughing-stock and a reproach. Do we falter, in view of these things? Let time answer. If we have been hitherto urgent, and bold, and denunciatory in our efforts,—hereafter we shall grow vehement and active with the increase of danger. We shall cry, in trumpet tones, night and day,—Wo to this guilty land, unless she speedily repent of her evil doings! The blood of millions of her sons cries aloud for redress! IMMEDIATE EMANCIPA- TION can alone save her from the vengeance of Heaven, and cancel the debt of ages!

9

"Guilt of New-England"

January 7, 1832

Garrison demanded that the North recognize its culpability in allowing slavery to continue. It was an important part of his moral mission and rhetorical strategy that the so-called free states realize that slavery was a crime for which they, too, were responsible.

See also "Prospectus of the Liberator. Volume III," December 8, 1832. For defenses of abolitionist style and strategy: January 31, 1835 and September 5, 1835 (Letters 1:437, 496, 510.)

As a people, we, of New-England, are lamentably ignorant of the subject of slavery, but even our ignorance is exceeded by our apathy. When we hear of the cruel conduct of the slaveholders, we often kindle into a flame, and our judgments tell us that they are without excuse. We can hardly believe that such beings exist in our land. This is a righteous indignation; these feelings of abhorrence are creditable to our humanity. But what if it should appear, on a candid examination, that we are as guilty as the slave owners? that we uphold and protect a system which is full of cruelty and blood? that the chains which bind the limbs of the slaves have been rivetted by us? Let us see whether we are indeed implicated in this bloody business.

In its origin, slavery was a common crime; it is equally so in its continuance, as well as a common curse; in its removal, we are all bound to assist. The foundation of the system was laid in Massachusetts and Virginia. Other colonies immediately began to build thereon; and if the free states have since overturned the wings of the superstructure, they have also assisted in furnishing materials to enlarge the main edifice. For thirty-two years after the Declaration of Independence, the ships of New England were actively engaged in stealing victims on the coast of Africa, by the desire and authority of the nation; and even at the present day, many of their vessels, manned with American officers and seamen, but under foreign colors, are undoubtedly engaged in the horrid traffic. Moreover, the transportation of domestic slaves (a trade equally atrocious with the foreign) is almost exclusively effected in eastern vessels. It is proverbial at the south, that the Yankees who become residents among them, are generally the most eager to acquire slaves, the most unmerciful in their treatment, and the last to engage in the work of emancipation. All proverbs are not true; but Solomon never uttered a truer, perhaps, than the one related. How, then, shall we boast of our innocence in this matter?

Every reader will recollect the beautiful panegyric upon England by Cowper:[1]

> Slaves cannot breathe in England: if their lungs
> Receive our air, that moment they are free;
> They touch our country, and their shackles fall.

But who exonerates her from blame in permitting slavery to exist in her West India Colonies? She is answerable to God and the world for that pernicious toleration. The foul stain, black and broad as an eclipse of the sun, covers her whole island, and the blood of the slaves rests upon all her people. The consciousness of this universality of guilt immediately calls forth the interrogation of the amiable poet:

> We have no slaves at home, *then why abroad?*

[1]William Cowper (1731–1800), British poet. See "The Timepiece," in *The Task,* bk. 2, l. 40.

How much more criminal is America, who retains the evil in her own bosom!

We are involved in the crime of slavery by the delicate ties of consanguinity. We are constantly marrying and giving in marriage with the south; and the more slaves we can get, as a wedding dowry, the more fervent and abiding is our love. There may be—I do not know, I hope the case is otherwise—there may be those in this city, who have jumped into a *black fortune* in this manner, or whose brother or sister, or father or mother, or uncle or aunt,—no matter which,—has made such a jump, and who boast of that wealth or of that relation. This is what may be called *marriageable guilt;* and a great many come to the wedding.

It is in vain that we profess to be opposed to the continuance of slavery, while our insincerity is so manifest. Look at the District of Columbia, over which we have ample control! *There* is a black monument of American tyranny, towering up into the sky; and more workmen are engaged in its completion, than were employed upon the tower of Babel—ten millions at the lowest calculation. The Bunker Hill Monument gets up very slowly, because the patriotism of this world is very liable to shocks of paralysis; but self-interest—or what is mistaken for self-interest—is immortal, and defies disease.

There is no sophistry or device which can give us absolution in this disreputable business. We have a right, and it is our duty, to lift up our voices against the existence of slavery in that District. Why may not the present sessions of Congress demolish it at a blow? It has certainly a legitimate right so to do; and is only waiting to receive a national impulse.

Why is it—if we are *really* hostile to oppression—why is it, that so few petitions go into Congress on this subject? The population of the free states now amounts to more than seven millions. Do we average five petitions, annually, to one million of inhabitants? It really seems as if we are enamored, instead of being disgusted with slavery.

So long as we continue one body—a union—a nation—the compact involves us in the guilt and danger of slavery. If the slaves, goaded to desperation by their cruel masters, should rise *en masse* to obtain redress, do the citizens of New-England reflect that they are constitutionally bound to assist the southern taskmasters in subduing or exterminating the blacks, and are liable to be drafted at a moment's warning? Perhaps we imagine, that there is little danger of a general insurrection among the slaves—(the recent events at the south to the contrary, notwithstanding)—but does this circumstance remove the responsibility from our shoulders? No matter what is the *probability* in this case. The question is, whether we are not solemnly pledged to put down a black rebellion in the south? At the present moment, indeed, appearances seem to indicate a double rebellion in that section of the Union; a rebellion against the Government by the whites, and a rebellion against the whites by the blacks; so that the "tug of war" may be nearer than the people of the free states imagine. What protects the south from instant destruction?

OUR PHYSICAL FORCE. Break the chain which binds her to the Union, and the scenes of St. Domingo[2] would be witnessed throughout her borders. She may affect to laugh at this prophecy; but she knows that her security lies in northern bayonets. Nay, she has repeatedly taunted the free states with being pledged to protect her: tyrannise long and cruelly as she may, they are bound to save her life, and, if necessary, to slaughter her slaves. How, then, do we make the inquiry, with affected astonishment, "what have we to do with the guilt of slavery?" Is this a novel view of the subject? Must we now begin to inquire, for the first time, what are our duties and responsibilities as American citizens?

Perhaps we internally resolve never to march against the blacks— never to bear arms south of the Potomac. But such a decision would be full of treachery to the people of the south. Let us give them fair warning when we intend to leave them to their fate; and let us not practise studied cruelty and deceit. Hear the language of a Representative from Massachusetts (Mr. Dwight) in the Congressional session of 1827:

> In an internal commotion in Georgia, where should its white population seek a shelter? Not, certainly, in the little fort of Savannah. In such an event, (and he hoped the day was far distant,) they would not look to the forts erected for maritime defence, but to the *stout hearts* and *sympathetic feelings* of their *northern brethren;* and he did not hazard too much in saying, that in such a case the north will *pour out its blood like water* to assist the south!

Are these indeed our sentiments? Can we cover ourselves with laurels in a war of oppression? What! ready to pour out our blood like water, in order that a large portion of our fellow countrymen may be kept in servile bondage!

It is awful to reflect, that it is solely by the authority of the free states slavery is tolerated in our land. The south is only our agent. We form a powerful combination which cannot be resisted, and give her a broad license to kidnap, plunder and oppress; promising our united aid, in case she is in personal danger! Yet we complacently wipe our mouths, and say, "We commit no evil—the south is the victim to be sacrificed." This is certainly an improvement upon the Holy Alliance.[3] We are guilty—all guilty—horribly guilty.

[2] See Document 1, note 9.
[3] Agreement among the emperors of Russia and Austria and the king of Prussia in 1815; it became a symbol for reactionary defense of the social order.

10

On the Constitution and the Union

December 29, 1832

This was one of Garrison's earliest critiques of the Constitution and the "Union" that it established—though it was not until the 1840s that Garrison made his case for "disunion" with full force. He argued that the Constitution was a proslavery document that provided slaveholders with guarantees (such as the three-fifths clause; see Document 1, note 5) for their wicked institution. For Garrison, moral principle always came first: if preservation of the Union required slavery, then the Union should be dissolved.
See also "Human Governments," June 23, 1837.

There is much declamation about the sacredness of the compact which was formed between the free and slave states, on the adoption of the Constitution. A sacred compact, forsooth! We pronounce it the most bloody and heaven-daring arrangement ever made by men for the continuance and protection of a system of the most atrocious villany [*sic*] ever exhibited on earth. Yes—we recognize the compact, but with feelings of shame and indignation; and it will be held in everlasting infamy by the friends of justice and humanity throughout the world. It was a compact formed at the sacrifice of the bodies and souls of millions of our race, for the sake of achieving a political object—an unblushing and monstrous coalition to do evil that good might come. Such a compact was, in the nature of things and according to the law of God, null and void from the beginning. No body of men ever had the right to guarantee the holding of human beings in bondage. Who or what were the framers of our government, that they should dare confirm and authorise such high-handed villany—such a flagrant robbery of the inalienable rights of man—such a glaring violation of all the precepts and injunctions of the gospel—such a savage war upon a sixth part of our whole population?—They were men, like ourselves—as fallible, as sinful, as weak, as ourselves. By the infamous bargain which they made between themselves, they virtually dethroned the Most High God, and trampled beneath their feet their own solemn and heaven-attested Declaration, that all men are created equal, and endowed by their Creator with certain inalienable rights—among

Dec. 29, 1832, 207.

which are life, liberty, and the pursuit of happiness. They had no lawful power to bind themselves, or their posterity, for one hour—for one moment—by such an unholy alliance. It was not valid then—it is not valid now. Still they persisted in maintaining it—and still do their successors, the people of Massachusetts, of New-England, and of the twelve free States, persist in maintaining it. A sacred compact! a sacred compact! What, then, is wicked and ignominious?

This, then, is the relation in which we of New-England stand to the holders of slaves at the south, and this is virtually our language toward them—"Go on, most worthy associates, from day to day, from month to month, from year to year, from generation to generation, plundering two millions of human beings of their liberty and the fruits of their toil—driving them into the fields like cattle—starving and lacerating their bodies— selling the husband from his wife, the wife from her husband, and children from their parents—spilling their blood—withholding the bible from their hands and all knowledge from their minds—and kidnapping annually sixty thousand infants, the offspring of pollution and shame! Go on, in these practices—we do not wish nor mean to interfere, for the rescue of your victims, even by expostulation or warning—we like your company too well to offend you by denouncing your conduct—'although we know that by every principle of law which does not utterly disgrace us by assimilating us to pirates, that they have as good and as true a right to the equal protection of the law as we have; and although we ourselves stand prepared to die, rather than submit even to a fragment of the intolerable load of oppression to which we are subjecting them—yet, never mind— let that be—they have grown old in suffering and we iniquity—and we have nothing to do now but to speak *peace, peace,* to one another in our sins. We are too wicked ever to love them as God commands us to do—we are so resolute in our wickedness as not even to desire to do so—and we are so proud in our iniquity that we will hate and revile whoever disturbs us in it. We want, like the devils of old, to be let alone in our sin. We are unalterably determined, and neither God nor man shall move us from this resolution, that our colored fellow subjects never shall be free or happy in their native land.' Go on, from bad to worse—add link to link to the chains upon the bodies of your victims—add constantly to the intolerable burdens under which they groan—and if, goaded to des-peration by your cruelties; they should rise to assert their rights and redress their wrongs, fear nothing—we are pledged, by a sacred com-pact, to shoot them like dogs and rescue you from their vengeance! Go on—we never will forsake you, for 'there is honor among thieves'—our swords are ready to leap from their scabbards, and our muskets to pour forth deadly vollies, as soon as you are in danger. We pledge you our physical strength, by the sacredness of the national compact — a compact by which we have enabled you already to plunder, persecute and destroy two millions of slaves, who now lie beneath the sod; and by which we now give you the same piratical license to prey upon a much larger number of victims and all their posterity. Go on — and by this sacred instrument, the Constitution of the United States, *dripping as it is with human blood,* we solemnly pledge you our lives, our fortunes, and our sacred honor, that we will stand by you to the last."

People of New-England, and of the free States! is it true that slavery is no concern of yours? Have you no right even to protest against it, or to seek its removal? Are you not the main pillars of its support? How long do you mean to be answerable to God and the world, for spilling the blood of the poor innocents? Be not afraid to look the monster SLAVERY boldly in the face. He is your implacable foe — the vampyre who is sucking your life-blood — the ravager of a large portion of your country, and the enemy of God and man. Never hope to be a united, or happy, or prosperous people while he exists. He has an appetite like the grave — a spirit as malignant as that of the bottomless pit — and an influence as dreadful as the corruption of death. Awake to your danger! the struggle is a mighty one — it cannot be avoided — it should not be, if it could.

It is said that if you agitate this question, you will divide the Union. Believe it not; but should disunion follow, the fault will not be yours. You must perform your duty, faithfully, fearlessly and promptly, and leave the consequences to God: that duty clearly is, to cease from giving countenance and protection to southern kidnappers. Let them separate, if they can muster courage enough — and the liberation of their slaves is certain. Be assured that slavery will very speedily destroy this Union, *if it be let alone;* but even if the Union can be preserved by treading upon the necks, spilling the blood, and destroying the souls of millions of your race, we say it is not worth a price like this, and that it is in the highest degree criminal for you to continue the present compact. Let the pillars thereof fall — let the superstructure crumble into dust — if it must be upheld by robbery and oppression.

"Declaration of the National Anti-Slavery Convention"

December 14, 1833

This is Garrison's manifesto setting out the aims of the American Anti-Slavery Society, formed in Philadelphia in December 1833.

For the Preamble, Constitution, and Address of the New England Anti-Slavery Society, see February 18, 1832.

The Convention, assembled in the City of Philadelphia to organize a National Anti-Slavery Society, promptly seize the opportunity to promulgate the following DECLARATION OF SENTIMENTS, as cherished by them in relation to the enslavement of one-sixth portion of the American people.

More than fifty-seven years have elapsed since a band of patriots convened in this place, to devise measures for the deliverance of this country from a foreign yoke. The corner-stone upon which they founded the TEMPLE OF FREEDOM was broadly this—"that all men are created equal; that they are endowed by their Creator with certain inalienable rights; that among these are life, LIBERTY, and the pursuit of happiness." At the sound of their trumpet-call, three millions of people rose up as from the sleep of death, and rushed to the strife of blood; deeming it more glorious to die instantly as freemen, than desirable to live one hour as slaves.—They were few in number—poor in resources; but the honest conviction that TRUTH, JUSTICE, and RIGHT were on their side, made them invincible.

We have met together for the achievement of an enterprise, without which, that of our fathers is incomplete, and which, for its magnitude, solemnity, and probable results upon the destiny of the world, as far transcends theirs, as moral truth does physical force.

In purity of motive, in earnestness of zeal, in decision of purpose, in intrepidity of action, in steadfastness of faith, in sincerity of spirit, we would not be inferior to them.

Their principles led them to wage war against their oppressors, and to spill human blood like water, in order to be free. *Ours* forbid the doing of evil that good may come, and lead us to reject, and to entreat the oppressed to reject, the use of all carnal weapons for deliverance from bondage—relying solely upon those which are spiritual, and mighty through God to the pulling down of strong holds.

Their measures were physical resistance—the marshalling in arms—the hostile array—the mortal encounter. *Ours* shall be such only as the opposition of moral purity to moral corruption—the destruction of error by the potency of truth—the overthrow of prejudice by the power of love—and the abolition of slavery by the spirit of repentance.

Their grievances, great as they were, were trifling in comparison with the wrongs and sufferings of those for whom we plead. Our fathers were never slaves—never bought and sold like cattle—never shut out from the light of knowledge and religion—never subjected to the lash of brutal taskmasters.

But those, for whose emancipation we are striving, — constituting at the present time at least one-sixth part of our countrymen, — are recognised by the laws, and treated by their fellow beings, as marketable commodities—as goods and chattels—as brute beasts; — are plundered daily of the fruits of their toil without redress; — really enjoy no constitutional nor legal protection from licentious and murderous outrages upon their persons; — are ruthlessly torn asunder—the tender babe from the arms of its frantic mother—the heart-broken wife from her weeping husband—at the caprice or pleasure of irresponsible tyrants; — and, for the crime of having a dark complexion, suffer the pangs of hunger, the infliction of stripes, and the ignominy of brutal servitude. They are kept in heathenish darkness by laws expressly enacted to make their instruction a criminal offence.

These are the prominent circumstances in the condition of more than TWO MILLIONS of our people, the proof of which may be found in thousands of indisputable facts, and in the laws of the slaveholding States.

Hence we maintain—

That in view of the civil and religious privileges of this nation, the guilt of its oppression is unequalled by any other on the face of the earth; — and, therefore,

That it is bound to repent instantly, to undo the heavy burden, to break every yoke, and to let the oppressed go free.

We further maintain—

That no man has a right to enslave or imbrute his brother—to hold or acknowledge him, for one moment, as a piece of merchandise—to keep back his hire by fraud—or to brutalize his mind by denying him the means of intellectual, social and moral improvement.

The right to enjoy liberty is inalienable. To invade it, is to usurp the prerogative of Jehovah. Every man has a right to his own body—to the products of his own labor—to the protection of law—and to the common advantages of society. It is piracy to buy or steal a native African, and subject him to servitude. Surely the sin is as great to enslave an AMERICAN as an AFRICAN.

Therefore we believe and affirm—

That there is no difference, *in principle,* between the African slave trade and American slavery;

That every American citizen, who retains a human being in involuntary bondage, is [according to Scripture] a MAN-STEALER;

That the slaves ought instantly to be set free, and brought under the protection of law;

That if they had lived from the time of Pharaoh down to the present period, and had been entailed through successive generations, their right to be free could never have been alienated, but their claims would have constantly risen in solemnity;

That all those laws which are now in force, admitting the right of slavery, are therefore before God utterly null and void; being an audacious usurpation of the Divine prerogative, a daring infringement on the law of nature, a base overthrow of the very foundations of the social compact, a complete extinction of all the relations, endearments and obligations of mankind, and a presumptuous transgression of all the holy commandments—and that therefore they ought to be instantly abrogated.

We further believe and affirm—

That all persons of color who possess the qualifications which are demanded of others, ought to be admitted forthwith to the enjoyment of the same privileges, and the exercise of the same prerogatives, as others; and that the paths of preferment, of wealth, and of intelligence, should be opened as widely to them as to persons of a white complexion.

We maintain that no compensation should be given to the planters emancipating their slaves—

Because it would be a surrender of the great fundamental principle that man cannot hold property in man;

Because SLAVERY IS A CRIME, AND THEREFORE IT IS NOT AN ARTICLE TO BE SOLD;

Because the holders of slaves are not the just proprietors of what they claim;—freeing the slaves is not depriving them of property, but restoring it to the right owner;—it is not wronging the master, but righting the slave—restoring him to himself;

Because immediate and general emancipation would only destroy nominal, not real property: it would not amputate a limb or break a bone of the slaves, but by infusing motives into their breasts, would make them doubly valuable to the masters as free laborers; and

Because if compensation is to be given at all, it should be given to the outraged and guiltless slaves, and not to those who have plundered and abused them.

We regard, as delusive, cruel and dangerous, any scheme of expatriation which pretends to aid, either directly or indirectly, in the emancipation of the slaves, or to be a substitute for the immediate and total abolition of slavery.

We fully and unanimously recognise the sovereignty of each State, to legislate exclusively on the subject of the slavery which is tolerated within its limits. We concede that Congress, *under the present national compact,* has no right to interfere with any of the slave States, in relation to this momentous subject.

But we maintain that Congress has a right, and is solemnly bound, to suppress the domestic slave trade between the several States, and to abolish slavery in those portions of our territory which the Constitution has placed under its exclusive jurisdiction.

We also maintain that there are, at the present time, the highest obligations resting upon the people of the free States, to remove slavery by moral and political action, as prescribed in the Constitution of the United States. They are now living under a pledge of their tremendous physical force to fasten the galling fetters of tyranny upon the limbs of millions in the southern States; — they are liable to be called at any moment to suppress a general insurrection of the slaves; — they authorise the slave owner to vote for three-fifths of his slaves as property, and thus enable him to perpetuate his oppression; — they support a standing army at the south for its protection; — and they seize the slave who has escaped into their territories, and send him back to be tortured by an enraged master or a brutal driver.

This relation to slavery is criminal and full of danger; IT MUST BE BROKEN UP.

These are our views and principles — these, our designs and measures. With entire confidence in the overruling justice of God, we plant ourselves upon the Declaration of our Independence, and upon the truths of Divine Revelation, as upon the EVERLASTING ROCK.

We shall organize Anti-Slavery Societies, if possible, in every city, town and village of our land.

We shall send forth Agents to lift up the voice of remonstrance, of warning, of entreaty and rebuke.

We shall circulate, unsparingly and extensively, anti-slavery tracts and periodicals.

We shall enlist the PULPIT and the PRESS in the cause of the suffering and the dumb.

We shall aim at a purification of the churches from all participation in the guilt of slavery.

We shall encourage the labor of freemen over that of the slaves, by giving a preference to their productions; — and

We shall spare no exertions nor means to bring the whole nation to speedy repentance.

Our trust for victory is solely in GOD. *We* may be personally defeated, but our principles never. TRUTH, JUSTICE, REASON, HUMANITY, must and will gloriously triumph. Already a host is coming up to the help of the Lord against the mighty, and the prospect before us is full of encouragement.

Submitting this DECLARATION to the candid examination of the people of this country, and of the friends of liberty all over the world, we hereby affix our signatures to it; — pledging ourselves that, under the guidance and by the help of Almighty God, we will do all that in us lies, consistently with this Declaration of our principles, to overthrow the most execrable system of slavery that has ever been witnessed upon earth — to deliver our land from its deadliest curse — to wipe out the foulest stain which rests upon our national escutcheon — and to secure to the colored population of the United States all the rights and privileges which belong to them as men and as Americans — come what may to our persons, our interests, or our reputations — whether we live to witness the triumph of JUSTICE, LIBERTY and HUMANITY, or perish untimely as martyrs in this great, benevolent and holy cause.

12

The Progress of Antislavery
January 23, 1836

This is taken from a January 17, 1836, letter that Garrison sent to his friend and fellow abolitionist Samuel J. May (1797–1871), Unitarian clergyman and agent of the Underground Railroad, and that he reprinted in The Liberator.

Compare with "Triumph of Mobocracy in Boston," November 7, 1835, on the Boston mob that attacked Garrison, and "A Martyr for Liberty," November 24, 1837, on the murder of abolitionist editor Elijah Lovejoy by a mob in Alton, Illinois, on November 7, 1837.

Jan. 23, 1836, 15; *Letters* 2:19–20.

It is indeed a mighty conflict, my dear brother, through which we are called to pass, and we shall assuredly be overcome, unless we are sustained by the energy of a divine love, and impressed with a fear of God that shall make all other fears contemptible. Remember that, but a little while since, we had to commence the work of converting the entire nation, (so thoroughly had slavery corrupted it,) beginning at Boston, as did the apostles at Jerusalem. Surprisingly has the truth made progress, and multitudinous are the converts to it. Still, though much has been done, more remains to be accomplished. The church is yet stained with "the blood of the souls of the poor innocents"[1]—it is yet the hiding-place and sanctuary of the ruthless monster that feeds upon human flesh, and battens upon human agony and degradation. The decidely pro-slavery tone of a large majority of our newspapers; the numerous public meetings that have been held in all parts of the free States, unanimously coinciding with the corrupt sentiments of the south; the slavish language uttered in every hall of legislation; the despotic recommendations of certain Governors in their recent messages, particularly of Gov. Marcy of New-York; the indifference, nay, the positive approbation with which propositions are received by the people, to destroy the liberty of speech and of the press, and annul the right of petitioning government, that protection and perpetuity may be given to slavery; the attitude assumed in Congress, by northern and southern representatives, respecting the abolition of slavery and the slave trade in the District of Columbia; the sanction given to the robbery and censorship of the mail; the impunity with which some of our northern citizens, convicted of no crime, have been seized at the south, and without a legal trial, publicly lacerated, or cast into prison, or ignominiously put to death; the rewards offered by the south for the abduction of certain freemen of the north; the demand of southern executives upon our own, to deliver over the same individuals to a murderous fate; the proposition of the south to the north, to imprison, or put to death "without benefit of clergy," all of us who shall dare to hint that slavery is inconsistent with humanity, justice and religion, or who shall refuse to subscribe to the monstrous dogma, that "domestic slavery is the cornerstone of our republican edifice";[2] the countenance which is given to mobs against the friends of emancipation, by men of high standing, both in Church and State; the impious justification of slavery by the southern

---

[1] Jeremiah 2:33–34 emphasizes that Israel has been faithless and will be condemned by God.

[2] Here Garrison quotes the words of Governor George McDuffie (1790–1851) of South Carolina, in his 1835 message to the legislature. Garrison reprinted the message in the December 12, 1835, issue of *The Liberator*.

clergy and churches; the general insensibility or perverseness of religious newspapers and periodicals; the unanimous declaration of southern oppressors, that they will never consent to the emancipation of their slaves, either immediately or ultimately, either for union or money, either for God or man; the dangers and difficulties which attend all our public attempts to plead the cause of our fettered, bleeding, guiltless countrymen; the brand of fanaticism, or treason, or robbery, which is put upon all the commandments and precepts of the bible, and upon the plainest maxims of republicanism: — these and other indications of the ferocious attachment of the people to the system of slavery, and to the company of slaveholders, portend that we are engaged in one of the mightiest moral struggles which the world has ever witnessed, and how how necessary it is that we all should have the endurance of the man of Uz,[3] the faith of Gideon, the meekness of Moses, and the intrepidity of the youthful David.

But I must pause. Brethren, "cease from man";[4] beware of a worldly policy; do not compromise principle; fasten yourselves to the throne of God; and lean upon the arm of Omnipotence. Let your doings be characterised by the loftiness of christian independence, and by the compassion of the Son of God. In your prayers, your resolutions, your speeches, make mention of our brethren GEORGE THOMPSON and CHARLES STUART,[5] and of all our brethren in England — and, above all things, fail not now and at all times to BE BOLD FOR GOD.

Yours, with brotherly affection,

Wm. Lloyd Garrison

---

[3]Job, the Old Testament figure.

[4]Isaiah 2:22 describes God's judgment on idolators.

[5]George Thompson (1804–1878) and Charles Stuart (1783–1865) were important English abolitionists, both of whom Garrison admired, though he later criticized Stuart for disagreeing with Garrison's stands on women's rights and nonresistance. He remained close friends with Thompson, who lectured in the United States in 1834–35, 1850, and 1864.

13

"Rights of Woman"
January 12, 1838

Women's rights were an important concern for Garrison; he attended many meetings and wrote often on this subject. He faced resistance, however, from abolitionists who judged that agitating for women's rights distracted from the primary mission of ending slavery and threatened the stability of marriage and the family. But Garrison persisted in advocating sexual equality and was contemptuous of the claim that rights for women would endanger social order.

In this selection Garrison reports on a debate that took place under the auspices of the Boston Lyceum. The lyceum movement—named after Aristotle's school in ancient Athens—was very popular in the nineteenth century and was an important institution in encouraging social reform. It was designed as a program for adult education and was the setting for lectures, concerts, discussion groups, and debates on major issues.

For more on the role of women in antislavery and the resistance to their work, see July 14, 1832 and May 25, 1838. Also see "The Woman Question," November 12, 1841. On dissension within the antislavery ranks, see May 22 and May 29, 1840.

On Thursday of last week, a large assemblage of both sexes filled the spacious Odeon, to listen to a debate on the part of the Boston Lyceum, whether it would be better for society if equal rights and duties were enjoyed by women as well as men. Two individuals spoke on the affirmative, and three on the negative side of the question. It was almost unanimously decided against the women—of course; although, if we can appreciate simple truth and sound logic, in our opinion those who sustained the affirmative (Messrs. Amasa Walker and J. A. Bolles) were victorious in every point of view. The speech of Mr. Walker was a mass of pertinent facts and forcible illustrations, in vindication of the intellectual, moral and social equality of woman with man. The question under discussion, he said, was a bold one, affecting as it did the happiness and interest of one half of the human race directly; but what question of reform had ever been

Jan. 12, 1838, 7.

proposed to mankind, that was not at first regarded as a bold one? He related an anecdote that is worth preservation. Some twelve years since, a few individuals held a meeting in Boston for the purpose of considering the practicability of not only forming but sustaining a Lyceum. A distinguished citizen, who was present, seemed to regard the project as Utopian; it would answer very well in theory, but not in practice; it might survive a few months, but as soon as its novelty was lost, it would go down. The reply to him was, "We intend to hitch on to it a powerful locomotive, — viz. the attendance and influence of woman, — and then it will be sure to go ahead." This was a new idea. Up to that time, it had not entered into the minds of men, that women could be either interested in or benefitted by scientific lectures. The plan was adopted, and the result had far surpassed the prediction. Mr. Walker said that women had always been found on the side of humanity and religion, foremost in every good work; and the nearer they approximated to an equality of rights with the men, the better it would be for society.

Mr. Bolles made a very neat, ingenious, and argumentative speech. It was claimed, he said, that priority of creation established the superiority of man over woman. If that were true, then the beasts of the field were superior to Adam; for they had precedence in creation over him. Adam was made from the dust of the ground; but it was not until the breath of Jehovah had quickened his inanimate form, and immortality had been united to that which was mortal, that Eve was created from his side. The order of creation was from the imperfect to the perfect. The climax of divine wisdom and benevolence was attained in the creation of woman. He reminded the audience, that the translators of the Bible did not attach to the words, "*help* meet for him," the Yankee meaning of "help"—that is, a servant or domestic—but simply a companion and equal. The idea was not that Eve was to be useful merely in doing the kitchen and chamber work in Paradise, but that she should be the solace, the "better half," of the twain made one. As to the eating of the forbidden fruit, Mr. B. said it was a remarkable circumstance, that Eve was induced to eat thereof, in consequence of her strong intellectual aspirations. The language of the serpent to her was—"Ye shall not surely die: for God doth know, that in the day ye eat thereof, then your eyes shall be opened; and ye shall be as gods, knowing good and evil." But Adam ate of the fruit obviously to gratify his appetite, or manifest his affection for his wife. To the objection that the punishment of Eve was that her desire should be to her husband, and he should rule over her, Mr. B. replied, that this punishment was *hers*, not necessarily or justly her *posterity*, by transmission or bequest of personal guilt, (and here he clashed with certain doctrinal notions)—and again, that it went only to show, that no such subjection to man was enjoined in Paradise, and consequently, in the restoration of our race from the fall by a common Savior, all inequalities, the fruits of that fall, ought to cease between the sexes. "In Christ Jesus, there is neither male nor female, neither bond nor free, but all are ONE." The instructions of Paul, on this subject, he argued, were clearly local and temporary in their application. Who were disposed to regard the apostle, when he said, "He that giveth in marriage doeth well, but he that giveth not in marriage doeth better," as enjoining celibacy, in preference to matrimony, upon people of every nation, and through all time? "For myself," said Mr. B., "I am one of those *unfortunate* men who have been able only to *do well.* I leave those who contend on the negative side of this question to *do better,* if they can."

Mr. B. said that an equality of rights is not an identity of duties. The duties of men and women might be correlative, reciprocal, equal, but are not necessarily identical. There are some employments, which men can better follow than women. The average physical strength, and muscular energy of men exceed those of the other sex; and yet women, in some countries, perform nearly all the drudgery and toil. But, as a moral and intellectual being, woman is entitled to exercise the same rights and enjoy the same privileges as man.

Whether Mr. B. argued merely for the occasion, as a disputant, or with sincere convictions of the truth of what he uttered we do not know; but his speech was a good one.

Those who spoke in the negative were very careful to express a high regard for woman—of course; but then, she must keep (one of them said, in his haste, "she ought to be *made to keep*") in her "appropriate sphere,"—a phraseology too indefinite to enable anyone to know how much or how little was intended by it, except by observing the spirit of these impounders of stray women. Bad illustrations and worse witticisms supplied the place of sound arguments; and "chimeras dire"[1] were conjured up as the inevitable consequences that must arise in admitting the sex to equal rights and privileges. It was thought a capital joke to suppose a frigate "manned, no, *womanned*" for a cruise upon the ocean. It was asked, how would it look to see the delicate hands of women managing thirty-two pounders in a conflict with the enemy, and these feminine warriors wading up to their knees in blood? Why, shockingly, no doubt. And so it is a shocking sight to see *men* engaged in such a horrid work. But the gospel of peace forbids our race, without distinction of sex, fighting under any circumstances. It commands every human being to love, not to

[1]Wild, dreadful fancies and fantasies.

kill his enemies; and when smitten by the hand of violence on one cheek, to turn the other also. The argument was a barbarous one, and therefore not entitled to christian consideration. We were told that woman's empire is the heart, in which it is her privilege to sway the sceptre of dominion. A most unmeaning flourish of words! Can any reason be given, why a man may not jointly rule in the same empire? why he should not govern solely by love as well as woman?

Though the arguments, in the discussion, were all on the side of the women, yet these were powerless against the prejudices, the pride and love of supremacy, the monopoly of power, on the part of the men. The unanimity with which the question was decided in the negative, and the uncourteous exultation which followed the decision, only revealed how feebly Christianity—that grand leveller of arbitrary and unnatural distinctions,—is apprehended even in republican, Christian America. Observe—women were not allowed to speak or vote on the occasion. There were at least two present (A. E. and S. M. Grimké,)[2] who, if they could have been permitted to speak on behalf of their sex, would have made a noble defence. It was like a meeting of slaveholders to discuss with all gravity the question, whether their slaves, if emancipated, would be in a better condition than if kept in bondage: and having muzzled their victims, so that their wishes could not be expressed or known, coming to the rational conclusion that to extend their "appropriate sphere" beyond the boundaries of a plantation, would be injurious to them and destructive to the welfare of society!

However, there is nothing like agitation. Free discussion will finally break all fetters, and put down all usurpation. The discussion of this question respecting the Rights of Woman is very important—its decision, at the Odeon, is of no consequence. Both sexes are ultimately to stand upon the dead level of humanity, equal in rights, in dominion, in honor, in dignity, in renown. They are far from occupying this position now. Even by the laws of this boasted republic, women are almost regarded as nonentities, as household appendages.—Their rights and liberties are entrusted, to a fearful extent, to proud and tyrannical men. If they would be emancipated, they must achieve their own deliverance; for when have the usurpers of mankind voluntarily surrendered their ill-gotten power? They must respect themselves; learn to despise outward ornament, and

---

[2]The Grimké sisters, Angelina Emily (1805–1879) and Sarah Moore (1792–1873), were members of a slaveholding family in Charleston, South Carolina, who became stalwart abolitionists and advocates of women's rights. They were attacked in the press and from the pulpit for presuming to speak in public—a violation of conventional female roles that disturbed many abolitionists as well.

covet inward worth; cultivate their minds, and inform their under-standings; and vindicate their cause in the light of a pure and resplendent Christianity.

14

"Declaration of Sentiments Adopted by the Peace Convention"

September 28, 1838

Garrison wrote this document for the Peace Convention (attended by about 160 delegates) that met in Boston on September 18, 1838. It was held to establish a Non-Resistance Society that would repudiate civil government and declare allegiance to Christ's rule alone. The "Declaration" is important not only as a statement of Garrison's extreme pacifism, but also as a sign of his opposition to political abolitionism. If all civil governments were corrupt, he asked, then how could the political system serve as a moral instrument for the antislavery cause? This was the objection that Garrison raised against all efforts to turn abolitionist activity, including the work of the American Anti-Slavery Society, toward the political arena of law-making.

See also "Mr. Garrison on Peace," September 8, 1837 (Letters 2:276); "Prospectus of The Liberator, *Volume VIII," on slavery, peace, religious perfectionism, December 15, 1837; and "Peace on Earth," March 8, 1839.*

ASSEMBLED in Convention, from various sections of the American Union, for the promotion of peace on earth and good-will among men, we, the undersigned, regard it as due to ourselves, to the cause which we love, to the country in which we live, and to the world, to publish a DECLARA-TION, expressive of the principles we cherish, the purposes we aim to accomplish, and the measures we shall adopt to carry forward the work of peaceful, universal reformation.

We cannot acknowledge allegiance to any human government; neither can we oppose any such government by a resort to physical force. We

Sept. 28, 1838, 154.

recognize but one KING and LAWGIVER, one JUDGE and RULER of mankind. We are bound by the laws of a kingdom which is not of this world; the subjects of which are forbidden to fight; in which MERCY and TRUTH are met together, and RIGHTEOUSNESS and PEACE have kissed each other; which has no state lines, no national partitions, no geographical boundaries; in which there is no distinction of rank, or division of caste, or inequality of sex; the officers of which are PEACE, its exactors RIGHTEOUSNESS, its walls SALVATION, and its gates PRAISE; and which is destined to break in pieces and consume all other kingdoms.

Our country is the world, our countrymen are all mankind. We love the land of our nativity only as we love all other lands. The interests, rights, liberties of American citizens are no more dear to us than are those of the whole human race. Hence, we can allow no appeal to patriotism, to revenge any national insult or injury. The PRINCE OF PEACE, under whose stainless banner we rally, came not to destroy, but to save, even the worst of enemies. He has left us an example, that we should follow his steps. GOD COMMENDETH HIS LOVE TOWARD US, IN THAT WHILE WE WERE YET SINNERS, CHRIST DIED FOR US.

We conceive, that if a nation has no right to defend itself against foreign enemies, or to punish its invaders, no individual possesses that right in his own case. The unit cannot be of greater importance than the aggregate. If one man may take life, to obtain or defend his rights, the same license must necessarily be granted to communities, states, and nations. If *he* may use a dagger or a pistol, *they* may employ cannon, bomb-shells, land and naval forces. The means of self-preservation must be in proportion to the magnitude of interests at stake and the number of lives exposed to destruction. But if a rapacious and bloodthirsty soldiery, thronging these shores from abroad, with intent to commit rapine and destroy life, may not be resisted by the people or magistracy, then ought no resistance to be offered to domestic troublers of the public peace or of private security. No obligation can rest upon Americans to regard foreigners as more sacred in their persons than themselves, or to give them a monopoly of wrong-doing with impunity.

The dogma, that all the governments of the world are approvingly ordained of God, and that THE POWERS THAT BE in the United States, in Russia, in Turkey, are in accordance with his will, is not less absurd than impious. It makes the impartial Author of human freedom and equality, unequal and tyrannical. It cannot be affirmed that THE POWERS THAT BE, in any nation, are actuated by the spirit or guided by the example of Christ, in the treatment of enemies; therefore, they cannot be agreeable to the will of God; and therefore, their overthrow, by a spiritual regeneration of their subjects, is inevitable.

We register our testimony, not only against all wars, whether offensive or defensive, but all preparations for war; against every naval ship, every arsenal, every fortification; against the militia system and a standing army; against all military chieftains and soldiers; against all monuments commemorative of victory over a fallen foe, all trophies won in battle, all celebrations in honor of military or naval exploits; against all appropriations for the defence of a nation by force and arms, on the part of any legislative body; against every edict of government requiring of its subjects military service. Hence, we deem it unlawful to bear arms, or to hold a military office.

As every human government is upheld by physical strength, and its laws are enforced virtually at the point of the bayonet, we cannot hold any office which imposes upon its incumbent the obligation to compel men to do right, on pain of imprisonment or death. We therefore voluntarily exclude ourselves from every legislative and judicial body, and repudiate all human politics, worldly honors, and stations of authority. If *we* cannot occupy a seat in the legislature or on the bench, neither can we elect *others* to act as our substitutes in any such capacity.

It follows, that we cannot sue any man at law, to compel him by force to restore anything which he may have wrongfully taken from us or others; but if he has seized our coat, we shall surrender up our cloak, rather than subject him to punishment.

We believe that the penal code of the old covenant, AN EYE FOR AN EYE, AND A TOOTH FOR A TOOTH, has been abrogated by JESUS CHRIST; and that, under the new covenant, the forgiveness instead of the punishment of enemies has been enjoined upon all his disciples, in all cases whatsoever. To extort money from enemies, or set them upon a pillory, or cast them into prison, or hang them upon a gallows, is obviously not to forgive, but to take retribution. VENGEANCE IS MINE—I WILL REPAY, SAITH THE LORD.

The history of mankind is crowded with evidences proving that physical coercion is not adapted to moral regeneration; that the sinful dispositions of men can be subdued only by love; that evil can be exterminated from the earth only by goodness; that it is not safe to rely upon an arm of flesh, upon man whose breath is in his nostrils, to preserve us from harm; that there is great security in being gentle, harmless, long-suffering, and abundant in mercy; that it is only the meek who shall inherit the earth, for the violent who resort to the sword are destined to perish with the sword. Hence, as a measure of sound policy—of safety to property, life, and liberty—of public quietude and private enjoyment—as well as on the ground of allegiance to HIM who is KING OF KINGS and LORD OF LORDS, we cordially adopt the non-resistance principle; being confident that it provides for all possible consequences, will ensure all things needful to us, is armed with omnipotent power, and must ultimately triumph over every assailing force.

We advocate no jacobinical[1] doctrines. The spirit of jacobinism is the spirit of retaliation, violence, and murder. It neither fears God nor regards man. *We* would be filled with the spirit of CHRIST. If we abide by our principles, it is impossible for us to be disorderly, or plot treason, or participate in any evil work; we shall submit to every ordinance of man, FOR THE LORD'S SAKE; obey all the requirements of Government, except such as we deem contrary to the commands of the gospel; and in no case resist the operation of law, except by meekly submitting to the penalty of disobedience.

But, while we shall adhere to the doctrine of non-resistance and passive submission to enemies, we purpose, in a moral and spiritual sense, to speak and act boldly in the cause of GOD; to assail iniquity, in high places and in low places; to apply our principles to all existing civil, political, legal and ecclesiastical institutions; and to hasten the time when the kingdoms of this world will have become the kingdoms of our LORD and of his CHRIST, and he shall reign for ever.

It appears to us a self-evident truth, that, whatever the gospel is designed to destroy at any period of the world, being contrary to it, ought now to be abandoned. If, then, the time is predicted when swords shall be beaten into ploughshares,[2] and spears into pruning-hooks, and men shall not learn the art of war any more, it follows that all who manufacture, sell or wield those deadly weapons, do thus array themselves against the peaceful dominion of the SON OF GOD on earth.

Having thus briefly, but frankly, stated our principles and purposes, we proceed to specify the measures we propose to adopt, in carrying our object into effect.

We expect to prevail through THE FOOLISHNESS OF PREACHING — striving to commend ourselves unto every man's conscience, in the sight of GOD. From the press, we shall promulgate our sentiments as widely as practicable. We shall endeavor to secure the co-operation of all persons, of whatever name or sect. The triumphant progress of the cause of TEMPERANCE and of ABOLITION in our land, through the instrumentality of benevolent and voluntary associations, encourages us to combine our own

---

[1]Related to political extremism or radical beliefs, used especially to refer to one who advocates terror and violence; derives from the radical democratic group that emerged during the French Revolution of 1789.

[2]Chapters 4 and 5 of the Old Testament book of Micah refer to the glories that lie ahead for Israel, including that "they shall beat their swords into plowshares" (4:3) and thus exchange war for peace and prosperity. See also Isaiah 2:4 and Joel 3:10.

means and efforts for the promotion of a still greater cause. Hence, we shall employ lecturers, circulate tracts and publications, form societies, and petition our State and national governments, in relation to the subject of UNIVERSAL PEACE. It will be our leading object to devise ways and means for effecting a radical change in the views, feelings, and practices of society, respecting the sinfulness of war and the treatment of enemies.

In entering upon the great work before us, we are not unmindful that, in its prosecution, we may be called to test our sincerity, even as in a fiery ordeal. It may subject us to insult, outrage, suffering, yea, even death itself. We anticipate no small amount of misconception, misrepresentation, calumny. Tumults may arise against us. The ungodly and violent, the proud and pharisaical,[3] the ambitious and tyrannical, principalities and powers, and spiritual wickedness in high places, may combine to crush us. So they treated the MESSIAH, whose example we are humbly striving to imitate. If we suffer with him, we know that we shall reign with him. We shall not be afraid of their terror, neither be troubled. Our confidence is in the LORD ALMIGHTY, not in man. Having withdrawn from human protection, what can sustain us but that faith which overcomes the world? We shall not think it strange concerning the fiery trial which is to try us, as though some strange thing had happened unto us; but rejoice, inasmuch as we are partakers of CHRIST'S sufferings. Wherefore, we commit the keeping of our souls to GOD, in well-doing, as unto a faithful Creator. FOR EVERY ONE THAT FORSAKES HOUSES, OR BRETHREN, OR SISTERS, OR FATHER, OR MOTHER, OR WIFE, OR CHILDREN, OR LANDS, FOR CHRIST'S SAKE, SHALL RECEIVE A HUNDRED FOLD, AND SHALL INHERIT EVERLASTING LIFE.

Firmly relying upon the certain and universal triumph of the sentiments contained in this DECLARATION, however formidable may be the opposition arrayed against them—in solemn testimony of our faith in their divine origin—we hereby affix our signatures to it; commending it to the reason and conscience of mankind, giving ourselves no anxiety as to what may befall us, and resolving in the strength of the LORD GOD calmly and meekly to abide the issue.

---

[3]Related to the rigid observance of outward forms. See Document 28, note 1.

15

"Abolition at the Ballot-Box"
June 28, 1839

Here Garrison stated his priorities. Eventually, abolition might indeed make its presence felt at the ballot box, but voters must first undergo a moral transformation. They should not vote until their souls were cleansed and they became wholly committed to Christ in all phases of life.

See also November 11, 1842, and January 20, 1843, for attacks on the Liberty Party (formed in Albany, New York, in April 1840 and based on an abolitionist platform) and the two-part commentary "Political Abolitionism," August 29 and September 5, 1845. On the Constitution and political action, see April 17, April 24, and May 1, 1846.

Once more, I beg not to be misapprehended. I have always expected, I still expect, to see abolition at the ballot-box, renovating the political action of the country—dispelling the sorcery influences of party—breaking asunder the fetters of political servitude—stirring up the torpid consciences of voters—substituting anti-slavery for pro-slavery representatives in every legislative assembly—modifying and rescinding all laws which sanction slavery. But this political reformation is to be effected solely by a change in the moral vision of the people—not by attempting to prove that it is the duty of every abolitionist to be a voter, but that it is the duty of every voter to be an abolitionist. By converting electors to the doctrine that slavery ought to be immediately abolished, a rectified political action is the natural consequence; for where this doctrine is received into the soul, the soul-carrier may be trusted any where, that he will not betray the cause of bleeding humanity. As to the height and depth, the length and breadth of CHRISTIANITY, it is not the province of abolition to decide; but only to settle one point—to wit, that slaveholding is a crime under all circumstances, leaving those who believe in the doctrine to carry out their principles, with all fidelity, in whatever sphere they may be called upon to act, but not authoritatively determining whether they are bound to be members of the church, or voters at the polls. It has never been a difficult matter to induce men to go to the ballot-box; but the grand difficulty ever has been, and still is, to persuade them to carry a good conscience thither, and act as free moral agents, not as the tools of party.

June 28, 1839, 102; *Letters* 2:481–84.

1841–1850:
"NO UNION WITH SLAVEHOLDERS!"

16

On Frederick Douglass
July 1, 1842

Garrison's relationship with Frederick Douglass (1817–1895) was complex, tense, and painful. After his escape from slavery in September 1838, Douglass traveled first to New York City and soon settled in New Bedford, Massachusetts. He read and subscribed to The Liberator *and first heard Garrison speak on August 9, 1841, at an antislavery meeting in New Bedford. Each man admired the other's rhetorical gifts and moral convictions. But by the late 1840s, the friendship between them suffered strains as Douglass launched his own newspaper and began to disagree with his mentor on antislavery policy and tactics. Douglass came to conclude that the Constitution was an antislavery document and that abolitionists could in good conscience enter the field of politics. By the 1850s, the Garrison-Douglass friendship had shattered.*

For the reprint of Garrison's preface to Douglass's Narrative, *see May 9, 1845. It is included in Douglass,* The Narrative of the Life, *ed. David W. Blight (Boston: Bedford Books, 1993), 29–35. See also the report of Douglass's speech at the May 6–8, 1845, American Anti-Slavery Society meeting, May 16, 1845, and comments on and reviews of and extracts from the* Narrative, *May 23, May 30, and June 6, 1845. For a defense of the truthfulness of Douglass's book, see February 20, 1846. The Liberator of the mid-1840s includes many reports on Douglass's activities abroad and reprints his speeches and letters. See, too, January 15, 1847, and March 5, 1847, for editorials in defense of "the ransom of Douglass." Here Garrison supported Douglass's purchase of his freedom—a plan some abolitionists opposed because it seemed to them to imply that slavery could be a legitimate transaction. On Garrison's dismay at Douglass's plans to edit his own newspaper, see July 23, 1847.*

July 1, 1842, 102.

Our first meeting was at Barnstable [Massachusetts], on Thursday, the 16th, on the subject of non-resistance. I was two hours behind the appointed time, (owing to the causes above stated,) but the audience behaved with exemplary patience, and they appeared to take a deep interest in the discussion that subsequently took place. Henry C. Wright was expected to be present, but was detained by his appointments in Maine. After I had spoken at some length, I was followed by two witnesses on the side of non-resistance, who, of all others, have the most cause to repudiate the doctrine, if it be dangerous to adopt it in practice. The first was Frederick Douglass. He stood there as a slave—a runaway from the southern house of bondage—not safe, for one hour, even on the soil of Massachusetts—with his back all horribly scarred by the lash—with the bitter remembrances of a life of slavery crowding upon his soul—with every thing in his past history, his present condition, his future prospects, to make him a fierce outlaw, and a stern avenger of outraged humanity! He stood there, not to counsel retaliation, not to advocate the right of the oppressed to wade through blood to liberty, not to declaim after the manner of worldly patriotism—O no!—but with the spirit of christian forgiveness in his heart, with the melting accents of charity on his lips, with the gentleness of love beaming in his eyes! His testimony was clear and emphatic. The cause of non-resistance he declared to be divine, and essential to the overthrow of every form of oppression on earth. It was so plain to his vision, it was so palpably in accordance with the genius of Christianity, that he found it difficult to argue the question. I could not help thinking how incomparably superior was this "chattel," in all the great qualities of the soul, to any warrior whose deeds are recorded on the page of history; and that here was a remarkable instance of christian magnanimity, and martyr-like devotion to the cause of humanity.—Unquestionably, above all men living, the slaves of this country would be justified in resisting their relentless tyrants unto blood. They find themselves stripped of all their heaven-derived rights, and ranked among the brutes that perish. Their bodies are lacerated with whips, or bound with chains, or scarred with branding-irons. They see their children sold on the auction-block, in company with cattle and swine—their wives scourged and polluted before their own eyes—their claim to be ranked among the intelligent creatures of God rejected with contempt. If, under such terrible provocations, it would be sinful for them to rise against their oppressors, and exact burning for burning, wound for wound, life for life; if, thus degraded, insulted, trampled on, they may not lift a hand or strike a blow in self defense; who will dare claim, for themselves, the right to use carnal weapons for their own protection? It is worthy of remark, that, in the case of their slave population, the American people admire the doctrine of non-resistance: in other words, they maintain that an insurrection against their bloody despotism would be an act of indescribable criminality. O base and shameless hypocrites! They can glory in the rebellion of 1776, and exult in the slaughter that was then made of the enemies of liberty; but they say it would be contrary to the teachings of the christian religion for those who are suffering from their tyranny to raise the standard of revolt, and cry liberty or death. The teachings of the christian religion! What do they care for any thing that is taught by that religion, if it conflict with their selfishness, ambition, lust, and love of dominion? But let them beware! They have a long account to settle with the God of justice — with him who is no respecter of persons, and who will by no means clear the guilty — with him who sank Pharaoh and his hosts beneath the waters of the Red Sea! Of what avail is their strength against his omnipotence? or their craftiness against his omniscience, or their show of freedom against his omnipresence?

17

"Address to the Slaves of the United States"
June 2, 1843

This is an example of Garrison's pledge of support to the slaves and affirmation of his own constancy and courage.

Take courage! Be filled with hope and comfort! Your redemption draws nigh, for the Lord is mightily at work in your behalf. Is it not frequently the darkest before day-break? The word has gone forth that you shall be delivered from your chains, and it has not been spoken in vain.

Although you have many enemies, yet you have also many friends — warm, faithful, sympathizing, devoted friends — who will never abandon your cause; who are pledged to do all in their power to break your chains; who are laboring to effect your emancipation without delay, in a peaceable manner, without the shedding of blood; who regard you as brethren and countrymen, and fear not the frowns or threats of your masters. They call themselves abolitionists. They have already suffered much, in various parts of the country, for rebuking those who keep you in slavery—for demanding your immediate liberation—for revealing to the people the horrors of your situation—for boldly opposing a corrupt public sentiment, by which you are kept in the great southern prison-house of bondage. Some of them have been beaten with stripes; others have been stripped, and covered with tar and feathers; others have had their property taken from them, and burnt in the streets; others have had large rewards offered by your masters for their seizure; others have been cast into jails and penitentiaries; others have been mobbed and lynched with great violence; others have lost their reputation, and been ruined in their business; others have lost their lives. All these, and many other outrages of an equally grievous kind, they have suffered for your sakes, and because they are your friends. They cannot go to the South, to see and converse with you, face to face; for, so ferocious and bloody-minded are your taskmasters, they would be put to an ignominious death as soon as discovered. Besides, it is not yet necessary that they should incur this peril; for it is solely by the aid of the people of the North, that you are held in bondage, and, therefore, they find enough to do at home, to make the people here your friends, and to break up all connexion with the slave system. They have proved themselves to be truly courageous, insensible to danger, superior to adversity, strong in principle, invincible in argument, animated by the spirit of impartial benevolence, unwearied in devising ways and means for your deliverance, the best friends of the whole country, the noblest champions of the human race. Ten years ago, they were so few and feeble as only to excite universal contempt; now they number in their ranks, hundreds of thousands of the people.—Then, they had scarcely a single anti-slavery society in operation; now they have thousands. Then, they had only one or two presses to plead your cause; now they have multitudes. They are scattering all over the land their newspapers, books, pamphlets, tracts, and other publications, to hold up to infamy the conduct of your oppressors, and to awaken sympathy in your behalf. They are continually holding anti-slavery meetings in all parts of the free States, to tell the people the story of your wrongs. Wonderful has been the change effected in public feeling, under God, through their instrumentality. Do not fear that they will grow weary in your service. They are confident of success, in the end. They know that the Lord Almighty is with them— that truth, justice, right, are with them—that you are with them. They know, too, that your masters are cowardly and weak, through conscious wrong doing, and already begin to falter in their course. Lift up your heads, O ye despairing slaves! Yet a little while, and your chains shall snap asunder, and you shall be tortured and plundered no more! Then, fathers and mothers, your children shall be yours, to bring them up in the nurture and admonition of the Lord. Then, husbands and wives, now torn from each other's arms, you shall be reunited in the flesh, and man shall no longer dare to put asunder those whom God has joined together. Then, brothers and sisters, you shall be sold to the remorseless slave speculator no more, but dwell together in unity. "God hasten that joyful day!" is now the daily prayer of millions.

The weapons with which the abolitionists seek to effect your deliverance are not bowie knives, pistols, swords, guns, or any other deadly implements. They consist of appeals, warnings, rebukes, arguments and facts, addressed to the understandings, consciences and hearts of the people. Many of your friends believe that not even those who are oppressed, whether their skins are white or black, can shed the blood of their oppressors in accordance with the will of God; while many others believe that it is right for the oppressed to rise and take their liberty by violence, if they can secure it in no other manner; but they, in common with all your friends, believe that every attempt at insurrection would be attended with disaster and defeat, on your part, because you are not strong enough to contend with the military power of the nation; consequently, their advice to you is, to be patient, long-suffering, and submissive, yet awhile longer—trusting that, by the blessing of the Most High on their labors, you will yet be emancipated without shedding a drop of your masters' blood, or losing a drop of your own.

The abolitionists of the North are the only true and unyielding friends on whom you can rely. They will never deceive nor betray you. They have made your cause their own, and they mean to be true to themselves and to you, whatever may be the consequence. They are continually increasing in number, in influence, in enterprise and determination; and, judging from the success which has already attended their measures, they anticipate that, in a comparatively short period, the entire North will receive you with open arms, and give you shelter and protection, as fast as you escape from the South. We, who now address you, are united with them in spirit and design. We glory in the name of abolitionists, for it signifies friendship for all who are pining in servitude. We advise you to seize every opportunity to escape from your masters, and, fixing your eyes on the North star, travel on until you reach a land of liberty. You are not the property of your masters. God never made one human being to be owned by another. Your right to be free, at any moment, is undeniable; and it is your duty, whenever you can, peaceably to escape from the plantations on which you are confined, and assert your manhood.

18

"The American Union"

January 10, 1845

Garrison frequently used harsh, violent language to indict America and advocate the imperative of "disunion."

For other examples of antislavery and disunion, see April 22, May 6, and June 10, 1842. See also "No Compromise with Slavery," January 19, 1844, May 24 and May 31, 1844; and "Address to the Friends of Freedom and Emancipation in the United States," May 31, 1844.

Tyrants of the old world! contemners of the rights of man! disbelievers in human freedom and equality! enemies of mankind! console not yourselves with the delusion, that REPUBLICANISM and the AMERICAN UNION are synonymous terms—or that the downfall of the latter will be the extinction of the former, and, consequently, a proof of the incapacity of the people for self-government, and a confirmation of your own despotic claims! Your thrones must crumble to dust; your sceptre of dominion drop from your powerless hands; your rod of oppression be broken; yourselves so vilely abased, that there shall be "none so poor to do you reverence." The will of God, the beneficent Creator of the human family, cannot always be frustrated. It is his will that every form of usurpation, every kind of injustice, every device of tyranny, shall come to nought; that peace, and liberty, and righteousness, shall "reign from sea to sea, and from the rivers to the ends of the earth"; and that, throughout the earth, in the fulness of a sure redemption, there shall be "none to molest or make afraid." Humanity, covered with gore, cries with a voice that pierces the heavens. *"His will be done!"* Justice, discrowned by the hand of violence, exclaims in tones of deep solemnity, "HIS WILL BE DONE!" Liberty, burdened with chains, and driven into exile, in thunder-tones responds, "HIS WILL BE DONE!"

Tyrants! know that the rights of man are inherent and unalienable, and therefore, not to be forfeited by the failure of any form of government, however democratic. Let the American Union perish; let these allied States be torn with faction, or drenched in blood; let this republic realize

---

Jan. 10, 1845, 5.

the fate of Rome and Carthage, of Babylon and Tyre;[1] still those rights would remain undiminished in strength, unsullied in purity, unaffected in value, and sacred as their Divine Author. If nations perish, it is not because of their devotion to liberty, but for their disregard of its requirements. Man is superior to all political compacts, all governmental arrangements, all religious institutions. As means to an end, these may sometimes be useful, though never indispensable; but that end must always be the freedom and happiness of man, INDIVIDUAL MAN. It can never be true that the public good requires the violent sacrifice of any, even the humblest citizen; for it is absolutely dependent on his preservation, not destruction. To do evil that good may come, is equally absurd and criminal. The time for the overthrow of any government, the abandonment of any alliance, the subversion of any institution, is, whenever it justifies the immolation of the individual to secure the general welfare; for the welfare of the many cannot be hostile to the safety of the few. In all agreements, in all measures, in all political or religious enterprises, in all attempts to redeem the human race, man, as an individual, is to be held paramount: —

"Him first, him last, him midst, and without end."

The doctrine, that the end sanctifies the means, is the maxim of profligates and impostors, of usurpers and tyrants. They who, to promote the cause of truth will sanction the utterance of a falsehood are to be put in the category of liars. So, likewise, they who are for trampling on the rights of the minority, in order to benefit the majority, are to be registered as the monsters of their race. Might is never right, excepting when it sees in every human being, "a man and a brother," and protects him with a divine fidelity. It is the recognition of these truths, the adoption of these principles, which alone can extirpate tyranny from the earth, perpetuate a free government, and cause the dwellers in every clime, "like kindred drops, to mingle into one."

Tyrants! confident of its overthrow, proclaim not to your vassals that the AMERICAN UNION is an experiment of Freedom, which, if it fail, will forever demonstrate the necessity of whips for the backs, and chains for the limbs of the people. Know that its subversion is essential to the triumph of justice, the deliverance of the oppressed, the vindication of the BROTHERHOOD OF THE RACE. It was conceived in sin, and brought forth in

---

[1] Rome, the center of the Roman Empire, was sacked by Germanic tribes in the fifth century; Carthage, a powerful ancient city in North Africa, was destroyed by Rome in the second century B.C., at the end of the Third Punic War; Babylon, the capital of the Babylonian Empire, was conquered by Persia in the sixth century B.C.; Tyre, the ancient city of Phoenicia on the Mediterranean coast, was besieged and sacked by Alexander the Great in the fourth century B.C.

iniquity; and its career has been marked by unparalleled hypocrisy, by high-handed tyranny, by a bold defiance of the omniscience and omnipotence of God. Freedom indignantly disowns it, and calls for its extinction; for within its borders are three millions of Slaves, whose blood constitutes its cement, whose flesh forms a large and flourishing branch of its commerce, and who are ranked with four-footed beasts and creeping things. To secure the adoption of the Constitution of the United States, it was agreed, first, that the African slave-trade, — till that time, a feeble, isolated colonial traffic, — should for at least twenty years be prosecuted as a national interest under the American flag, and protected by the national arm; — secondly, that a slaveholding oligarchy, created by allowing three-fifths of the slave population to be represented by their taskmasters, should be allowed a permanent seat in Congress; — thirdly, that the slave system should be secured against internal revolt and external invasion, by the united physical force of the country; — fourthly, that not a foot of national territory should be granted, on which the panting fugitive from Slavery might stand, and be safe from his pursuers — thus making every citizen a slave-hunter and slave-catcher. To say that this "covenant with death" shall not be annulled — that this "agreement with hell" shall continue to stand — that this "refuge of lies" shall not be swept away — is to hurl defiance at the eternal throne, and to give the lie to Him who sits thereon. It is an attempt, alike monstrous and impracticable, to blend the light of heaven with the darkness of the bottomless pit, to unite the living with the dead, to associate the Son of God with the prince of evil.

Accursed be the AMERICAN UNION, as a stupendous republican imposture!

Accursed be it, as the most frightful despotism, with regard to three millions of the people, ever exercised over any portion of the human family!

Accursed be it, as the most subtle and atrocious compromise ever made to gratify power and selfishness!

Accursed be it, as a libel on Democracy, and a bold assault on Christianity!

Accursed be it, as stained with human blood, and supported by human sacrifices!

Accursed be it, for the terrible evils it has inflicted on Africa, by burning her villages, ravaging her coast, and kidnapping her children, at an enormous expense of human life, and for a diabolical purpose!

Accursed be it, for all the crimes it has committed at home — for seeking the utter extermination of the red men of its wildernesses — and for enslaving one-sixth part of its teeming population!

Accursed be it, for its hypocrisy, its falsehood, its impudence, its lust, its cruelty, its oppression!

Accursed be it, as a mighty obstacle in the way of universal freedom and equality!

Accursed be it, from the foundation to the roof, and may there soon not be left one stone upon another, that shall not be thrown down!

Henceforth, the watchword of every uncompromising abolitionist, of every friend of God and liberty, must be, both in a religious and political sense—"NO UNION WITH SLAVEHOLDERS!"

19

"American Colorphobia"

June 11, 1847

Garrison called not only for abolition but also for equal rights and the end of racial prejudice. He was responding here to a shockingly racist article by the Irish political operative Mike Walsh,[1] which Garrison reprinted on the front page of the June 4, 1847, Liberator. *Walsh derided the "disgusting intimacy" between a white woman and the "black vagabond" and "semi-baboon" Frederick Douglass that, he said, included a sexual liaison aboard a steamship.*

A friend in New-York, in a private note to us, expresses regret that we should have descended so far as to notice the scurrilous attack of the notorious Mike Walsh upon FREDERICK DOUGLASS, and especially that we copied into the last number of the Liberator, Walsh's brutal and defamatory article. We are not sure that our friend is not right in his judgment in this matter. Though the "REFUGE OF OPPRESSION" is a department of our paper, the express object of which is to make permanent record of the various forms of hostility to the anti-slavery cause, its faithful advocates, and the free colored population, — and though we have found it necessary to print in it, numerous malignant and ferocious articles, to

[1] Walsh (1815–1859) was an Irish immigrant and a printer, journalist, and political agent and agitator in New York City. He denounced abolitionists for caring more about black slaves in the South than about white laborers and factory workers, the "wage slaves" of the North.

illustrate the character and spirit of our opponents, — yet there are limits even to an indulgence of this kind; and some of these attacks are either so puerile and paltry, or so indecent and revolting, as to forbid their publication even in a department consecrated to infamy.

Reluctant as we felt to insert the offensive article alluded to, it so undisguisedly expressed the venomous hatred which so generally prevails in this country toward the free colored people — mark! in exact proportion as they become enlightened and refined — (none is cherished toward the slave population, for they are completely crushed, and excite no fear of rivalry) — that we were satisfied it not only carried its own antidote with it, but would help to overthrow, by reaction, the odious spirit of complexional caste which it was designed to eternize.

In another column, a letter will be found from Mr. Douglass, in denial and refutation of the foul charge brought against him, (this was quite needless,) and in particular reference to an article in the Albany "Switch," a paper so habitually obscene and libellous, we understand, as to have no tangible proprietor, publisher, or editor.

The only thing we regret is, that one of the best and noblest of her sex, in her humane anxiety to secure for Mr. Douglass the usual accommodations granted to white travellers on the Hudson river, that his health might not be perilled by exposure, should have effected her purpose by a violation of the rules of the boat, which preclude any colored person from occupying a state room, or obtaining a comfortable berth. These rules are most unreasonable and cruel; but they are not to be subverted by stealth, which only irritates and hardens the spirit which framed them. They must be conquered openly, and through much suffering. We highly appreciate her generous self-forgetfulness, and the humane impulses by which she was actuated; but we think she committed an error of judgment. With the harmlessness of the dove, she did not in this instance blend the wisdom of the serpent; and thus she subjected herself and friend to foul reproaches and frenzied maledictions. It shows that too much heed cannot be given to the apostolic admonition, to shun the very appearance of evil. It happens, unfortunately, that Capt. Cruttenden, of the Hendrick Hudson, is peculiarly inimical to the abolitionists, and raving with colorphobia; and hence, there is no lack of disposition on his part to put the vilest construction upon an act as pure, as disinterested, and as benevolent, as was ever conceived by the human heart, or executed by human will. We are told that he formerly kept the City Hotel in New-York, and derived no small amount of patronage from Southern sojourners in that city. Possibly he is a slave-owner; or, if not, it is not, we opine, on account of any scruples of conscience. Let him and his boat be remembered by the friends of justice and humanity, as they travel up or down the Hudson river, and both be shunned as far as practicable.

There is nothing which excites more unfeigned astonishment in the old world, than the prejudice which dogs the footsteps of the man of color in this pseudo republic. True, there are many absurd, criminal, aristocratic distinctions abroad, which ought to cease; but these are also found, to a great extent, in the United States, and have been common to all countries, and in every age. They originate in the pride of wealth, in successful enterprise, in educational superiority, in official rank, in civil, military, and ecclesiastical rule. For these, there may be framed some plausible excuses. But to enslave, brutalize, scorn and insult human beings solely on account of the hue of the skin which it has pleased God to bestow on them; to pronounce them accursed, for no crime on their part; to treat them substantially alike, whether they are virtuous or vicious, refined or vulgar, rich or poor, aspiring or grovelling; to be inflamed with madness against them in proportion as they rise in self-respect, and improve in their manners and morals; this is an act so unnatural, a crime so monstrous, a sin so God-defying, that it throws into the shade all other distinctions known among mankind. Thank God, it is confined to a very small portion of the globe; though, strange to tell, it is perpetrated the most grossly, and in a spirit the most ferocious and inexorable, in a land claiming to be the pattern-land of the world—the most enlightened, the most democratic, the most Christian. Complexional caste is tolerated no where excepting in the immediate vicinage of slavery. It has no foundation in nature, reason, or universal custom. But, as the origin of it is to be traced to the existence of slavery, so its utter eradication is not to be expected until that hideous system be overthrown. Nothing but the removal of the cause can destroy the effect. That, with all its desperate efforts to lengthen its cords and strengthen its stakes, the Slave Power is continually growing weaker, is most clearly demonstrated in the gradual abatement of the prejudice which we have been deploring; for strong and terrible as that prejudice now is, it has received a very perceptible check within the last ten years, especially in New England.

No one can blame the intelligent and virtuous colored American for turning his back upon the land of his nativity, and escaping from it with the precipitancy that marked the flight of Lot out of Sodom. To remain in it is to subject himself to continual annoyance, persecution, and outrage. In fifteen or twenty days, he can place his feet on the shores of Europe—in Great Britain and Ireland—where, if he cannot obtain more food or better clothing, he can surely find that his complexion is not regarded as a crime, and constitutes no barrier to his social, intellectual, or political advancement. He who, with this powerful temptation to become an exile before him, is resolved to remain at home, and take his lot and portion with his down trodden brethren—to lay his comfort, reputation and hopes on the altar of freedom—exhibits the true martyr spirit, and is deserving of a world's sympathy and applause. Such a man, in an eminent degree, is FREDERICK DOUGLASS. Abroad, beloved, honored, admitted to the most refined circles, and eulogised by the Jerrolds, the Howitts,[2] and a host of Britain's brightest intellects;—at home, not without numerous friends and admirers, it is true, yet made the object of popular contumely, denied the customary rights and privileges of a man, and surrounded by an atmosphere of prejudice which is enough to appal the stoutest heart, and to depress the most elastic spirit. Such is the difference between England and America; between a people living under a monarchical form of government, and a nation of boasting republicans!—O what crimes are perpetrated under the mask of democratic liberty! what outrages are consummated under the profession of Christianity!

> Fleecy locks and dark complexion
> Cannot forfeit Nature's claim;
> Skins may differ, but affection
> Dwells in white and black the same.

[2] Douglas William Jerrold (1803–1857) was an English man of letters and playwright; William (1792–1879) and Mary (1799–1888) Howitt were English Quakers and popular writers and translators.

20

Mob Attack on Douglass
August 20, 1847

This is taken from an August 9, 1847, letter that Garrison wrote to his wife and that he reprinted in The Liberator. *In it he describes the hostility that Douglass encountered as a free black man traveling in Pennsylvania and speaking to an audience there.*

On Saturday morning, Douglass and I bade farewell to our kind friends in Philadelphia, and took the cars for this place [Harrisburg], a distance of 106 miles. Before we started, an incident occurred which evinced something of that venomous pro-slavery spirit which pervades the public sentiment in proportion as you approach the borders of the slave States. There is no distinction made at Philadelphia in the cars on account of complexion, though colored persons usually sit near the doors. Douglass took a seat in one of the back cars before I arrived; and, while quietly looking out at the window, was suddenly accosted in a slave-driving tone, and ordered to "get out of that seat," by a man who had a lady with him, and who might have claimed the right to eject any other passenger for his accommodation with as much propriety. Douglass quietly replied, that if he would make his demand in the form of a gentlemanly request, he would readily vacate his seat. His lordly commander at once laid violent hands upon him, and dragged him out. Douglass submitted to this outrage unresistingly, but told his assailant that he behaved like a bully, and therefore precluded him (D.) from meeting him with his own weapons. The only response of the other was, that he would knock D.'s teeth down his throat if he repeated the charge. The name of this man was soon ascertained to be John A. Fisher of Harrisburg, a lawyer; and the only palliation (if it be one) that I hear offered for his conduct is, that he was undoubtedly under the influence of intoxicating liquor. This was a foretaste of the violence to be experienced on our attempting to lecture here, and which I anticipated even before I left Boston.

Though the cars (compared with our Eastern ones) look as if they were made a century ago, and are quite uncomfortable, yet the ride was far from being irksome, on account of the all-pervading beauty and opulence of the country through which we passed, so far as a fine soil and natural scenery are concerned. We passed through the counties of Philadelphia, Chester, Lancaster, and a portion of Dauphin, and, through the whole distance, saw but a single spot that reminded us of our rocky New England. Arriving at 3 o'clock, we found at the depot, awaiting our coming, Dr. Rutherford, an old subscriber to the Liberator, and his sister-in-law, Agnes Crane, both of them true and faithful to the anti-slavery cause in the midst of a perverse and prejudiced people; and also several of our colored friends, with one of whom (Mr. Wolf, an intelligent and worthy man) Douglass went home, having previously engaged to do so; while I went with Dr. Rutherford, and received a cordial welcome from his estimable lady.

The Court House had been obtained for us for Saturday and Sunday evenings. Hitherto, nearly all the anti-slavery lecturers have failed to gather any considerable number together; but, on this occasion, we had the room filled, some of the most respectable citizens being present. At an early period of the evening, before the services commenced, it was evident that mischief was brewing and an explosion would ultimately follow. I first addressed the meeting, and was listened to, not only without molestation, but with marked attention and respect, though my remarks were stringent, and my accusations severe. As soon, however, as Douglass rose to speak, the spirit of rowdyism began to show itself outside of the building, around the door and windows. It was the first time that a "nigger" had attempted to address the people of Harrisburg in public, and it was regarded by the mob as an act of unparalleled audacity. They knew nothing at all of Douglass, except that he was a "nigger." They came equipped with rotten eggs and brickbats, firecrackers, and other missiles, and made use of them somewhat freely—breaking panes of glass, and soiling the clothes of some who were struck by the eggs. One of these bespattered my head and back somewhat freely. Of course there was a great deal of yelling and shouting, and of violent exclamation—such as, "Out with the damned nigger," etc., etc. The audience at first manifested considerable alarm, but I was enabled to obtain a silent hearing for a few moments, when I told the meeting that if this was a specimen of Harrisburg decorum and love of liberty, instead of wasting our breath upon the place, we should turn our backs upon it, shaking off the dust of our feet, etc., etc.

21

The Death of President Polk
June 22, 1849

James K. Polk (1795–1849), Democrat from Tennessee, was elected president in 1844. Garrison believed that Polk had instigated the Mexican War (1846–1848) to gain more territory for slavery. By the terms of the Treaty of Guadalupe Hidalgo (February 2, 1848), Mexico had ceded two-fifths of its territory to the United States, and this had sparked intense national debate about whether slavery should be allowed to expand into the West and Southwest. To Garrison, Polk's presidency showed the complete control over the national government that expansionist slaveholding interests had acquired.

June 22, 1849, 98.

The death of the late Ex-President of the United States is announced to have taken place last Friday night, near Nashville, Tennessee. His complaint was chronic diarrhea. The transition from the Presidential chair to the grave has been swift and startling. Neither humanity, nor justice, nor liberty, has any cause to deplore the event. He probably died an unrepentant man-stealer. His administration has been a curse to the country, which will extend to the latest posterity.

22
John C. Calhoun, Daniel Webster, and the Compromise of 1850
March 15, 1850

Garrison denounced the Southern Senator Calhoun for his proslavery stand, but like many antislavery advocates in the North, he was especially angered by the conduct of Daniel Webster (1782–1852), senator from Massachusetts, who had spoken on March 7, 1850, in favor of the "compromise" measures of 1850.

The Compromise of 1850 included provisions favorable to antislavery: the slave trade was prohibited in the District of Columbia, and California was admitted to the Union as a free state. But the Compromise also enacted a new, more severe fugitive slave law (passed on September 18, 1850) that denied a jury trial to and prohibited the testimony of escaped slaves and that imposed severe penalties on anyone who aided them.

Webster was not only an admired lawyer and statesman, but also a brilliant orator. His support for the Compromise of 1850 struck Garrison and others as an act of moral treason. They were indeed preoccupied, even obsessed, by Webster's action. It exemplified to them the complete abandonment of principle, the surrender of Webster's great powers of eloquence to an evil cause.

On Calhoun, see also "The Debate in Congress," May 5, 1848, and January 26 and February 2, 1849.

For more on Webster, see "The Great Apostate," December 27, 1850, and November 21, 1851, and May 28, 1852. Note, too, "The Death of

Webster" (by Edmund Quincy), October 29, 1852, and Garrison's own commentary, December 3, 1852. There are many letters, commentaries, and addresses on Webster by Theodore Parker, Thomas Wentworth Higginson, Wendell Phillips, Samuel J. May, and others in the 1850–1855 issues. Garrison remarked on Webster in "Webster's Birthday," January 27, 1854, and returned to him yet again in "Man-Worship," January 25, 1856.

Among the half a dozen men in Congress, the utterance of whose sentiments, in times of deep excitement, command the national attention, and exert in all sections of the country a strong influence over the popular mind, for good or evil, Mr. Calhoun stands prominent. Yet he has no breadth of character, no greatness of spirit, no generosity of purpose, no comprehensiveness of view. No man was ever more sectional in his feelings and aims. In no aspect does he present an *American* front; he is a Southern man as against the North; the welfare of the South, not of the republic, is the object of his solicitude; the extension and perpetuity of slavery, not the enlargement and preservation of liberty, are the ends of his public labors. To be simply an American; to go, in the grandiloquent language of Mr. Webster, for "our country, our whole country, and nothing but our country"—or, in the profligate declaration of Mr. Winthrop,[1] for "our country, however bounded"—is to present to the world a very small pattern of a man; but to be, in affection, interest, honor, absorbed by a fractional portion of the land of one's nativity, to the utter unconsciousness of any other relations or duties, is a reduction to pigmean littleness. Intellectually, it is universally conceded tht Mr. Calhoun is much above mediocrity; but a strong intellect, miserably perverted, is neither an object of admiration, nor creditable to its possessor; certainly, it is a calamity to the race. The real dimensions of a man are to be known by the size of his heart, rather than by the volume of his brain. But where or what is the heart of John C. Calhoun? Who has felt its warmth? who can testify to its pulsation? who perceives in it any vitality? There is no blood in him; he is as cold as a corpse. He is made of iron, not flesh; he is hybridous, not natural. There never has been his match or parallel on earth, in his consecration as a public man to the hideous system of chattel slavery—its safety, advancement, perpetuation. His statesmanship is nothing better, nothing less, than demonship. He is demonized by a principle or passion that destroys all human affinity, and saps the foundation of all morality. He

[1] The reference here is probably to Robert Winthrop (1809–1894), lawyer, orator, legislator, and congressman from Massachusetts.

believes, and acts in accordance with that belief, that it is "better to reign in hell than serve in heaven." Damnation suits his taste and temperament, he being uppermost among the damned, invested with full powers of mastery. Where there are no chains, no torments, no enforced degradation, no contempt of moral obligation, he could not, and would not dwell at ease. Universal peace, equality, purity, happiness, would be to him an intolerable state of society. Like Satan, as described in Milton's Paradise Lost, he exclaims —

> Farewell, happy fields,
> Where joy for ever dwells! hail, horrors! hail,
> Infernal world! and thou, profoundest hell,
> Receive thy new possessor! One, who brings
> A mind not to be chang'd by place or time.
> The mind is its own place, and in itself
> Can make a heaven of hell, a hell of heaven.
> What matter where, if I be still the same,
> And what I should be, all but less than he
> Whom thunder hath made greater? Here at least
> We shall be free; the Almighty hath not built
> Here for his envy; will not drive us hence;
> Here we may reign secure; and in my choice
> To reign is worth ambition, though in hell.

— The beams of the sun of liberty are as hateful to him as were those of the natural sun to Lucifer, after his overthrow: —

> O thou! that with surpassing glory crown'd,
> Look'st from thy sole dominion like the god
> Of this new world; at whose sight all the stars
> Hide their diminish'd heads; to thee I call,
> But with no friendly voice, and add thy name,
> O sun! to tell thee how I hate thy beams,
> That bring to my remembrance from what state
> I fell; how glorious once above thy sphere;
> Till pride and worse ambition threw me down,
> Warring in heaven against heaven's matchless King.

For three centuries, chattel slavery has had its advocates and defenders; but rather as a temporary expedient than as a permanent system. Few persons, of any note, have been so lost to shame as to vindicate it as in itself right, and worthy of perpetuity. Washington, Patrick Henry, Jefferson, all the distinguished men of the South identified with "the times that tried men's souls," invariably deplored its existence as an evil, and contemplated its gradual but certain extirpation. But Mr. Calhoun — in utter disregard of testimonies like these, in absolute contempt of the self-evident truths set forth in the Declaration of Independence, in bold defiance of the sentiments of a world still low in its estimate of human liberty, in violence of all the instincts of his nature—asserts it to be a blessing, the noblest of all institutions, the source of national prosperity, the corner-stone of the temple of republican freedom!! Living, he contends for it as though existence without it would be insupportable; and dying, he is resolved to bequeath it to posterity as the richest legacy that can be given! Is this unadulterated wickedness or downright insanity? If he is a sane man, on this subject; if his brain is not diseased to an extent that destroys accountability; then he is among the wickedest of men—of his father, the devil, whose work he delights to do. His conscience is "seared as with a hot iron." In point of cruelty, he is more to be abhorred than Caligula; on the score of tyranny, he is worse than Pharaoh.[2] His villanies [sic] are innumerable and stupendous. He commits atrocities on a gigantic scale. He is not merely an adulterer, a thief, a barbarian, an oppressor, a man-stealer, in an individual sense, on a private scale, but comprehensively, multitudinously, by wholesale. He is not to be judged by the number of slaves actually on his plantation, under his special treatment. As the shameless robber of their rights, the remorseless foe to their emancipation and improvement, he is to be ranked as a criminal of no ordinary dye. But he goes for the enslavement of millions of his race, and their posterity to the end of time; and whatever that bondage requires, — or whips, or chains, or instruments of torture, or bloodhounds, or merciless penal laws, — for its unimpaired exercise, he is ready to advocate and enforce. He is destitute of virtue; for he denies to these millions the marriage institution, and enforces universal prostitution. He is without natural affection; for he is in favor of a wholesale and retail traffic in human flesh, and sells the babes of mothers as readily as the progeny of swine. He is fraudulent to the last degree; keeping back the hire of the laborers who reap down his fields, and plundering them of every possession. His impiety cannot be transcended; for to his miserable victims he says, — "*I am God, and beside me there is none else*"—and to the command to let the oppressed go free, he says, in the language of the Egyptian tyrant, "Who is the Lord, that I should obey his voice, to let Israel go? I know not the Lord, neither will I let Israel go."

If, on the other hand, Mr. Calhoun is diseased on this subject to an

---

[2] Caligula (A.D. 12–41) was the cruel and extravagant emperor of Rome from 37 to 41. Pharaoh was the god-king of ancient Egypt; the term was used especially in reference to Rameses II, the pharaoh of the Exodus, the Old Testament account of the Hebrews' flight to freedom from Egyptian captivity.

insane degree, and so is not to be held accountable for his sayings and doings, then his proper place is in an Insane Asylum, and not in the Senate of the United States,—though it is true, since the addition of Foote and Clemens[3] to that body, the Senate has partaken largely of the characteristics of Bedlam. But this excuse is not to be gravely urged, and therefore Mr. Calhoun, in a right moral estimate, is deserving the condemnation we have bestowed upon him.

On our first page, we have given a large portion of the speech of Mr. Calhoun, (and next week we shall publish the remainder,) which, in consequence of his feeble state of health, was read in the Senate, at his request, on the 4th instant. If we had time, we have not room to notice it at length in our present number; but its sum and substance are easily stated in a few words.

He bitterly complains, (and here he seems to give plausible evidence of insanity,) that while the North and the South, at the adoption of the Constitution, had almost an equal population, and an equal division of the States, the North has since been rapidly distancing the South, in point of numbers, political strength, prosperity, &c. &c., so that the equilibrium is lost, on which alone the Union can be maintained!! This striking disparity between the two sections he perversely declares has been owing to the preponderance of Northern influence in the management of the government; whereas, it is merely the difference between free labor and slave labor; and, moreover, it is notorious that the government has been wholly controlled by the Slave Power for the last fifty years.

How can the Union be preserved? Only by stopping the anti-slavery agitation, and keeping Liberty within the dimensions of the Procrustean bedstead of Slavery!! What can be more rational than this? what more easily effected? It is a demand for a repeal of the law of gravitation, and the extinction of the human mind!

> Tyrants! in vain ye trace the wizard ring;
> In vain ye limit Mind's unwearied spring!
> What! can ye lull the winged winds asleep,
> Arrest the rolling world, or chain the deep?
> No—the wild wave contemns your sceptered hand:
> It rolled not back when Canute[4] gave command![5]

---

[3] Henry Foote (1804–1880), Democratic senator from Mississippi; Jeremiah Clemens (1814–1865), Democratic senator from Alabama.

[4] Canute was an eleventh-century king of England, Denmark, and Norway who, it is said, tried to make the tide recede—a story that was taken to show human weakness compared with the power of God.

[5] From the 1799 poem "The Pleasures of Hope," 1.429–434, by Scottish poet Thomas Campbell (1777–1844).

Let the People Speak

What if DANIEL WEBSTER has betrayed the cause of liberty, bent his supple knees anew to the Slave Power, and dishonored the State which he was sent to Congress faithfully to represent? Is he *Massachusetts*—and as he moves, is she to follow, even to the lowest depth of moral degradation? No—he is only one of eight hundred thousand, many of whom are incomparably his superior, if not in intellectual ability, at least in all those moral qualities and generous affections which bless and preserve society. On the great question of slavery extension or slavery prohibition, now before the country, the "common people"—the farmers, mechanics, and working classes generally—are as capable of forming their own opinions, each for himself, as Daniel Webster or John C. Calhoun. It is for them to speak and act with promptness at this crisis, (when so many public men are yielding to the power of corruption,) in a manner worthy of the glorious cause of liberty. Let it be shown, on their part, by a movement almost as rapid as that of the lightning of heaven, that Mr. Webster receives no endorsement at their hands; that he has not spoken their sentiments; and that they regard him as worthy of official censure. To facilitate such a movement, the following memorial to the Legislature has been drawn up for signatures, not in condemnation of his whole speech, as such, (though it has not a redeeming feature in it,) but in reference to two or three points on which the people of Massachusetts, without distinction of party, are overwhelmingly united in sentiment. Let this memorial be quickly circulated, signed, and presented to the Legislature; and we trust that that body will fearlessly discharge its duty by responding to the prayer of the memorialists, in an emphatic manner.

1851–1860: DECADE OF CRISIS:
THE COMING OF THE CIVIL WAR

23

Review of Harriet Beecher Stowe's Novel
Uncle Tom's Cabin
March 26, 1852

Harriet Beecher Stowe's extremely popular and influential antislavery novel Uncle Tom's Cabin *appeared first in serialized form from June 1851 to April 1852 in the Washington, D.C.–based* The National Era *(1847–1860), the official weekly journal of the American and Foreign Anti-Slavery Society. This society had formed in May 1840 in opposition to Garrison. Its leaders included Lewis Tappan (1788–1873), James Birney (1792–1857), and others who judged that Garrison had mistakenly involved the American Anti-Slavery Society in the cause of women's rights and, in addition, had curtailed the impact of abolitionism by remaining opposed to political action.*

In his review Garrison challenged the meekness and subservience that Stowe (1811–1896) depicted in the martyred slave Tom, and he briefly noted his disapproval of the Liberian colonization plan that Stowe endorsed in her final chapters (especially chapters 43 and 45).

See the reprint of chapter 7 of the novel (Eliza's escape and crossing of the Ohio River on chunks of ice), April 2, 1852; and the brief comment on Stowe's book, June 11, 1852. For an editorial, "Anti-Slavery Novels," see January 5, 1855. See also Document 5.

In the execution of her very difficult task, Mrs. Stowe has displayed rare descriptive powers, a familiar acquaintance with slavery under its best and its worst phases, uncommon moral and philosophical acumen, great facility of thought and expression, feelings and emotions of the strongest character. Intimate as we have been, for a score of years, with the features and operations of the slave system, and often as we have listened to the recitals of its horrors from the lips of the poor hunted fugitives, we confess to the frequent moistening of our eyes, and the making of our heart grow

Harriet Beecher Stowe in 1852, the year in which *Uncle Tom's Cabin* was published

liquid as water, and the trembling of every nerve within us, in the perusal of the incidents and scenes so vividly depicted in her pages. The effect of such a work upon all intelligent and humane minds coming in contact with it, and especially upon the rising generation in its plastic condition, to awaken the strongest compassion for the oppressed and the utmost abhorrence of the system which grinds them to the dust, cannot be estimated: it must be prodigious, and therefore eminently serviceable in the tremendous conflict now waged for the immediate and entire suppression of slavery on the American soil.

The appalling liabilities which constantly impend over such slaves as have "kind and indulgent masters," are thrillingly illustrated in various personal narratives; especially in that of "Uncle Tom," over whose fate every reader will drop the scalding tear, and for whose character the highest reverence will be felt. No insult, no outrage, no suffering, could ruffle the Christlike meekness of his spirit, or shake the steadfastness of his faith. Towards his merciless oppressors he cherished no animosity, and breathed nothing of retaliation. Like his Lord and Master, he was willing to be "led as a lamb to the slaughter," returning blessing for cursing, and anxious only for the salvation of his enemies. His character is sketched with great power and rare religious perception. It triumphantly exemplifies the nature, tendency, and results of CHRISTIAN NON-RESISTANCE.

We are curious to know whether Mrs. Stowe is a believer in the duty of non-resistance for the white man, under all possible outrage and peril, as well as for the black man; whether she is for self-defence on her own part, or that of her husband or friends or country, in case of malignant assault, or whether she impartially disarms all mankind in the name of Christ, be the danger or suffering what it may. We are curious to know this, because our opinion of her, as a religious teacher, would be greatly strengthened or lessened as the inquiry might terminate. That all the slaves of the South ought, "if smitten on the one cheek, to turn the other also,"—to repudiate all carnal weapons, shed no blood, "be obedient to their masters," wait for a peaceful deliverance, and abstain from all insurrectionary movements— is everywhere taken for granted, because the VICTIMS ARE BLACK. *They* cannot be animated by a Christian spirit and yet return blow for blow, or conspire for the destruction of their oppressors. *They* are required by the Bible to put away all wrath, to submit to every conceivable outrage without resistance, to suffer with Christ if they would reign with him. None of *their* advocates may seek to inspire *them* to imitate the example of the Greeks, the Poles, the Hungarians,[1] our Revolutionary sires; for such teaching would evince a most unchristian and bloodthirsty disposition. For *them* there is no hope of heaven unless *they* give the most literal interpretations to the non-resisting injunctions contained in the Sermon on the Mount, touching the treatment of enemies. It is for *them,* though despoiled of all their rights and deprived of all protection, to "threaten not, but to commit the keeping of their souls to God in well-doing, as unto a faithful Creator."

---

[1] Garrison refers here to countries in which revolutions had arisen. The campaign against slavery and for freedom in the United States coincided not only with the abolitionist movement abroad (in 1833 Parliament ordered the abolition of slavery in the British colonies by Aug. 1, 1834) but also with political rebellion and reaction in nearly every European nation.

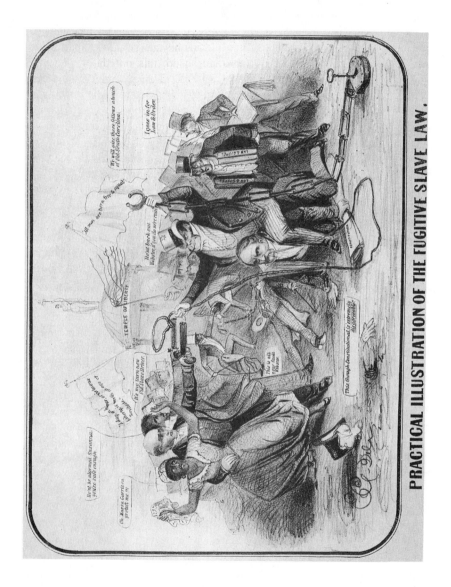

PRACTICAL ILLUSTRATION OF THE FUGITIVE SLAVE LAW.

Nothing can be plainer than that such conduct is obligatory upon *them;* and when, through the operations of divine grace, they are enabled to manifest a spirit like this, it is acknowledged to be worthy of great commendation, as in the case of "Uncle Tom." But, for those whose skin is of a different complexion, the case is materially altered. When they are spit upon and buffeted, outraged and oppressed, talk not then of a non-resisting Saviour—it is fanaticism! Talk not of overcoming evil with good—it is madness! Talk not of peacefully submitting to chains and stripes—it is base servility! Talk not of servants being obedient to their masters—let the blood of the tyrants flow! How is this to be explained or reconciled? Is there one law of submission and non-resistance for the black man, and another law of rebellion and conflict for the white man? When it is the whites who are trodden in the dust, does Christ justify them in taking up arms to vindicate their rights? And when it is the blacks who are thus treated, does Christ require them to be patient, harmless, long-suffering, and forgiving? And are there two Christs?

The work, towards its conclusion, contains some objectionable sentiments respecting African colonization, which we regret to see.

Left: This contemporary cartoon shows how the Fugitive Slave Law was seen to have degraded the principles of freedom and equality. A brutish slave catcher rides Daniel Webster, the famous orator and U.S. senator from Massachusetts who had angered abolitionists and many citizens in the North when he urged passage of the law as part of the Compromise of 1850. Garrison is portrayed here defending a female slave, yet curiously he is fending off the slave catchers with a pistol—not something that the real-life nonresister Garrison would have done.

24

Women's Rights

October 28, 1853

Garrison introduced these resolutions on October 5, 1853, at the Fourth Annual National Woman's Rights Convention in Cleveland, Ohio.

On Wednesday evening, Wm. Lloyd Garrison presented the following series of resolutions to the Convention:—

1. *Resolved,* That the natural rights of one human being are those of every other; in all cases equally sacred and inalienable; hence, the boasted "Rights of Man," about which we hear so much, are simply the "Rights of Woman," about which we hear so little; or, in other words, they are the Rights of Humankind, neither affected by or dependent upon sex or condition.

2. *Resolved,* That those who deride the claims of woman to a full recognition of her civil rights and political equality, exhibit the spirit which tyrants and usurpers have displayed in all ages towards the mass of mankind—strike at the foundation of all truly free and equitable government—contend for a sexual aristocracy, which is as irrational and unjust in principle, as that of wealth or hereditary descent—and show their appreciation of liberty to be wholly one-sided and supremely selfish.

3. *Resolved,* That for the men of this land to claim for themselves the elective franchise, and the right to choose their own rulers, and enact their own laws, as essential to their freedom, safety and welfare, and then to deprive all the women of all those safe guards, solely on the ground of a difference of sex, is to evince the pride of self-esteem, the meanness of usurpation, and the folly of a self-assumed superiority.

4. *Resolved,* That woman, as well as man, has a right to the highest mental and physical development—to the most ample educational advantages—to the occupancy of whatever position she can reach in Church and State, in science and art, in poetry and music, in painting and sculpture, in civil jurisprudence and political economy, and in the varied departments of human industry, enterprise and skill—to the elective franchise—and to a voice in the administration of justice and the passage of laws for the general welfare.

Oct. 28, 1853, 172; *Letters* 4:259–60.

5. *Resolved,* That to pretend that the granting of these claims would tend to make woman less amiable and attractive, less regardful of her peculiar duties and obligations as wife and mother, a wanderer from her proper sphere, bringing confusion into domestic life, and strife into the public assembly, is the cant of Papal Rome, as to the discordant and infidel tendencies of the right of private judgment in matters of faith[1]—is the outcry of legitimacy of the incapacity of the people to govern themselves—is the false allegation which selfish and timid conservatism is ever making against every new measure of Reform—and has no foundation in reason, experience, fact or philosophy.

6. *Resolved,* That the consequences arising from the exclusion of woman from the possession and exercise of her natural rights and the cultivation of her mental faculties have been calamitous to the whole human race—making her servile, dependent, unwomanly—the victim of a false gallantry on the one hand, and of tyrannic subjection on the other—obstructing her mental growth, crippling her physical development, and incapacitating her for general usefulness, and thus inflicting an injury upon all born of woman; and cultivating in man a lordly and arrogant spirit; a love of dominion, a disposition to lightly disregard her comfort and happiness, all of which have been indulged in to a fearful extent, to the curse of his own soul, and the desecration of her nature.

7. *Resolved,* That so long as the most ignorant, degraded and worthless men are freely admitted to the ballot-box, and practically acknowledged to be competent to determine who shall be in office, and how the government shall be administered, it is preposterous to pretend that women are not qualified to use the elective franchise, and that they are fit only to be recognized, politically speaking, as *non compos mentis.*[2]

---

[1] Garrison refers to the "infallibility" doctrine of the Catholic Church, which affirms the Pope's rightness of judgment in all matters of religious faith.

[2] Latin for "not of sound mind."

25

Uncle Tom's Cabin *Reconsidered*
December 23, 1853

Garrison wrote this letter to Harriet Beecher Stowe but did not identify her as the addressee when he printed it in The Liberator. *Nor did he tell her in advance that he intended to publish it.* Stowe had been invited to attend the *twentieth anniversary meeting of the American Anti-Slavery Society, but she refused, saying that while she admired both the society's work and* The Liberator, *she could not accept Garrison's religious radicalism. She was especially dismayed by Garrison's refusal to accept the divine authority of Scripture. In a note to Garrison, she stated that she feared he would "take from poor Uncle Tom his Bible, and give him nothing in his place" (*Letters *4:286).*

Boston, Nov. 30, 1853

Esteemed Friend:

You frankly say—"In regard to you, your paper, and in some measure your party, I am in an honest embarrassment. I sympathise with you in many of your positions: others I consider erroneous, hurtful to liberty and the progress of humanity." Still, you believe us to be "honest and conscientious" in our opinions.

What those erroneous opinions are, you do not state. I am not able, therefore, to make any reply, on that score. The ground we occupy, as abolitionists, is simply this:—*"Immediate emancipation is the duty of the master, and the right of the slave."* Our motto is, *"No Union with Slaveholders, religiously or politically."* This is only the practical application of our principles to whatever sanctions or upholds slavery, in Church or State. I am not disposed to conclude that you regard such sentiments as "hurtful to liberty and the progress of humanity"; and yet, as these are comprehensively all that we entertain and promulgate, for the overthrow of the slave system, I can only vaguely conjecture to what else you have reference. Believing, as I do, that none of the positions assumed by the American Anti-Slavery Society can be successfully assailed,—and de-

---

Dec. 23, 1853, 202; *Letters* 4:280–86.

sirous of having them tested as severely as possible,—permit me to say that if, in any particular, you think they are indefensible, I shall esteem it both an honor and a privilege to publish whatever you may feel inclined to write, by way of animadversion or protest.

Of THE LIBERATOR you speak in a friendly spirit, and profess to admire "its frankness, fearlessness, truthfulness and independence." I thank you for this tribute. "At the same time," you add, "I regard with apprehension and sorrow much that is in it." Why are you thus apprehensive? It seems to me a suspicious symptom. Are not the righteous "as bold as a lion"? The Psalmist could exclaim—"The Lord is my light and my salvation; whom shall I fear? The Lord is the strength of my life; of whom shall I be afraid?" Your alarm indicates a want of confidence in the truth; nay, I will not say in the truth, but in the soundness of your own opinions. In the truth, your mind is serene; in regard to certain theological views, it is confessedly perturbed. In saying that there is much in THE LIBERATOR which you "regard with apprehension and sorrow," am I not correct in surmising that you make no reference to the pro-slavery matter which occupies so liberal a portion of its columns? You would not, I think, have me refuse a hearing to slaveholders or their abettors. I doubt not you appreciate my paper all the more for granting them fair play, and feel no solicitude as to the effect of this course upon the popular mind. "Let the discussion go on," you will exclaim, and "God speed the right." And, yet, what heresy has ever been broached in THE LIBERATOR, which, for impiety and barbarity, will compare with the defence of man-stealing as a divine institution? And why are you not troubled on this account? Shall I answer my own question? It is because of your faith in the absolute and eternal rectitude of the anti-slavery cause: you are sure that no weapon that is formed against it can prosper. It is only the slaveholder who is alarmed in view of a full investigation of this subject. He wishes only his side of it presented. Now, how does it happen, my friend, that, touching the discussion of another subject, you participate in his uneasiness? I mean nothing invidious by this illustration. It seems to me that what, in THE LIBERATOR, you "regard with apprehension and sorrow," should fill your bosom with composure, and elicit from you high commendation—namely, that I allow no topic to be introduced into its columns, without giving both sides an impartial hearing. To this rule I have adhered with such fidelity, that no one charges me with its violation. Especially have I ever taken pains to lay before my readers, whatever I have found in print in opposition to my own views, whether relating to Anti-Slavery, Non-Resistance, the Bible, the Sabbath, Woman's Rights, &c. &c. In what do you discover the

"frankness, fearlessness, truthfulness and independence" of THE LIBER-
ATOR, if not in this treatment of all conflicting opinions? That you occa-
sionally find in the paper sentiments distasteful to you, at variance with
your ideas of right, is not at all surprising. *So do I*. But what then? Is not
this inseparable from free discussion? And may not "error of opinion be
safely tolerated, where truth is left free to combat it"? Your objection
is fatal to the freedom of the human mind—to the existence of a free
press.

You say—"Were the *Liberator* circulated only among intelligent, well-
balanced minds, able to discriminate between good and evil, I should not
feel so much apprehension." So says the Romish Church in regard to the
indiscriminate circulation of the Bible among the laity. So says Absolutism,
respecting the diffusion of intelligence among the masses. I am surprised
at the narrowness of your limitation. Are the people not to be trusted? Are
the Pope, and Nicholas, and Francis Joseph,[1] right in the conclusions to
which they come? Would you have the laws of nature repealed, because
they are so often violated, either ignorantly or wilfully? Shall not a beneficent Creator continue to spread the table of his bounty for all, because
so many surfeit themselves? Does he err in causing his sun to rise on the
evil and on the good, and his rain to fall on the just and on the unjust?
Besides, I believe the patrons of THE LIBERATOR will be found to possess
remarkably "intelligent, well-balanced minds," and to be interested in all
the great reforms of the age; and I have yet to hear of any person who has
been made less humane, just, Christ-like, by his candid perusal of it. On
the contrary, thousands gratefully acknowledge that they have been deeply indebted to it for higher and nobler views of God, of human brotherhood, of life and duty. What other journal in this country is so feared and
hated, so proscribed and anathematized, by slave-traffickers and slave-
owners, trimming politicians and profligate demagogues, hireling priests
and religious formalists, mercenary journalists and servile publishers, —all
that is tyrannical in the Government, and corrupt in the Church? How is it
habitually characterized by "the Satanic press"—*Bennett's Herald,* the
New York Observer, the *New York Express,* &c., &c.? Can such a journal
be "hurtful to liberty and the progress of humanity," in any rational sense?
Can it be safely trusted only "among intelligent, well-balanced minds, able
to discriminate between good and evil"?

---

[1] The Pope is the supreme authority of the Roman Catholic Church; Pius IX (1792–1878)
was pope from 1846 to 1878. Nicholas I (1796–1855) was the despotic emperor of Russia
from 1825 to 1855. Francis Joseph (1830–1916), emperor of Austria and king of Hungary,
was noted for severely suppressing the hopes of the various nationalities of his empire.

Ah! here is the cause of your disquietude!—"What I fear is, that it will take from poor Uncle Tom his Bible, and give him nothing in its place." And you say significantly, "You understand me—do you not?" Frankly, I do not. First—I do not understand, if the Bible be all that you claim for it, and if every adverse criticism upon it in THE LIBERATOR is allowed to be met by a friendly one, why you should be anxious as to its just appreciation. The more the anti-slavery coin is rubbed, the brighter it shines—does it not? The more "Uncle Tom's Cabin" is assailed, the more impregnable it is seen to be. And the more the Bible is sifted, the more highly it will be prized, if it be all holy and true.

Second—I do not understand how any one can "take from poor Uncle Tom his Bible," if that book be really a lamp to his feet, and a light to his path, and the word of the living God to his soul; and it seems to me that you throw positive discredit upon his religious experience and inward regeneration, by making such a[n] opposition. If the infernal cruelty of a Legree could not shake his trust in his God and Saviour, do you really think a full discussion of the merits of the Bible, pro and con, might induce him to throw that volume away?

Third—I do not understand how it follows, even if Uncle Tom, or any body else, should be led astray by reading THE LIBERATOR, because it allows both sides of every question to be discussed in its columns, that such a "frank, fearless, truthful and independent" sheet, as you concede it to be, ought no longer to possess these characteristics, but should be one-sided, narrow, partial.

Finally—I do not understand why the imputation is thrown upon THE LIBERATOR as tending to rob "Uncle Tom" of his Bible. I know of no writer in its pages, who wishes to deprive him of it, or of any comfort he may derive from it. It is for him to place whatever estimate he can upon it; and for you and me to do the same; but for neither of us to accept any more of it than we sincerely believe to be in accordance with reason, truth, eternal right. How much of it is true and obligatory, each one can determine only for himself; for on Protestant ground, there is no room for papal infallibility.[2] All Christendom professes to believe in the inspiration of the volume; and, at the same time, all Christendom is by the ears as to its real teachings. Surely, you would not have me disloyal to my conscience. How do you prove that you are not trammelled by educational or traditional notions as to the entire sanctity of the book? Indeed, it seems to me very

---

[2] Papal infallibility is the doctrine of the Catholic church that affirms the Pope's rightness of judgment in all matters of religious faith. See Document 24, note 1.

evident that you are not free in spirit, in view of the "apprehension and sorrow" you feel, because you find your conceptions of the Bible controverted in THE LIBERATOR. Else why such disquietude of mind? "Thrice is he armed who hath his quarrel just."

Again you say—"It is a grief and sorrow of heart to me, that any who are distinguished in the Anti-Slavery cause should be rejecters of that Bible, on which I ground all my hopes of the liberties, not only of the slave, but of the whole human race." Remember that the Anti-Slavery platform is one to which all are cordially invited, without regard to their scriptural or theological opinions, and on which no person is to be arraigned for anything else but compromising the rights of the slave. Who shall oracularly decide what constitutes a rejection of the Bible? Not you or me—not anybody. Who are the rejecters of that book, to whom you refer? I know of none. If, however, there are such, it is not as abolitionists, but as men. The widest dissent from your opinion, or from mine, in regard to the authority and value of the Bible, it is not necessarily heresy,—unless the great Protestant right of private judgment be heretical, as Papal Rome says it is. You and I are as likely to err as others, and may make no higher claim to infallibility than others. I must respectfully protest, therefore, against your invidious thrust at "any who are distinguished in the Anti-Slavery cause," or who are not distinguished, because they do not endorse your opinions concerning the plenary inspiration of the Bible. You might as properly express "grief and sorrow of heart," because there are Unitarians, Universalists, Quakers, &c. &c.,—those who reject the ordinances, those who deny the doctrine of everlasting punishment, those who do not believe in the trinity,—to be found among the abolitionists, and all are not Orthodox.

You say it is on the Bible you ground all your hopes of the liberties, not only of the slave, but of the whole human race. How does it happen, then, that, in a nation professing to place as high an estimate upon that volume as yourself, and denouncing as infidels all who do not hold it equally sacred, there are three millions and a half of chattel slaves, who are denied its possession, under severe penalties? Is not slavery sanctioned by the Bible, according to the interpretation of it by the clergy generally, its recognized expounders? What, then, does the cause of bleeding humanity gain by all this veneration for the book?

My reliance for the deliverance of the oppressed universally is upon the nature of man, the inherent wrongfulness of oppression, the power of truth, and the omnipotence of God—using every rightful instrumentality to hasten the justice.

Again you say—"I cannot but regard the admission, by some abolition-ists, that the Bible sanctions slavery, as equally unwise and groundless." But if this is their honest conviction, would you not have them express it? And, thus believing, are they not to be commended for their unswerving fidelity to principle, in refusing to accept it as the inspired word of God? If such were your understanding of any portion of the book, would you not reject it as barbarous and immoral—especially if it consigned you, and your husband, and your children, and your father and mother, and your brothers and sisters, and all your relatives and friends, to the horrible doom of "Uncle Tom"? I am sure you would, even though you should be branded as infidel by all the clergy and all the churches of Christendom.

For myself, I do not know of a single member of the American Anti-Slavery Society, who admits that the Bible sanctions such a system as that of American slavery. In any meeting of that Society, I believe such an interpretation of the Bible would be unanimously rejected. Ever since its organization, it has uniformly wielded that volume against the impious practice of chattelizing men, women and children and one of its heaviest and most frequent accusations against the slave system has been, that it makes the Bible an unlawful book in the hands of the slaves.

Possibly, in this particular, you may be better informed than I am as to the Biblical views of the "Garrisonian abolitionists." Possibly, some of them may believe that American slavery is sanctioned in some parts of the Bible; yes, in both the Old and New Testament. What then? First—in this opinion, they are sustained by nine-tenths of the evangelical clergy in the United States, and so cannot be heretical, if the latter are soundly ortho-dox. Second—so believing, they (unlike the clergy) declare the record to be *false to that extent,* and hold it to be "a self-evident truth, that all men are created equal, and endowed by their Creator with an inalienable right to liberty." They fill you with "grief and sorrow," and you cannot refer to them without registering your protest against their course. But you can, and do, recognize the clergy aforesaid as the ministers of Jesus Christ, and sit at the same communion table with them, and have never called for their expulsion from the pulpit or the church, though they say and teach, first, that chattel slavery is sanctioned by the Bible; and, second, that therefore it cannot be sinful. How marvellously inconsistent is your conduct, as between these parties! Third—whatever may be the convictions of a few individuals in the anti-slavery ranks, as to the pro-slavery character of some parts of the Bible, the American Anti-Slavery Society entertains no such views of the book, as all its official proceedings will testify. A few years since, it twice offered to place five thousand dollars in the treasury of the American Bible Society, provided that Society would agree to expend that sum, with some additional appropriations, in circulating the Bible among the slave population; but the offer was rejected. Moreover, it is a remarkable fact, that the American Anti-Slavery Society is the only organization in this country, that has ever caused to be written, and circulated broadcast through the land, a defence of the Bible against all its pro-slavery interpreters. . . . Ought not your solicitude, as to the book, to be given to the American Bible Society, and to the great body of the Orthodox clergy, rather than to the American Anti-Slavery Society, or to any of its friends?

You do me but simple justice in expressing your belief that I shall be well-pleased with your frankness and sincerity; and I will cherish the hope that you will be equally well-pleased with mine, as exhibited in this reply.

Yours, with high regards,

Wm. Lloyd Garrison

26

The Bible and Women's Rights

January 12, 1855

Garrison made these remarks at the Fifth Annual National Woman's Rights Convention in Philadelphia, October 18–20, 1854. He showed again his support for women's rights and also his reliance on conscience rather than on the literal text of the Bible.

Wm. L. Garrison commenced his review of the Scripture argument. He believed men and women were equal in the sight of God, as to their rights and responsibilities. The mass of the people in this country profess to believe that the Bible comes from God, and that whatever that book decrees should be the rule of right. They would be converts to the doctrine of woman's rights, if it were not for the Bible difficulty. But why go to the Bible to settle this question, when we, as a nation, have precluded such an appeal by our Declaration of Independence, in which we assert the equality of mankind to be a self-evident truth? The Bible has never yet settled any question. It has filled the world with theological discussions, growing out of the various interpretations given to the book. The human soul is greater than any book. If there is truth in the Bible, we take it; if error, we discard it. In this country, the Bible has been used to support slavery and capital punishment, while in the old countries, it has been used to support all manner of tyranny and persecution. We must take things independently. We find woman endowed with certain capabilities; we must accept her as nature has endowed her. Would his friend Henry Grew deny Lucretia Mott the capacity to preach?

LUCRETIA MOTT wished Henry's own daughter's name (MARY GREW) substituted for hers.[1]

W. L. GARRISON thought things ought to be tried by the eternal rule of right, and not by appealing to any book as absolute and conclusive authority.

[1] At the World's Anti-Slavery Convention in London in June 1840, the Philadelphia minister and abolitionist Henry Grew (1781–1862) had opposed the seating of women delegates, though his daughter Mary was one of them. Garrison himself had attended the convention and had sat in the balcony in solidarity with the women delegates who had not been allowed to participate. Lucretia Mott (1793–1880) was a Quaker abolitionist from Philadelphia and one of the women who had not been allowed to take her seat during the 1840 convention.

27

Disunion

June 15, 1855

Garrison's critics pressed him to explain how "disunion" should take place. In a section of a speech he presented at the May 31, 1855, New England Anti-Slavery Convention, Garrison suggested that disunion would be a simple matter once the American people were ready for it.

We are asked, "How is the dissolution of the Union to be effected? Give us your plan!" My answer is, whenever THE PEOPLE are ready for Disunion, they will easily find out a way to effect it. When this sentiment shall spread like a flame, as I trust in God it will, through the length and breadth of the free States, (cheers,) the people will come together in their primary assemblies, and elect such men to represent them in General Convention as they may deem best qualified to devise ways and means for effecting a separation, and to frame a new government, free from the spirit of bondage. In that hour, they will not ask for any plan of mine, or any of my associates on this platform: we shall be as drops in the Atlantic ocean. The chain once broken, the EVERETTS, the CHOATES, the WINTHROPS,[1] will then be as ready to obey the popular sentiment, and to take the lead in the cause of freedom, as they have hitherto been subservient to the will of the Slave Power. Our preliminary work is, not to construct a new government, but first of all to make every Northern man see and confess, that our boasted Union is a snare, a curse, and a degrading vassalage; — in strict verity, that *there is no Union for freedom to be dissolved*, but ONE TO BE CREATED! For where is the man who will venture to deny any one of the allegations contained in the resolution I have submitted to the Convention? Allow me to read it once more: —

"Resolved, That the American Union is the supremacy of the bowie knife, the revolver, the slave-driver's lash, and lynch law, over freedom of speech, of the press, of conscience, of locomotion, in more than one half of the nation" — [Is it not so? — "Yes, yes";] — "and the degrading vassalage of the entire North to the accursed Slave Power"; [Is not that true? — "Yes, yes";] "that such a Union" — [mark you! *"such a Union"* — not an ideal one — not something yet to be realized] — "that such a Union is to be resisted, denounced and repudiated by every lover of liberty, until its utter overthrow shall be consummated; and that, to effect this glorious object, there should be one united shout of *"No Union with Slaveholders, religiously or politically!"*

This declaration cannot be gainsayed. Let us, then, not waste our time in verbal criticism, or legal hair-splitting, as to the meaning of words. DOWN WITH SUCH A UNION! (Cheers, and a few hisses in the gallery.)

Mr. Chairman, this question does not concern me, or the Abolitionists in particular: it concerns every one who means to be a MAN, and to carry a heart in his bosom—every Whig, every Democrat, every Know Nothing,[2] every Free Soiler. I take it for granted, whether they have any

---

[1] Edward Everett (1794–1865), Unitarian clergyman, orator, president of Harvard College (1846–49), and senator from Massachusetts (1853–54); Rufus Choate (1799–1859), Massachusetts lawyer and statesman; Robert Winthrop, lawyer and legislator from Massachusetts (see Document 22, note 1). All were prominent members of the Whig party, the major rival national party to the Democrats until it was destroyed by internal disagreements over the slavery crisis and how to respond to it.

[2] The American, or Know-Nothing, party was a powerful political force for a brief period from the early to mid-1850s. It stood opposed to immigration and to the election of Catholics to political office; and it stayed somewhat distant from the slavery question. By the middle of the decade, however, the Know-Nothings quickly faded with the emergence of the Republican party, which was opposed to slavery extension.

bowels of mercy for those in slavery, or not, they mean to assert their own right to freedom of speech and locomotion, in every section of the land; or, if not, then they are dastards. Now, is this a right that they possess? Who, of them all, dares venture south of Mason and Dixon's line, and fearlessly rebuke the slaveholder to his face, and openly declare that his sympathies are with the enslaved? In vain shall he make his appeal to the "higher law"! The Southern substitute for this, in all such cases, is "lynch law." In vain shall he assert his constitutional right to speak his own sentiments: the Constitution is powerless! He will fare no better than the most radical Disunion Abolitionist. That being so, where is our Northern manhood? Do we always mean to cower under the Southern lash? Is it coolly said by any in reply, "We do not want to agitate the subject of slavery"? But what if you did? You cannot with impunity. Men are apt to change their minds; and the Whig, or Democrat, or Know Nothing, who to-day cares nothing for those in bonds, may to-morrow feel constrained to plead their cause, even at the South. In that case, he too becomes an outlaw. Ay, the very men who bow down to the Slave Power here—who fill our pulpits and our editorial chairs—who denounce the anti-slavery movement as undeserving of any support or countenance—are them-selves, *as the friends of impartial liberty,* as much outlaws in the South as any of us. Is such a Union to be perpetuated? By all that is just and equal, no!

Mr. Chairman, declamation and rhetoric, on so grave an issue, are worth little; but facts are irresistible. We are demanding extraordinary action of the people of the North; and in order to induce them to take that action, boldly and understandingly, they need to be shown what are the real facts in the case, especially as affecting their own rights and liberties at the South.

Undeniably, it is a provision of the Constitution of the United States, that "the citizens of each State shall be entitled to all the privileges and immunities of citizens" in the several States. There are no less than eight thousand recognised colored "citizens" in Massachusetts, taxed and rep-resented as such; many of them legal voters, eligible to every office in the gift of the people; all of them to be protected in their rights by the combined power of the Commonwealth, as much as ABBOTT LAWRENCE, or Chief Justice SHAW, or Governor GARDNER[3]—for in Massachusetts one citizen is, by our Bill of Rights, equal to every other; and the faith of the whole people is pledged to stand by each other to the end. Now, there is

[3] Abbott Lawrence (1792–1855), Massachusetts merchant and manufacturer; Lemuel Shaw (1781–1861), Massachusetts legislator and chief justice from 1830–1860; Henry Gardner (1818–1892), successful Know-Nothing candidate for governor of Massachusetts in 1855.

not one of that large number of citizens who can enter the slave States, whether on business, or in quest of health and recreation, without subjecting himself to fine and imprisonment, and even the liability to be sold on the auction-block into perpetual slavery.

28

"The 'Infidelity' of Abolitionism"
December 21, 1855

Here Garrison located abolition within the history of reform movements, in particular noting that reformers had always faced a hostile response from the institutions of church and state.

See also Garrison's speech at a meeting of African Americans, December 28, 1855.

Every great reformatory movement, in every age, has been subjected alike to popular violence and to religious opprobrium. The history of one is essentially that of every other. Its origin is ever in obscurity; its earliest supporters are destitute of resources, uninfluential in position, without reputation; it is denounced as fanatical, insane, destructive, treasonable, infidel. The tactics resorted to for its suppression are ever the same, whether it be inaugurated by the prophets, by Jesus and his apostles, by Wickliffe, Luther, Calvin, Fox,[1] or any of their successors. Its opponents have scornfully asked, as touching its pedigree, "Is not this the carpenter's son?" They have patriotically pronounced it a seditious attempt to play into the hands of the Romans, to the subversion of the State and nation. They have piously exclaimed against it as open blasphemy. They have branded it as incomparably more to be feared and abhorred than robbery and murder.

---

[1] John Wycliffe (c. 1328–1384), Martin Luther (1483–1546), John Calvin (1509–1564), and George Fox (1624–1691) were Protestant reformers and dissenters persecuted for their religious views. Fox was the founder of the Society of Friends in the late 1660s — though it is slightly possible that Garrison's reference is not to him, but to John Foxe (1516–1587), the English clergyman and author of the *Book of Martyrs* (1554, 1559), which records the history of the persecution of Protestant reformers.

Dec. 21, 1855, 202.

No other result has been possible, under the circumstances. The wrong assailed has grown to a colossal size: its existence not only implies, but demonstrates, universal corruption. It has become organic—a part of the habits and customs of the times. It is incorporated into the State; it is nourished by the Church. Its support is the test of loyalty, patriotism, piety. It holds the reins of government with absolute mastery—rewarding the venal, stimulating the ambitious, terrifying the weak, inflaming the brutal, satisfying the pharisaical,[2] ostracising the incorruptible. It has its temple, its ritual, its priesthood, its divine paternity, in the prevailing religion, no matter what may be the title or pretension thereof.

Such, then, was the system,—so buttressed and defended,—to be assailed and conquered by the Abolitionists. And who were they? In point of numbers, as drops to the ocean; without station or influence; equally obscure and destitute of resources. Originally, they were generally members of the various religious bodies, tenacious of their theological views, full of veneration for the organized church and ministry, but ignorant of the position in which these stood to "the sum of all villanies [*sic*]." What would ultimately be required of them by a faithful adherence to the cause of the slave, in their church relations, their political connections, their social affinities, their worldly interest and reputation, they knew not. Instead of seeking a controversy with the pulpit and the church, they confidently looked to both for efficient aid to their cause. Instead of suddenly withdrawing from the pro-slavery religious organizations with which they were connected, they lingered long and labored hard to bring them to repentance. They were earnest, but well-balanced; intrepid, but circumspect; importunate, but long-suffering. Their controversy was neither personal nor sectional; their object, neither to arraign any sect nor to assail any party, primarily. They sought to liberate the slave by every righteous instrumentality—nothing more. But, to their grief and amazement, they were gradually led to perceive, by the terrible revelations of the hour, that the religious forces on which they had relied were all arrayed on the side of the oppressor; that the North was as hostile to emancipation as the South; that the spirit of slavery was omnipresent, invading every sanctuary, infecting every pulpit, controlling every press, corrupting every household, and blinding every vision; that no other alternative was presented to them, except to wage war with "principalities, and powers, and spiritual wickedness in high places," and to separate themselves from every slaveholding alliance, or else to daub with untempered mortar, substitute

---

[2] Resembling the Pharisees, the sect among the ancient Jews noted for their rigid observance of outward forms and ceremonies and, in the New Testament, for their opposition to Jesus (see, for instance, Mark 3, 7, 10; Matthew 23; John 11).

compromise for principle, and thus betray the rights and liberties of the millions in thraldom, at a fearful cost to their own souls.

29

"Southern Degradation"

September 19, 1856

Garrison concentrated on the horrors of slavery for blacks, but he also dramatized the effects of slavery on the white population. Slavery, he argued, ruined the morality and subverted the freedom of the whites who sustained it.

Like many abolitionists, Garrison pointed to Preston S. Brooks (1819– 1857), congressman from South Carolina, as an example of the corrupting effects of slavery. Brooks beat Massachusetts Senator Charles Sumner (1811–1874) over the head with a cane on the Senate floor on May 22, 1856, two days after Sumner's "Crime against Kansas" speech, a fierce attack on slavery extension into the Kansas territory that included Sumner's sharp, insulting words about Brooks's distant relative Andrew P. Butler (1796– 1857), Democratic senator from South Carolina.

Also see "Liberty and Slavery Contrasted," November 21, 1856; "No 'Covenant with Death,' " Dec. 5, 1856; and a review of and editorial on George Fitzhugh's proslavery treatise Cannibals All!, *March 6 and March 13, 1857. On the hardening of Southern sentiment on the slavery question, see "Southern Testimonies against Slavery," April 23, 1858.*

Although the African slave trade is adjudged by the law of the land to be PIRACY—an act to which the penalty of DEATH is affixed—it is a common subterfuge of the slaveholders, in order to shield themselves from the just condemnation of an indignant world, to claim that the transfer of the Africans from their native land to our own has greatly improved their condition. As if the true method to civilize the ignorant and to enlighten the superstitious were to ravage their coasts—give their dwellings to the consuming fire—shoot down all who offer any resistance—seize and manacle such as can make no defence—drag them on board of slave ships—pack them to suffocation in the holds of those "floating hells"—

subject them to all the horrors of "the middle passage"—drive the survivors to unrequited toil under the lash, denying to them all the rights of our common humanity, forbidding them to learn to read the name of God, legally affirming them to be "goods and chattels, to all intents, purposes and constructions whatsoever," and trafficking in them as in cattle and swine! Why then prohibit the African slave trade, under such a penalty? Why not give unlimited encouragement to it? Why not let Christian philanthropy be as broad as the Atlantic, and Africa be depopulated afresh? What! put to death those benevolent men who kidnap benighted heathens for their good! What! brand those as pirates who forcibly remove the natives of Guinea[1] to the plantations of Carolina, seeing the result will be their temporal and everlasting welfare! Is not this the command of Christ—"Go ye into all Africa, and seize as many of its wretched inhabitants as ye can by fraud and violence, that they may be taken to slaveholding America, where my gospel is proclaimed!"

One thing is at least certain. However beneficial slavery may have proved to the slaves of the South, it has most fearfully debased and deteriorated the slaveholders, and the entire white population of the slave States; cursing them in their basket and in their store, in their cities and in their fields, in the fruits of their bodies and the fruits of their ground, in the increase of their kine[2] and the flocks of their sheep, when they come in and when they go out, when they rise up and when they lie down; in the usefulness of their hands and the productions of their brains; in their manners and morals; in every thing pertaining to body, mind, soul, or estate; giving them over to unrestrained licentiousness, filthy amalgamation, incurable laziness, profligate wastefulness, satanic pride, pitiable ignorance, hardness of heart, atrocious barbarity; setting their passions "on fire of hell," blending in their character the conceit of the peacock with the ferocity of the tiger, and making their condition the most hopeless of any portion of the human race. It has destroyed in them all sense of justice, all perception of right, all knowledge of virtue, all regard for humanity; so that, habitually, they put darkness for light, and light for darkness, and call good evil, and evil good. "Their hands are defiled with blood, and their fingers with iniquity; they trust in vanity, and speak lies; they conceive mischief, and bring forth iniquity; they hatch cockatrice's eggs, and weave the spider's web; their feet run to evil, and they make haste to shed innocent blood; their works are works of iniquity, and there is no judgment in their goings."[3] Such have been the industrial, in-

---

[1] From the coast of West Africa.
[2] Archaic plural for *cow*.
[3] Quotation from Isaiah 59:3–8.

tellectual, and moral effects of this all-pervading curse upon them, which covers them like a garment.

Take South Carolina, for instance, with more than half of her population in chains! Without invention, enterprise, art, science, industry, thrift, education, refinement, strength, or promise, how boundless is her conceit, how swollen her pomposity, how active her combativeness, how ludicrous her assumed superiority, how unproductive her head, how evil her heart, how cowardly and brutal her spirit! What a frightful revelation she has made of herself, in the case of Preston S. Brooks! What honors she is heaping upon that dastard, — almost a murderer, — for his stealthy assault upon the helpless, unsuspecting, unarmed Sumner! How she glories in what fills the civilized world with astonishment, indignation and horror! No audible dissent is allowed upon her soil; her public approbation of the vile deed amounts to perfect unanimity. What hope is there of the regeneration of such a State? Where conscience is outlawed, and speech suppressed, and the press shackled, and all protection denied, and Lynch law in constant operation, how can the truth be uttered, or right find a foothold? Accursed slavery! thus to have wrought all this ruin, — a ruin which appears to be remediless!

30

Dred Scott and Disunion
March 12, 1858

The Supreme Court handed down its decision in the Dred Scott case on March 6, 1857. Dred Scott (1795?–1858) was a black slave in the state of Missouri who accompanied his master in the 1830s first to Illinois, a free state, and later to a section of the Wisconsin territory where slavery had been prohibited by the Missouri Compromise of 1820. (Until it was repealed by the Kansas-Nebraska Act of 1854, this Compromise had prohibited slavery in the territory of the Louisiana Purchase north of the 36°30' line.) After his master's death in 1846, Scott sued for his freedom, arguing that residence in a free state and free territory had ended his bondage.

In the Court opinion for the majority, Chief Justice Roger Taney (1777–1864) ruled that Scott remained a slave. But Taney went further, stating that neither slaves nor the free descendants of slaves were citizens and that

Congress could not prohibit slavery in the territories of the United States. Along with many abolitionists, and many more in the antislavery Republican party, Garrison condemned the decision. He counseled resistance to it and reiterated that "disunion" was the only possible response to slavery's grip on the government.

The following is taken from a speech that Garrison presented at a March 5, 1858, antislavery meeting in Faneuil Hall, Boston, in commemoration of the March 5, 1770, Boston Massacre, at which a black man named Crispus Attucks had been one of those killed by British soldiers.

We are here to enter our indignant protest against the Dred Scott decision—against the infamous Fugitive Slave Law—against all unjust and oppressive enactments, with reference to complexional distinctions—against the alarming aggressions of the Slave Power upon the rights of the people of the North—and especially against the existence of the slave system at the South, from which all these have naturally sprung, as streams of lava from a burning volcano. We are here to reiterate the self-evident truths of the Declaration of Independence, and to call for their practical enforcement throughout our land. We are here to declare that the men who, like CRISPUS ATTUCKS, were ready to lay down their lives to secure American Independence, and the blessings of liberty—who, in every period of our history, at all times, and in all parts of the country, on the land and on the sea, have ever been prompt in the hour of peril to fill "the deadly, imminent breach," pour out their blood like water, and repel the minions of foreign tyranny from our shores—are not the men to be denied the claims of human nature, or the rights of citizenship. Alas! what have they reaped for all their patriotic toils and sufferings but contumely, proscription, ostracism? O, shame on this cruelly unjust and most guilty nation! I trust in God that no colored men will ever again be found ready to fight under its banner, however great the danger that may menace it from abroad, until their rights are first secured, and every slave be set free. If they have no scruples in using the sword in defence of liberty, let them at least refuse to draw it in behalf of those who depise and oppress them.

Our work is before us. It is to disseminate light—to change public opinion—to plead every man with his neighbor—to insist upon justice—to demand equal rights—to "crush out" slavery wherever it exists in the land. Let Massachusetts lead the van. Let her be true to the cause of freedom, cost what it may. She has done well in saying that the Fugitive Slave Law shall not be executed on her soil—at least, not without the intervention of a jury trial. That is one step in the right direction. She has decreed, that none of her official servants shall at the same time be a Slave

Commissioner under the United States; and hence the duty of removing Judge Loring[1] for disobedience and contumacy. I am confident we shall all soon have the satisfaction of seeing him walk the plank overboard. (Loud cheering.) But there is one thing more to be done. Massachusetts must not tolerate a slave-hunter on her soil—nor a Slave Commissioner—nor allow a human being to be put on trial to decide whether he has a right to himself, or is the property of another—but she must transform every slave into a free man as soon as he comes within her borders. (Renewed cheering.)

We shall be told that this is equivalent to a dissolution of the Union. Be it so! Give us Disunion with liberty and a good conscience, rather than Union with slavery and moral degradation. What! shall we shake hands with those who buy, sell, torture, and horribly imbrute their fellow-creatures, and trade in human flesh! God forbid! Every man should respect himself too much to keep such company. We must break this wicked alliance with men-stealers, or all is lost. By all the sacred memories of the past—by all that was persistent, courageous, unconquerable in the great struggle for American Independence—by the blood of ATTUCKS and his martyred associates in King Street—by the death of WARREN and the patriotic slain on Bunker Hill[2]—by the still higher and better examples of ancient apostles and martyrs—let us here renew our solemn pledge, that, come what may, we will not lay down our arms until liberty is proclaimed throughout all the land, to all the inhabitants thereof. (Prolonged applause.)

[1] Edward G. Loring (1802–1890) was the U.S. commissioner of the Circuit Court in Massachusetts who, in line with the Fugitive Slave Law of 1850, ordered the return to slavery of Thomas Sims (April 1851) and Anthony Burns (May–June 1854). His decisions in these two cases in Boston led abolitionists to demand his removal from office as probate judge of Suffolk County. Garrison and others agitated for this for years, circulating petitions and arguing before the Massachusetts legislature. Loring was removed from office in 1858.

[2] A black man named Crispus Attucks (1750?–1770) was one of those killed by British soldiers in the March 5, 1770. Boston Massacre; Joseph Warren (1741–1775), political leader in the American Revolution, was killed in the Battle of Bunker Hill (see Document 32, note 1); Bunker Hill, an important early battle (in fact, it took place on Breed's Hill) in the American Revolution, was fought in Boston on June 17, 1775 (see Document 2, note 2).

31

"Depravity of the American Press"
September 17, 1858

In this editorial Garrison lashed the popular press for its coverage of anti-slavery speeches, meetings, and activities. He said that reporters and editors deliberately distorted the truth and lied outright because they wished to pander to common prejudices about abolitionism and reaffirm the views of those in power.

See also, on freedom of the press, January 30, 1846, and April 2, 1847.

The American press is, to a fearful extent, in the hands of a cowardly, mercenary and unprincipled class of men, who have no regard for truth in dealing with what is unpopular; who cater to the lowest passions of the multitude, and caricature every movement aiming at the overthrow of established wrong; who are as destitute of all fairness in controversy as they are lacking in self-respect; and whose columns are closed against any reply that may be proffered to their libellous accusations. It is true, these men represent the prevailing public sentiment, either in the locality in which they reside, or in the country at large; but, fearfully demoralized as that sentiment is, in many particulars, they aim to make it still more corrupt, rather than to change it for the better. They not only publish all the lies they can pick up, in opposition to the struggling cause of humanity, but they busy themselves in coining lies, which they audaciously present to their credulous readers as reliable truths. There is no end to their deception and tergiversation.[1] Such men are far more dangerous to society than burglars, incendiaries and highwaymen. Occupying a position of solemn trust, and almost awful responsibility, — exerting a potent influence over a large class of ignorant and unreflecting minds, who look up to them as teachers and guides, however deficient in brains or vicious in morals, — they have it alike in their power and in their disposition to deceive, mislead, circumvent, and demoralize, to a ruinous extent. Each of them is a local authority; and of their many readers, comparatively few think of questioning the authenticity of what is laid before them, from day to day, or from week to week.

[1]Evasion, equivocation, reversal of opinion.

Sept. 17, 1858, 150.

In what part of the country—in what town or village—can an anti-slavery meeting be held, of an uncompromising character, even after a struggle of twenty-five years, without being basely misrepresented by the press, or treated with silent contempt? Yes, for a quarter of a century, abolitionism—the denial of the right to make man the property of man—has been lampooned, anathematized, vilified, unceasingly and universally, by the journals of the day, both religious and secular—its advocates have been held up as crazy fanatics and wild disorganizers—and its meetings represented as unworthy of countenance by sane and decent men! Every other unpopular movement, however noble and good, has been treated in the same manner—and "the end is not yet."

We feel competent thus to arraign the American press generally—first, because we have been familiar with its course for the last forty years—and second, because we have the consciousness of publishing a free, independent, impartial journal, in the columns of which all sides have ever been allowed a fair hearing, and which seeks to make known "the truth, the whole truth, and nothing but the truth," at whatever cost or hazard. How such a paper—advocating the noblest cause that can engage the attention of man, and giving auxiliary support to other great reformatory movements—is appreciated and sustained, is seen in its petty subscription list, in its limited circulation, in the covert and open effort every where made for its suppression; and how other papers, which espouse the side of the oppressor, make falsehood and jesuitism[2] their stock in trade, and resist every attempt to reform society by removing old abuses, are encouraged and upheld, may be seen in the wide circulation and richly remunerative income of Bennett's *Herald,* the New York *Observer,* the *Journal of Commerce,* and many others of a similar stamp. What does all this indicate as to the state of the country?

---

[2] Relating to the Jesuits, a Catholic religious society founded in the sixteenth century, known for missionary and educational work; the term was used disparagingly to imply cunning, intrigue, and equivocation.

32

"The Tragedy at Harper's Ferry"
October 28, 1859

The radical abolitionist John Brown (1800–1859) and his twenty-one followers attacked the federal arsenal in Harpers Ferry, Virginia, on October 16, 1859. His intention was to liberate and arm slaves, establish strongholds with them in the mountains, kindle insurrections among them, and thereby strike deadly blows against slavery in the heart of the South. This attempt to spur slave resistance and revolt fell apart on the morning of October 18, when a number of Brown's men were killed and he was wounded and captured by U.S. troops under the command of Robert E. Lee (1807–1870), who later became the Confederacy's leading general.

We have devoted a large portion of our present number to the publication of such particulars of the well-intended but sadly misguided effort of Capt. John Brown and his score of confederates, at Harper's Ferry, to liberate the slaves in Virginia, and ultimately throughout the South, as have been received; with the comments of various Democratic and Republican journals upon this outbreak, which are characterized by an equal mixture of ferocity and cowardice.

As to the plot itself, it is evident that few or none were privy to it, except the little band directly engaged in it; for though Capt. Brown had many to sympathize with him, in different parts of the country, in view of his terrible bereavements, perils and sufferings in Kansas, in defence of the freedom of that territory against Border Ruffian invasion, and were disposed to contribute not only to relieve his necessities, but also to facilitate the escape of slaves through his instrumentality to Canada, still an enterprise so wild and futile as this could not have received any countenance in that direction.

As to Capt. Brown, all who know him personally are united in the conviction that a more honest, conscientious, truthful, brave, disinterested man, (however misguided or unfortunate,) does not exist; that he possesses a deeply religious nature, powerfully wrought upon by the trials through which he has passed; that he as sincerely believes himself to have been raised up by God to deliver the oppressed in this country, in the

---

Oct. 28, 1859, 170.

way he has chosen, as did Moses in relation to the deliverance of the captive Israelites; that when he says, he aims to be guided by the Golden Rule, it is no cant from his lips, but a vital application of it to his own soul, "remembering those that are in bonds as bound with them"; that when he affirms, that he had no other motive for his conduct at Harper's Ferry, except to break the chains of the oppressed, by the shedding of the least possible amount of human blood, he speaks "the truth, the whole truth, and nothing but the truth"; and that if he shall be (as he will speedily, beyond a peradventure) put to death, he will not die ignobly, but as a martyr to his sympathy for a suffering race, and in defence of the sacred and inalienable rights of man, and will therefore deserve to be held in grateful and honorable remembrance to the latest posterity by all those who glory in the deeds of a Wallace or Tell, a Washington or Warren.[1] Read his replies to the interrogatories propounded to him by Senator Mason[2] and others! Is there another man, of all the thirty millions of people inhabiting this country, who could have answered more wisely, more impressively, more courageously, or with greater moral dignity, under such a trying ordeal? How many hearts will be thrilled and inspired by his utterances! Read, too, his replies in court with reference to his counsel! Where shall a more undaunted spirit be found? In vain will the sanguinary tyrants of the South, and their Northern minions, seek to cover him with infamy—

> Courts, judges can inflict no brand of shame,
> Or shape of death, to shroud him from applause.

For, by the logic of Concord, Lexington and Bunker Hill, and by the principles enforced by this nation in its boasted Declaration of Independence, Capt. Brown was a hero, struggling against fearful odds, not for his own advantage, but to redeem others from a horrible bondage, to be justified in all that he aimed to achieve, however lacking in sound discretion. And by the same logic and the same principles, every slaveholder has forfeited his right to live, if his destruction be necessary to enable his victims to break the yoke of bondage; and they, and all who are disposed to aid them by force and arms, are fully warranted in carrying rebellion to any extent, and securing freedom at whatever cost.

[1] Sir William Wallace (1272?–1305), Scottish soldier and national hero; William Tell, legendary Swiss patriot; George Washington (1732–1799), commander-in-chief of the Continental Army in the American Revolution and first U.S. president; Joseph Warren (1741–1775), political leader in the American Revolution, killed in the battle of Bunker Hill (1775).

[2] James Mason (1798–1871), Virginia lawyer, legislator, and U.S. senator who interviewed Brown shortly after Brown's capture.

John Brown in 1856, three years before the raid at Harpers Ferry

It will be a terribly losing day for all Slavedom when John Brown and his associates are brought to the gallows. It will be sowing seed broadcast for a harvest of retribution. Their blood will cry trumpet-tongued from the ground, and that cry will be responded to by tens of thousands in a manner that shall cause the knees of the Southern slave-mongers to smite together as did those of Belshazzar[3] of old! O that they might avoid all this by a timely repentance!

---

[3] Sixth-century B.C. ruler of Babylon, who suffered divine punishment for sacrilege (Daniel 5:1–31).

33

John Brown and the Principle of Nonresistance
December 16, 1859

This is part of a speech that Garrison delivered at a meeting in Tremont Temple, Boston, on December 2, 1859, the day John Brown was executed for the Harpers Ferry raid.

Brown was greatly esteemed by many in the North for his dignified conduct during his imprisonment and trial and was portrayed by abolitionists as a selfless martyr for the antislavery cause. Like the different cases of David Walker, Nat Turner, and Uncle Tom, he prompted Garrison again to ponder the meanings of violent and nonviolent forms of resistance.

See also Garrison's speech on Harpers Ferry at the annual meeting of the Massachusetts Anti-Slavery Society, February 17, 1860. For earlier discussions of violent means, see February 29, 1856, and March 14 and March 28, 1856, and "Is It Right to Kill Our Enemies?," April 4, 1856.

A word upon the subject of Peace. I am a non-resistant—a believer in the inviolability of human life, under all circumstances; I, therefore, in the name of God, disarm John Brown, and every slave at the South. But I do not stop there; if I did, I should be a monster. I also disarm, in the name of God, every slaveholder and tyrant in the world. (Loud applause.) For wherever that principle is adopted, all fetters must instantly melt, and there can be no oppressed, and no oppressor, in the nature of things. How many agree with me in regard to the doctrine of the inviolability of human life? How many non-resistants are there here to-night? (A single voice— "I.") There is *one!* (Laughter.) Well, then, you who are otherwise are not the men to point the finger at John Brown, and cry "traitor"—judging you by your own standard. (Applause.) Nevertheless, I am a non-resistant, and I not only desire, but have labored unremittingly to effect the peaceful abolition of slavery, by an appeal to the reason and conscience of the slaveholder; yet, as a peace man—an "ultra" peace man—I am prepared to say, "Success to every slave insurrection at the South, and in every slave country." (Enthusiastic applause.) And I do not see how I compromise or stain my peace profession in making that declaration. Whenever there is a contest between the oppressed and the oppressor,—the weapons being equal between the parties, — God knows that my heart must be with the oppressed, and always against the oppressor. Therefore, whenever commenced, I cannot but wish success to all slave insurrections. (Loud applause.) I thank God when men who believe in the right and duty of wielding carnal weapons are so far advanced that they will take those weapons out of the scale of despotism, and throw them into the scale of freedom. It is an indication of progress, and a positive moral growth; it is one way to get up to the sublime platform of non-resistance; and it is God's method of dealing retribution upon the head of the tyrant. Rather than see men wearing their chains in a cowardly and servile spirit, I would, as an advocate of peace, much rather see them breaking the head of the tyrant with their chains. Give me, as a non-resistant, Bunker Hill, and Lexington, and Concord, rather than the cowardice and servility of a Southern slave plantation.

The verdict of the world, whether "resistance to tyrants is obedience to God," has been rendered in the affirmative in every age and clime. Whether the weapons used in the struggle against despotism have been spiritual or carnal, that verdict has been this: —

> Glory to those who die in Freedom's cause!
> Courts, judges, can inflict no brand of shame,
> Or shape of death, to shroud them from applause!
> No, manglers of the martyr's earthly frame,
> Your hangmen fingers cannot touch his fame!
> Long trains of ill may pass, unheeded, dumb —
> But Vengeance is behind, and Justice is to come!
>   (Loud applause.)

We have been warmly sympathizing with John Brown all the way through, from the time of his arrest till now. Now he no longer needs our sympathy, for he is beyond suffering, and wears the victor's crown. Are we to grow morbid over his death, to indulge in sentimental speech, to content ourselves with an outburst of emotional feeling, and not to come up to the work of abolishing slavery? I confess, I am somewhat apprehensive in regard to this powerful and wide-spread excitement, lest there may follow an exhaustion of the system, a disastrous reaction, in consequence of neglecting to make it directly subservient to the cause of emancipation by earnest and self-sacrificing effort. I see in every slave on the Southern plantation *a living John Brown* — one to be sympathized with far more than ever John Brown needed sympathy, whether in the jail or on the scaffold at Charlestown. I see *four millions of living John Browns* needing our thoughts, our sympathies, our prayers, our noblest exertions to strike off their fetters. And, by God's help, will we not do it? What can we do? I do not know that we can do any thing for Virginia. She seems past all salvation—to have been "given over to believe a lie that she may be damned." But here we stand, with our feet upon the old Pilgrim ground; and I ask the sons of the Fathers, are we not competent to make the old Bay State[1] free to all who tread its soil? (Enthusiastic applause.) Are we to have another Anthony Burns rendition?[2] ("No!" "No!") Shall we allow any more slave-hunting from Berkshire to Barnstable?[3] ("No!" "No!") No? How, then, will you prevent it? You must make that decree a matter of record, through your representatives in the State House; and if you want to do an effectual work tomorrow, and to consummate John Brown's object as far as you can, see to it that you put your names to the petition to the Legislature, now in circulation, asking that body to declare that, henceforth, no human being shall be regarded, tried or treated as a slave within the limits of this Commonwealth. (Immense applause.) But that is "treason," (laughter,) and John Brown was a "traitor." The Boston *Post* and the Boston *Courier* are very anxious to discover who were the instigators of the Harper's Ferry rebellion. Most disinterested and patriotic journals! When you read any of their editorials on this subject, just look at the bottom and see in staring capitals—"SOLD TO THE DEVIL, AND PAID FOR." (Laughter and applause.)

Who instigated John Brown? Let us see. It must have been Patrick Henry,[4] who said—and he was a Virginian—"*Give me liberty, or give me death!*" Why do they not dig up his bones, and give them to the consuming fire, to show their abhorrence of his memory? It must have been Thomas Jefferson—another Virginian—who said of the bondage of the Virginia slaves, that "one hour of it is fraught with more misery than ages of that which our fathers rose in rebellion to oppose"—and who, as the author of the Declaration of Independence, proclaimed it to be "a SELF-EVIDENT TRUTH, that all men are created equal, and endowed by their Creator with AN INALIENABLE RIGHT TO LIBERTY." (Applause.) Beyond all question, it must have been VIRGINIA HERSELF, who, by her coat of arms, with its terrible motto, "*Sic semper tyrannis,*"[5] asserts the right of the oppressed

---

[1]Massachusetts.

[2]Anthony Burns (1834–1862), fugitive slave, escaped from Richmond, Virginia, to Boston in February 1854. Burns was arrested as a fugitive on May 24, and, despite protests, rallies, and meetings and even a violent attempt by abolitionists to storm the courthouse where he was held, Burns was turned over to his master and sent back into slavery on June 2.

[3]Counties in western (Berkshire) and southeastern (Barnstable) Massachusetts.

[4]Patrick Henry (1736–1799) was the colonial orator and statesman who declared "Give me liberty or give me death!" in a speech at the Virginia Convention, Richmond, on March 23, 1775.

[5]Thus always to tyrants.

to trample their oppressors beneath their feet, and, if necessary, consign them to a bloody grave! Herein John Brown found the strongest incitement and the fullest justification.

Who instigated the deed at Harper's Ferry? The people whose motto is, "Resistance to tyrants is obedience to God"—and whose exulting talk is of Bunker Hill and Yorktown, and the deeds of their REVOLUTIONARY sires! Nay, we must go back to the source of life itself:—"So God created man in his own image; male and female created he them." Thus making an "irrepressible conflict" between the soul of man and tyranny *from the beginning,* and confirming what Lord Brougham[6] so eloquently uttered years ago—"Tell me not of rights; talk not of the property of the planter in his slaves. I deny the right; I acknowledge not the property. The principles, the feelings of our nature rise in rebellion against it. Be the appeal made to the understanding or to the heart, the sentence is the same that rejects it. In vain you tell me of laws that sanction such a claim. There is a law above all the enactments of human codes—the same throughout the world, the same in all time—it is *the law written by the finger of God upon the heart of man;* and by that law, unchangeable and eternal, while men despise fraud, and loathe rapine, and abhor blood, they will reject with indignation the wild and guilty phantasy that man can hold property in man." (Loud applause.)

We have a natural right, therefore, to seek the abolition of slavery throughout the globe. It is our special duty to make Massachusetts free soil, so that the moment the fugitive slave stands upon it, he shall take his place in the ranks of the free. God commands us to "hide the outcast, and bewray not him that wandereth." I say, LET THE WILL OF GOD BE DONE! That is "the head and front" of my "fanaticism"! That is the extent of my "infidelity"! That comprehends all of my "treason"! THE WILL OF GOD BE DONE! (Great applause.)

---

[6]Henry Peter Brougham (1778–1868), British lawyer, statesman, reformer, and critic of the slave trade.

34

Antislavery Progress
November 9, 1860

Garrison had long been convinced that the nation was dominated by what he and other abolitionists called the "Slave Power." Yet with the approach of the presidential election of 1860, which matched the Republican candidate Abraham Lincoln (1809–1865) against the Democrat Stephen A. Douglas (1813–1861), he nevertheless was heartened by the rising tide of antislavery feeling in the North—which he saw in such contrast to the public's indifference to slavery and disdain for abolitionists twenty-five years earlier.

The following letter was read to the meeting by Mr. McKim:—

Boston, October 11, 1860

My Dear Friend:

Since I promised to attend the anniversary of the Pennsylvania Anti-Slavery Society at Kennett, I have been suffering from a severe attack of bronchitis; and though at the present time it is considerably mitigated, I am under positive medical prohibition, in reference to public speaking, for some time to come; hence I must again disappoint my Pennsylvania friends—most deeply to my own regret and loss, for their magnetic presence is ever most delightful and strengthening to my spirit. I can only beg to be affectionately remembered to them all, and invoke upon their deliberations the blessing of the Infinite Father.

Twenty-five years ago this evening, I was in a cell in the Leverett street jail in this city—a device of the city authorities to save my life against the murderous designs of an infuriated mob of (so called) "gentlemen of property and standing," on account of my anti-slavery principles. Previous to my imprisonment, I was in the hands of the rioters for a time, who tore the clothes from my body as they dragged me through the streets, and who made the most desperate efforts to take me where they could apply a coat of tar and feathers, and commit such other outrages as their ungovernable malignity might suggest. Rescued at last, by the Mayor and his posse, it was deemed indispensable to my personal safety to commit me to prison! This was the only governmental protection that was vouchsafed to me. You remember all the circumstances of that memorable

Nov. 9, 1860, 178; *Letters* 4:697.

event, and I need not repeat them. Nearly all the prominent actors therein have been called to their final account, but the sacred and glorious cause which they madly attempted to overthrow is now shaping the destiny of the nation.

So far as the North is concerned, a marvellous change for the better has taken place in public sentiment in relation to the anti-slavery movement. The struggle for freedom of speech and of the press has every where been fought, and the victory won. A general enlightenment has taken place upon the subject of slavery. The opinions of a vast multitude have been essentially changed, and secured to the side of freedom. The conflict between free institutions and slave institutions is seen and acknowledged to be irrepressible—not of man's devising, but of God's ordering—and it is deepening in intensity daily, in spite of every effort of political cunning and religious sorcery to effect a reconciliation. The pending Presidential election witnesses a marked division between the political forces of the North and of the South; and though it relates, ostensibly, solely to the question of the further extension of slavery, it really signifies a much deeper sentiment in the breasts of the people of the North, which, in process of time, must ripen into more decisive action.

So far as the South is concerned, she has apparently waxed worse and worse—grown more and more desperate—revealed more and more of savage brutality and fiendish malignity, until her crimes and atrocities, not only as perpetrated upon her dehumanized slaves, but as inflicted upon Northern citizens and strangers within her limits, have become too numerous for record, and almost too horrible for belief.

But all this is the sign that the end is rapidly approaching. Peaceably, or by a bloody process, the oppressed will eventually obtain their freedom, and nothing can prevent it. Trusting that it may be achieved without the shedding of blood, I remain,

Yours, for liberty and equality for all mankind,

Wm. Lloyd Garrison

35

"Southern Desperation"
November 16, 1860

As Garrison pointed out, Abraham Lincoln did not attain national office as an abolitionist. Lincoln was opposed to the extension of slavery but— determined above all to preserve the Union—he had promised not to interfere with slavery where it already existed. Still, his assurances were not enough to prevent Southern outrage over the threat to slavery he represented.

See also "Southern Secessionists," April 19, 1861; for Garrison's editorial on the crisis, February 15, 1861; on Lincoln's inaugural address, March 8, 1861; on the "right of secession," April 12, 1861; and on the outbreak of the war, April 26, 1861.

The election of the Republican candidate, Abraham Lincoln, to the Presidency of the United States, has operated upon the whole slaveholding South in a manner indicative of the torments of the damned. The brutal dastards and bloody-minded tyrants, who have so long ruled the country with impunity, are now furiously foaming at the mouth, gnawing their tongues for pain, indulging in the most horrid blasphemies, uttering the wildest threats, and avowing the most treasonable designs. Their passions, "set on fire of hell," are leading them into every kind of excess, and they are inspired by a demoniacal phrenzy. To the South is strikingly applicable, at this hour, the language of the Revelator:[1]—"Babylon is fallen, is fallen, and is become the habitation of devils, and the hold of every foul spirit, and a cage of every unclean and hateful bird. Her sins have reached unto heaven, and God hath remembered her iniquities. In the cup which she hath filled, fill to her double. In her is found the blood of prophets and of saints. How much she hath glorified herself, and lived deliciously, so much torment and sorrow give her. Therefore shall her plagues come in one day, death, and mourning, and famine; and she shall be utterly burned with fire; for strong is the Lord God who judgeth her." So much for dealing in "slaves, and souls of men," trampling upon all

---

[1] Refers to the New Testament book of Revelation, which announces the doom of the city under divine judgment (18:2).

Nov. 16, 1860, 182.

human rights, defying God and his eternal law, and giving unlimited indulgence to every sensual and devilish inclination! "Rejoice over her, thou heaven, and ye holy apostles and prophets; for God hath judged the great whore, which did corrupt the earth with her fornication, and hath avenged the blood of his servants at her hand."

Never has the truth of the ancient proverb, "Whom the gods intend to destroy, they first make mad," been more signally illustrated than in the present condition of the Southern slaveholders. They are insane from their fears, their guilty forebodings, their lust of power and rule, their hatred of free institutions, their consciousness of merited judgments; so that they may be properly classed with the inmates of a lunatic asylum. Their dread of Mr. Lincoln, of his administration, of the Republican party, demonstrates their insanity. In vain does Mr. Lincoln tell them, "I do not now, nor ever did, stand in favor of the unconditional repeal of the Fugitive Slave Law"—"I do not now, nor ever did, stand pledged against the admission of any more Slave States into the Union"—"I do not stand pledged to the abolition of slavery in the District of Columbia"—"I do not stand pledged to the prohibition of the slave trade between the different States"—they rave just as fiercely as though he were another John Brown, armed for Southern invasion and universal emancipation! In vain does the Republican party present but one point of antagonism to slavery—to wit, no more territorial expansion—and exhibit the utmost cautiousness not to give offence in any other direction—and make itself hoarse in uttering professions of loyalty to the Constitution and the Union—still, they protest that its designs are infernal, and for them there is "sleep no more"! Are not these the signs of a demented people?

Nevertheless, there is "method" in their madness. In their wildest paroxysms, they know precisely how far to proceed. "Will they secede from the Union?" Will they jump into the Atlantic? Will they conflagrate their own dwellings, cut their own throats, and enable their slaves to rise in successful insurrection? Perhaps they will—probably they will not! By their bullying and raving, they have many times frightened the North into a base submission to their demands—and they expect to do it again! Shall they succeed?

1861–1865: THE FINAL PHASE
OF *THE LIBERATOR*: GARRISON AND LINCOLN

36

"The War—Its Cause and Cure"
May 3, 1861

In the early phases of the Civil War, many in the North stated that it was a war undertaken to maintain the Union, not to end the slavery system. This was Lincoln's position, too, in part because he truly believed in it and in part because he knew that public opinion was not ready for a military assault on slavery. Garrison insisted that the real cause of the conflict be acknowledged.

The 1861–1862 issues of The Liberator *include many discussions of secession, the causes of the war, and the duty of abolitionists. See especially the reprint of Garrison's address in New York City, "The Abolitionists and Their Relations to the War," January 24, 1862, and Garrison's letter to George Thompson, published in the March 7, 1862, issue of* The Liberator.

Eighty-five years ago, the war-cry of "INDEPENDENCE" rang throughout all the American Colonies, and a united people took up arms to sunder their connection forever with the mother country. The latter had been guilty of a long series of aggressions and usurpations toward the former, indicating "a design to reduce them under absolute bondage," and had haughtily disregarded all appeals to her sense of justice. As between the parties, they were in the right, and she flagrantly in the wrong. On the 4th of July, 1776, in justification of their course, they published their world-famous Declaration of Independence, in which they held "these truths to be self-evident:—that all men are created equal; that they are endowed by their Creator with certain inalienable rights; that among these are life, liberty, and the pursuit of happiness." At that time, they held in the galling chains of chattel servitude half a million of slaves! By the standard which they had erected, and by the eternal law of justice, their first duty obviously was to "proclaim liberty throughout all the land to all the

May 3, 1861, 70.

inhabitants thereof." Instead of doing this, they went through their seven years' struggle, mingling the clanking of fetters, and the crack of the slave whip, and the groans of their imbruted victims with their cries for liberty and their shouts of victory! It was a revolting spectacle, and a horrible paradox, admitting of no justification, or even apology. When their independence was achieved, and it became necessary for them to crystallize their several powers into one general government, instead of abolishing what Mr. Madison[1] justly characterized as "the most oppressive dominion ever exercised by man over man," they proceeded to make that oppression organic, by granting to it certain constitutional guaranties, whereby it should derive nourishment, defence and security from the whole body politic. This was the result of a compromise, in order to make the Union complete and enduring. . . .

What shall be said, then, of those who insist upon ignoring the question of slavery as not involved in this deadly feud, and maintain that the only issue is, the support of the government and the preservation of the Union? Surely, they are "fools and blind"; for it is slaveholders alone who have conspired to seize the one, and overturn the other. As long as the enslavement of a single human being is sanctioned in the land, the curse of God will rest upon it. That it may go well with us, let us break every yoke!

It alters nothing to say, that the South is guilty of unparalleled perfidy and treason. Granted! But why overlook *the cause of all this?* That cause is SLAVERY! If that be not removed, how is it possible to escape the consequences? Suppose we succeed in "conquering a peace," leaving things as they were; in due time, a still more fearful volcanic explosion will follow.

As between the North and the South, the conflict cannot long be doubtful; for, in point of numbers, resources, energy, courage, and valor, the latter can bear no comparison with the former. But, after the subjugation of the South, what then? Will that bring reconciliation? Is the old "covenant with death" to be renewed, and the "agreement with hell" to stand as hitherto? Is a slave representation still to be allowed on the floor of Congress? Are fugitive slaves still to be hunted as freely in the old Bay State[2] as in Carolina? Are slave insurrections still to be quelled by the strong arm of the general government, if required? Are the "stars and stripes" still to represent fifteen slave as well as nineteen free States, and still to wave over four millions of crouching, marketable human chattels? Is

---

[1] James Madison (1751–1836), U.S. statesman and fourth president (1809–1817). Though a slaveholder in Virginia, Madison decried slavery and favored gradual emancipation, accompanied by a plan for colonization.

[2] Massachusetts.

lynch law still to be administered to all Northern men at the South who prefer freedom to slavery? Is freedom of speech still to be mobbed afresh, and the moral agitation for the overthrow of slavery again branded as fanaticism, and forcibly suppressed if possible? If so, then better that the flag be forever furled! If so, then accursed be such a political structure, from foundation to top-stone! If so, then hundreds of millions of dollars will have been spent, and rivers of blood shed, to none other than an evil purpose!

It is true, Mr. Stephen A. Douglas[3] says, in a recent speech delivered at Columbus, Ohio — "The issue is not the negro; this question is above all the negroes in Christendom; it involves the freedom and independence of the ten millions, soon to be a hundred millions, of free white men in this valley." Other prominent men have uttered the same heartless and absurd declaration. As rationally might Pharaoh and the Egyptians have averred, while tormented with the lice, blains, murrain, and other judgments sent upon them for their cruel oppression of the children of Israel,[4] "The issue is *not the Jew*"! It *was* the Jew then, and it *is* the negro now — involving in his enslavement the most tremendous consequences to his enslavers, and a direful visitation to the whole country. "For the oppression of the poor, for the sighing of the needy, now will I arise, saith the Lord; I will set him in safety from him that puffeth at him."[5] Ours should be the penitent confession of the brethren of Joseph: "We are verily guilty concerning our brother, in that we saw the anguish of his soul, when he besought us, *and we would not hear;* THEREFORE IS THIS DISTRESS COME UPON US."[6]

Now, we solemnly maintain, that it is the most deplorable infatuation to aim to restore the old order of things. No blessing can attend it. God has frowned upon it, and, *through judgment, provided a way of escape.* Nothing is more clear than that an "irrepressible conflict" between slavery and freedom must continue. It is useless to deny that the Union is dissolved, and every slave State virtually in rebellion against the government. Let there be no more compromise. In humbling the Southern conspirators, let the government, UNDER THE WAR POWER, either *proclaim emancipation to all in bondage,* or else take measures for *a final and complete separation between the free and slave States.* Unquestionably, the former course would

---

[3] Stephen A. Douglas (1813–1861), Vermont-born lawyer, congressman, senator from Illinois, political rival to Lincoln, and Democratic presidential candidate in 1860.

[4] Garrison refers to the ten plagues that God inflicted upon the Egyptians to force them to grant the Israelites their freedom (see Exodus 7:14–12:36).

[5] Psalms 12:5 refers to the Lord's deliverance of his people.

[6] Genesis 42:21, spoken by Joseph's brothers in Egypt, in acknowledging their mistreatment of him.

be justified by the exigencies of the country, and be the readiest way to bring the war to a close, and the traitors to terms. It would also be the greatest boon that could possibly be bestowed upon the South. But if this measure be deemed questionable, then for a free, independent Northern republic, leaving the South to her fate!

Out of the slave system comes this terrible civil war, with whatever ghastly horrors may follow in its train. So Divine Justice has ordered it, that both North and South may be scourged for their transcendant [*sic*] iniquity in tolerating such a system in the land. Is it not so, Mr. Edward Everett, Mr. Millard Fillmore, Mr. Franklin Pierce,[7] Mr. Stephen Arnold Douglas—Democrats and Republicans all? Say, are they freemen or slaveholders who have perfidiously captured forts, arsenals, magazines, mints, revenue cutters, steamships, and custom-houses, and are now plotting the seizure of the Capital? Men of the North! is it not your mission, in this campaign, to make it possible for a free government and a glorious Union to exist, *by decreeing the extinction of slavery as utterly antagonistical to both?* No class of human beings living have such claims upon your sympathy, justice, and benevolent intervention, as the slaves of the South. No cause is so sacred as theirs. In Heaven's name, do nothing to keep them longer in their chains! Do everything rightfully in your power those chains to sunder!

If this war shall put an end to that execrable system, it will be more glorious in history than that of the Revolution. If it shall leave it unscathed, and in full operation,—even though Southern treason may for a time be "crushed out,"—there will be nothing to look for but heavier judgments and an irrevocable doom! "For the sword of the Lord shall devour from the one end of the land to the other: no flesh shall have peace. . . . O house of David, thus saith the Lord, Execute judgment in the morning, and deliver him that is spoiled out of the hand of the oppressor, lest my fury go out like fire, and burn that none can quench it, BECAUSE OF THE EVIL OF YOUR DOINGS. . . . Undo the heavy burdens, break every yoke, and let the oppressed go free; then shalt thou be like a watered garden, and like a fountain whose waters fail not; and they that shall be of thee shall build the old waste places; thou shalt be called, THE REPAIRER OF THE BREACH, THE RESTORER OF PATHS TO DWELL IN."[8]

---

[7] Edward Everett, Massachusetts political figure (see Document 27, note 1); Millard Fillmore (1800–1874), U.S. president (1850–1852), and candidate for president on the Know-Nothing party ticket in 1856 (see Document 27, note 2); Franklin Pierce (1804–1869), lawyer, Democrat, and U.S. president (1852–1856).

[8] "For the sword of the Lord": Jeremiah 12:12 refers to God's anger toward his enemies. O House of David: Jeremiah 21:12–14. Undo the heavy burdens: Isaiah 58:9–12.

37
"Why a Prolonged War"
January 30, 1863

Garrison contended that the war could have been brought to a successful end sooner if the government had taken two important steps — emancipation and the enlistment of black troops.

Lincoln's Emancipation Proclamation of January 1, 1863, issued in preliminary form on September 22, 1862, declared the slaves free in all states in rebellion against the Union. (It did not affect slaves in the border states of Delaware, Maryland, Kentucky, and Missouri, which had remained loyal to the Union.) The Proclamation also allowed blacks to enlist in the Union army.

When the electric wires conveyed with lightning speed the startling intelligence of the surrender of Fort Sumter, and therefore the actual commencement of deadly war upon the government by the confederate traitors of the South, all party distinctions at the North seemed to be merged, for the time being, in a common determination to uphold the national flag, and suppress the rebellion, at whatever cost of blood or treasure. Nor was the task considered a difficult one. At the worst, if a sharp, certainly a short conflict would settle the whole matter — summarily send to the gallows the leading conspirators — enforce the loyal recognition of the supremacy of the U.S. Constitution in every disaffected section — and bring back the old state of things, leaving scarcely a scar upon the face of the country. Nearly two years have passed away, and during that time colossal armies have been raised, a formidable navy created, desperate and bloody battles fought, fabulous sums of money expended, to ensure the triumph of the Federal government; yet the Union still remains divided, the piratical Confederate States still maintain their independence, the war still goes on with varying fortune, and what is to be the end of these things even the most sagacious and far-sighted hesitate to conjecture. It is undeniable that at no period since the outbreak have there been such anxiety of mind and heaviness of heart as to the final issue, as are now felt throughout the North.

It may be profitable to inquire into some of the causes of these sanguine expectations on the one hand, and these severe disappointments on the other.

Jan. 30, 1863, 18.

1. None but those who had thoroughly mastered the spirit, tendency and necessities of chattel slavery saw that from it proceeded the flames of this rebellious war as naturally as volcanic eruptions burst forth from Vesuvius or Etna. In vain they pointed to the line of division between the loyal and the disaffected, running precisely where the free institutions of the North found their geographical boundary, and the slave institutions of the South began—at least, so far as the dominating public sentiment was concerned on either side. In vain they arrayed impregnable evidence, demonstrating that just where the slave oligarchy were the most powerful, and slaves the most numerous, there the treasonable spirit was the most rampant—culminating as well as originating in thrice accursed South Carolina,—a large majority of whose entire population was owned as property, subjected to stripes and tortures, and herded with the beasts of the field. In vain they warned the government that no effective blow could be struck at the rebellion, which did not directly strike at the existence of slavery; that, whether it prosecuted the war expressly to free the fettered negro or not, the war was commenced and carried on for no other purpose, by the traitors, than to prevent the negro from getting his freedom. Month after month was allowed to pass away in abortive strategy or sanguinary conflict, under the delusion that the rebellion could be quelled not only without shaking the slave system to its foundation, but all the more quickly by letting slavery entirely alone. Never was delusion more complete or more disastrous! Every where prevailing, how was success possible under such circumstances? Therefore the war "dragged its slow length along." If the advice of the abolitionists had been followed, long ere this both slavery and the rebellion had been effectually suppressed, and peace restored from sea to sea. There is no such uncompromising loyalty to freedom and free institutions as theirs. They will be found true, inflexible, unconquerable, when all others, disclaiming the appellation, are found ready for compromise or capitulation.

2. Another reason why the war has lingered has been the unwillingness to employ the free colored and slave population in the military service of the government. The proposition to do this has stirred up an incredible amount of democratic (!) bile, and elicited from the lips of a hollow, tumid patriotism the indignant exclamation—"What! shall it be said that twenty millions of Northern freemen cannot overcome eight millions of Southern rebels, without the aid of the niggers! Shame on him who says to the contrary!" This was cowardly swaggering and not true bravery, and it has since received merited retribution. Moreover, if it proved any thing, it proved too much; for if it would be cowardly for twenty millions to call in negro help to subjugate eight millions, is it not also cowardly for twenty millions to bring all their forces to bear against eight millions? and should

they not, to place their courage beyond suspicion, tie one hand behind them, and fight only with the other, disdaining to meet the enemy beyond man for man? Yet, with all the advantage of numbers, resources, intelligence, and bravery on the part of the North, the South, —whatever her sufferings and sacrifices, —continues unsubdued, defiant, confident of ultimate triumph and permanent independence. Remember that, for more than eighteen months after the humbling of the "stars and stripes" at Sumter, the policy adopted by President Lincoln, in conducting the war, gave such satisfaction to the democratic press as to elicit from it the strongest laudations; nor did it cease to extol his honesty, independence and patriotic purpose until, in September last, he announced to the rebellious States that their slaves should be declared free, in case they did not return to their allegiance by the first of January, 1863. During all that time, why were not the rebels conquered—eight millions against twenty millions—if the aid of the negroes was not needed? Remember, moreover, that from first to last, the army of the Potomac and the army of the West have been led and controlled by democratic officers,[1] who have managed every thing in their own way, caring little or nothing for the wishes, requests or commands of the President, — as signally illustrated in the case of Gen. McClellan, around whom are gathering, by an unerring instinct, all the elements of sedition and ruffianism at the North for the most desperate purposes. Why, with the lion's share of office, emolument and power magnanimously conceded to them, did not these democratic leaders long since carry their armies through victoriously to the Gulf? Will the democratic press answer?

Of course—other things being equal—eight millions of people cannot successfully cope with twenty millions, of the same blood and nation as themselves. The disparity is so overwhelming that, in the sequel, they must be either subdued or exterminated. Other things being equal, we said—and here lies the rub; for in this struggle things are not equal, and so the comparison is as illogical as it is vain-glorious. In the first place, it is cool deception to talk of eight millions as constituting the sum total of the Confederate strength; whereas, to this number must be added four millions of slaves, who, under the iron dominion of their rebel masters, are as clay in the hands of the potter, and who, used in every conceivable way to carry on the rebellion, constitute a most formidable power to be hurled like a thunderbolt against an invading force. The Southern aggregate, then, is twelve millions.

There are other considerations, explanatory of the lingering nature of the war, which we must defer till another week.

---

[1] Members of the Democratic party.

38
Defense of Lincoln
May 20, 1864

Garrison spoke and wrote critically on many occasions about Lincoln's cautious wartime policies. Yet he admired the president, recognizing the difficult challenges that Lincoln confronted, and thus he disagreed with Wendell Phillips (1811–1884) and other abolitionists who wanted to support a more radical antislavery candidate in the 1864 election.

This passage is taken from comments that Garrison made in response to a speech by Phillips at the May 10–11, 1864, meeting in New York City of the American Anti-Slavery Society. Phillips had castigated the administration's tardiness in attacking slavery, its failure to "acknowledge the manhood" of blacks, and its timid early plans for reconstruction.

For critical commentaries on Lincoln, see the editorials on Lincoln's March 6, 1862, message, March 14 and March 21, 1862. Garrison denounced Lincoln's interest in colonization, August 22, August 29, and December 5, 1862. See also Garrison's dispute with Phillips on Lincoln, February 5 and February 26, 1864, June 10, 1864, and October 28, 1864. Garrison made a number of highly favorable statements about Lincoln in the issues of this period.

Grant that there are many sad things to look in the face; grant that the whole of justice has not yet been done to the negro; grant that here and there grievances exist which are to be deplored and to be redressed; still, looking at the question broadly, comprehensively, and philosophically, I think the people will ask another question—whether they themselves have been one hair's breadth in advance of Abraham Lincoln? (Applause.) Whether they are not conscious that he has not only been fully up with him, but, on the whole, a little beyond them? (Applause.) As the stream cannot rise higher than the fountain, so the President of the United States, amenable to public sentiment, could not, if he wished to do it, far transcend public sentiment in any direction. (Applause.) For my own part, when I remember the trials through which he has passed, and the perils which have surrounded him—perils and trials unknown to any man, in any age of the world, in official station—when I remember how fearfully pro-slavery was the public sentiment of the North, to say nothing of the

---

South—when I remember what he has had to deal with—when I remember how nearly a majority, even at this hour, is the seditious element of the North, and then remember that Abraham Lincoln has struck the chains from the limbs of more than three millions of slaves (applause); that he has expressed his earnest desire for the total abolition of slavery; that he has implored the Border States to get rid of it; that he has recognized the manhood and citizenship of the colored population of our country; that he has armed upwards of a hundred thousand of them, and recognized them as soldiers under the flag; when I remember that this Administration has recognized the independence of Liberia and Hayti;[1] when I remember that it has struck a death blow at the foreign slave trade by granting the right of search;[2] when I remember that we have now nearly reached the culmination of our great struggle for the suppression of the rebellion and its cause, I do not feel disposed, for one, to take this occasion, or any occasion, to say anything very harshly against Abraham Lincoln. (Loud and prolonged applause.)

[1]The colony of Liberia in western Africa was founded in 1822 as a homeland for former slaves and was constituted as the Free and Independent Republic of Liberia in 1847. Haiti was the site of a major slave rebellion in the 1790s, and it achieved independence from France in 1804.

[2]Refers to a June–July 1862 treaty with Great Britain that allowed war vessels of both the U.S. and Great Britain to search and confiscate merchant ships engaged in the slave trade.

39

"The Late Presidential Struggle"
November 18, 1864

Garrison rejoiced in Lincoln's victory over the former general of the Union army and Democratic candidate George B. McClellan (1826–1885) in November 1864. Until Union General William T. Sherman (1820–1891) captured Atlanta in September, his reelection had been in doubt—Lincoln himself believed he would lose. Garrison expressed pride in the surge of popular support for the North's cause that was evident in Lincoln's win— though McClellan did receive 45 percent of the popular vote.

Two decades earlier, Garrison had rejected politics and advocated disunion. (See, for example, Documents 14 and 18.) Now he perceived Lincoln's reelection as the striking result of antislavery strength at the ballot box and a sign of the highest form of civilization.

Nov. 18, 1864, 186.

The reelection of Mr. Lincoln, therefore, derives its significance and importance not only from its vast numerical power, but still more from the character and position of the mighty mass who gave him their suffrages. It is a decision from which there can be no appeal, except from the highest civilization to the lowest barbarism. It indicates incomparably greater attributes than can be found in mere physical supremacy—all of education, science, art, morality, religion in its best development, philanthropy in its highest aspirations, reform in its widest bearings. Hence, the government is stable beyond all precedent, notwithstanding the rebellious convulsions of the hour; and the administration of Mr. Lincoln has accorded to it a sanction and strength which no previous one—not excepting Washington's—has ever been able to secure.

The election has determined many things. First—it shows how great is the confidence of the people in the honesty, sagacity, administrative ability, and patriotic integrity of Abraham Lincoln. And yet, what efforts were left undone by some whose loyalty was unquestionable, and by all whose disloyalty was "palpable as a mountain," to utterly destroy that confidence, and cause his ignominious rejection? He was ridiculed and caricatured in every possible manner—represented (incoherently enough) as playing the part of tyrant and usurper, and yet being little better than an imbecile, having no mind of his own, but moulded by the abolition party, or by one or two members of his cabinet, "as clay in the hands of the potter"—as animated by a selfish desire to secure his re-election, no matter at what cost to the country—as disregarding all constitutional checks and limitations—as turning the war from its legitimate purpose to an unconstitutional end—as equally destitute of capacity and principle—as incurably afflicted with "nigger on the brain"—as oppressively bent on "subjugating" the rebellious South, and making conditions whereby union and peace were rendered impossible—as being too slow, and at the same time too fast—&c., &c. Moreover, it was said that he had lost the confidence of nearly all the prominent supporters of his administration, in Congress and out of it, who would in due time show their preference for another;—so that between such representations and the boastful predictions of his enemies, there seemed to be no chance for his success. As his most formidable loyal antagonist, General Fremont[1] was early hurried into the field, with a flourish of trumpets and an assurance of easy victory which the result makes too ridiculous to need any comment.

---

[1] In late May 1864, a week before the Republican convention was scheduled to begin in Baltimore, a number of Democrats and discontented Republicans had met in convention in Cleveland and had nominated explorer, soldier, and Republican presidential candidate in 1856, John C. Fremont (1813–1890) for president. Fremont later withdrew and gave grudging support to Lincoln's candidacy.

Either to preserve a show of consistency, or to indulge a mortified pride, there are some who stoutly insist that Mr. Lincoln's re-election by such immense odds is no evidence whatever of his popularity with the people, but only of their determination to see the rebellion put down, and the authority of the government vindicated! A nice distinction, and very easily made, but none the less unjust and foolish. In regard to all that has been said in disparagement of the President, the people have rendered their verdict in a manner that only sophistry can distort or effrontery deny.

Second—another thing settled by this election is, that no quarters are to be given to the rebellion, or to that accursed system of slavery from which it sprang, but both must expire together, and find the same ignominious grave, "lower than plummet ever sounded." Every loyal vote was an anti-slavery vote. It was the adoption of the Baltimore Platform,[2] in the fullness of its spirit and the strictness of its letter—sanctioning whatever has been done, whether by the President or Congress, to break the chains of the oppressed, and pledging the Union party to labor to secure an amendment to the Constitution of the United States, whereby slavery in every part of the republic shall be expressly and forever prohibited. The day of compromise is ended. The "covenant with death" is to be annulled, and the "agreement with hell" no longer permitted to stand. The spell is broken, the enchantment dissolved, and reason assumes its supremacy. "A house divided against itself cannot stand," as this rebellion shows. Years ago, Abraham Lincoln prophetically said— "This nation must be all slave or all free"—and the nation has just decided which it shall be. Woe to the man or to the party hereafter attempting to secure a truce for a traitorous slave oligarchy in arms, or a compromise for the longer continuance of slavery! They shall be smitten to the dust by an outraged public sentiment. The first business at the next session of Congress must be the renewal of the proposed anti-slavery amendment of the Constitution, and the speedy submission of it to the suffrages of an awakened people, who only wait for the legal opportunity to adopt it with a unanimity even greater than that which they have evinced in the re-election of Mr. Lincoln.

Third—another thing settled by this election is, the inherent vitality and strength of a republican form of government to meet and surmount the worst conceivable perils, with a firmness not to be shaken, an energy unparalleled, and an intelligent reference to the rights of human nature. Slavery is not the product of free institutions, but necessarily hostile to

---

[2]The Republican party, renamed the National Union party for the election, met in convention in Baltimore in early June 1864. Its platform stated that the war should continue until the surrender of the South and that a constitutional amendment should be passed to abolish slavery.

them; it constitutes no part of true democracy, any more than heathenism does of Christianity. It belongs to the despotisms of all ages—the crowning crime and curse of them all. That it is now in flaming rebellion is the clearest evidence of the growth of the spirit of liberty in our land. That it has not been more effectually grappled with is the consequence of the vast political influence wielded factiously by those whose birth was in a foreign land,[3] whose training was under aristocratic rule, and who, captivated by the name of "democracy," have been the dupes of cunning demagogues, and shamefully misled on all occasions—they alone making the experiment of a government like ours a matter of doubt and anxiety, through their general want of education and moral training. But the termination of slavery will be the enjoyment of personal freedom from sea to sea; and hand in hand with that freedom will go all those facilities for mental development which have made the North so intelligent, enterprising, prosperous and powerful. After that, European emigration will cease to be a source of uneasiness as to its bearings upon the welfare of the republic.

—But, however bright the omens, let it never be forgotten—"the price of Liberty is eternal vigilance."

[3] Five million persons immigrated to the United States between 1815 and 1860, about 40 percent of them from Ireland. Many Irish laborers, especially in the cities, supported the Democratic party, and they had bitterly (and sometimes violently) opposed the abolitionists (see Document 19, note 1).

40

The Death of Slavery

February 10, 1865

This forms part of an address that Garrison delivered at a Grand Jubilee Meeting, held on February 4, 1865, at the Music Hall in Boston, "to Rejoice over the Amendment prohibiting Human Slavery in the United States forever."

Lincoln had asked the Republican party at its convention in 1864 to call for a constitutional amendment that would prohibit slavery. On February 1, 1865, the Thirteenth Amendment was introduced in Congress.

Feb. 10, 1865, 22.

On the need to grant equal rights to the freed slaves, see "Reconstruction,"
December 2, 1864; "The Cause of the Freedmen," December 30, 1864; and
"Equal Political Rights," January 13, 1865.

When I was requested, by our honored chairman, to write upon a slip of paper some of the names of those who had made themselves conspicuous in the Anti-Slavery movement, but who had ascended to a higher sphere of existence, I had but a few moments in which to recall their memories. The list might be extended indefinitely; but I beg leave to add to it, on this occasion, the name of Professor Follen,[1] among the earliest and the truest, the friend and champion of impartial freedom in Europe and America; and him, whose "soul is marching on," John Brown. (Enthusiastic cheers.) — At this point, Major General Butler[2] came upon the platform, and was received with a storm of applause from the audience, who rose to their feet, and clapped their hands, and waved hats and handkerchiefs for several minutes. Quietude being restored, Mr. Garrison continued as follows: —

Mr. Chairman, Ladies and Gentlemen: — In the long course of history, there are events of such transcendant [*sic*] sublimity and importance as to make all human speech utterly inadequate to portray the emotions they excite. The event we are here to celebrate is one of these — grand, inspiring, glorious, beyond all power of utterance, and far-reaching beyond all finite computation. (Applause.)

At last, after eighty years of wandering and darkness, — of cruelty and oppression, on a colossal scale, towards a helpless and an unoffending race — of recreancy to all the Heaven-attested principles enunciated by our revolutionary sires in justification of their course; through righteous judgment and fiery retribution; through national dismemberment and civil war; through suffering, bereavement and lamentation, extending to every city, town, village and hamlet, almost every household in the land; through a whole generation of Anti-Slavery warning, expostulation and rebuke, resulting in wide-spread contrition and repentance; the nation, rising in the majesty of its moral power and political sovereignty, has decreed that

[1]Charles Follen (1796–1840), Unitarian clergyman, abolitionist, and first professor of German literature at Harvard. His connection to Harvard ended in 1835 because of his support for abolition.

[2]Benjamin Butler (1818–1893), lawyer, Union soldier, and politician, originally a Democrat but by war's end a staunch Republican. He was nicknamed "the Beast" in the South because of his harsh administration of New Orleans, beginning in May 1862, where he was commander of the Union forces occupying the city.

LIBERTY shall be "PROCLAIMED THROUGHOUT ALL THE LAND, TO ALL THE INHABITANTS THEREOF," and that henceforth no such anomalous being as slaveholder or slave shall exist beneath the "stars and stripes," within the domain of the republic. (Cheers.)

Sir, no such transition of feeling and sentiment, as has taken place within the last four years, stands recorded on the historic page; a change that seems as absolute as it is stupendous. Allow me to confess that, in view of it, and of the mighty consequences that must result from it to unborn generations, I feel to-night in a thoroughly methodistical[3] state of mind—disposed at the top of my voice, and to the utmost stretch of my lungs, to shout "Glory!" "Alleluia!" "Amen and amen!" (Rapturous applause—"Glory!" "Alleluia!" "Amen and amen!" being repeated with great unction by various persons in the audience.) Gladly and gratefully would I exclaim with one of old, "The Lord hath done great things for us, whereof we are glad." (Applause.) With the rejoicing Psalmist, I would say to the old and the young, "O give thanks unto the Lord, for he is good; for his mercy endureth forever. To him alone that doeth great wonders; for his mercy endureth forever. To him that overthrew Pharaoh and his host in the Red sea; for his mercy endureth forever. And brought out Israel from among them, with a strong hand, and with a stretched out arm; for his mercy endureth forever." (Loud applause.) "Let every thing that hath breath praise the Lord!"

Mr. Chairman, friends and strangers stop me in the streets, daily, to congratulate me on having been permitted to live to witness the almost miraculous change which has taken place in the feelings and sentiments of the people on the subject of slavery, and in favor of the long rejected but ever just and humane doctrine of immediate and universal emancipation. Ah, sir, no man living better understands or more joyfully recognizes the vastness of that change than I do. But most truly can I say that it causes within me no feeling of personal pride or exultation—God forbid! But I am unspeakably happy to believe, not only that this vast assembly, but that the great mass of my countrymen are now heartily disposed to admit that, in disinterestedly seeking, by all righteous instrumentalities, for more than thirty years, the utter abolition of slavery, I have not acted the part of a madman, fanatic, incendiary, or traitor, (immense applause,) but have at all times been of sound mind, (laughter and cheers,) a true friend of liberty and humanity, animated by the highest patriotism, and devoted to the welfare, peace, unity, and ever increasing prosperity and glory of my

---

[3]Laying great stress on method, systematic, but may also refer to Methodism, the Christian denomination founded by John Wesley (1703–1791).

native land! (Cheers.) And the same verdict you will render in vindication of the clear-sighted, untiring, intrepid, unselfish, uncompromising Anti-Slavery phalanx, who, through years of conflict and persecution— misrepresented, misunderstood, ridiculed and anathematized from one end of the country to the other—have labored "in season and out of season" to bring about this glorious result. (Renewed applause.) You will, I venture to think and say, agree with me, that only RADICAL ABOLITIONISM is, at this trial-hour, LOYALTY, JUSTICE, IMPARTIAL FREEDOM, NATIONAL SALVATION—the Golden Rule blended with the Declaration of Independence! (Great applause.)

Mr. Chairman, in the early days of the Anti-Slavery struggle, when those who ventured to espouse it were "few and far between," we endeavored to recruit our ranks by singing at our gatherings—

> Come, join the abolitionists,
>   The fair, the old, the young,
> And, with a warm and cheerful zeal,
>   Come, help the cause along!
>   O, that will be joyful, joyful, joyful,
>   When all shall proudly say,
> "This, this is FREEDOM's day! Oppression, flee away!"
>   Tis then we'll sing, and offerings bring,
>   When FREEDOM wins the day!

Thanks unto God, that day is here and now! Freedom is triumphant! THE PEOPLE have decreed the death of slavery! All the controlling elements of the country—national, state, religious, political, literary, social, economical, wealthy, industrial—are combined for its immediate extinction. There is no longer occasion, therefore, for the repetition of that persuasive song. As Jefferson said, in his inaugural message to Congress, "We are all Federalists, we are all Republicans"—so, in view of the dominant Anti-Slavery sentiment of the land, it may now be comprehensively declared, "We are all abolitionists, we are all loyalists, to the back-bone." (Loud applause.)

Fellow-citizens, we are here, moved as by one electric impulse, to commemorate a radical change in the Constitution of the United States— so radical that, whereas, for more than seventy years, it served as a mighty bulwark for the slave system, giving it national sanction and security, now it forbids human slavery in every part of the republic!

41

"Valedictory: The Last Number of The Liberator"

December 29, 1865

The final issue of The Liberator *coincided with the announcement by Secretary of State William H. Seward (1801–1872) that the necessary number of states had ratified the Thirteenth Amendment abolishing slavery. Garrison preceded his "Valedictory" editorial with a reprint of the statement of intention (see Document 2) with which he began the paper on January 1, 1831.*

> The last! the last! the last!
> O, by that little word
> How many thoughts are stirred—
> That sister of THE PAST!

The present number of the *Liberator* is the completion of its thirty-fifth volume, and the termination of its existence.

Commencing my editorial career when only twenty years of age, I have followed it continuously till I have attained my sixtieth year—first, in connection with *The Free Press,* in Newburyport, in the spring of 1826; next, with *The National Philanthropist,* in Boston, in 1827; next, with *The Journal of the Times,* in Bennington, Vt., in 1828–9; next, with *The Genius of Universal Emancipation,* in Baltimore, in 1829–30; and, finally, with the *Liberator,* in Boston, from the 1st of January, 1831, to the 1st of January, 1866;—at the start, probably the youngest member of the editorial fraternity in the land, now, perhaps, the oldest, not in years, but in continuous service,—unless Mr. Bryant, of the New York *Evening Post,* be an exception.

Whether I shall again be connected with the press, in a similar capacity, is quite problematical; but, at my period of life, I feel no prompting to start a new journal at my own risk, and with the certainty of struggling against wind and tide, as I have done in the past.

I began the publication of the *Liberator* without a subscriber, and I end it—it gives me unalloyed satisfaction to say—without a farthing as the pecuniary result of the patronage extended to it during thirty-five years of unremitted labors.

Dec. 29, 1865, 206.

From the immense change wrought in the national feeling and sentiment on the subject of slavery, the *Liberator* derived no advantage at any
time in regard to its circulation. The original "disturber of the peace,"
nothing was left undone at the beginning, and up to the hour of the late
rebellion, by Southern slaveholding villany [*sic*] on the one hand, and
Northern pro-slavery malice on the other, to represent it as too vile a
sheet to be countenanced by any claiming to be Christian or patriotic; and
it always required rare moral courage or singular personal independence to
be among its patrons. Never had a journal to look such opposition in the
face—never was one so constantly belied and caricatured. If it had
advocated all the crimes forbidden by the moral law of God and the
statutes of the State, instead of vindicating the sacred claims of oppressed
and bleeding humanity, it could not have been more vehemently denounced or more indignantly repudiated. To this day—such is the force of
prejudice—there are multitudes who cannot be induced to read a single
number of it, even on the score of curiosity, though their views on the
slavery question are now precisely those which it has uniformly advocated.
Yet no journal has been conducted with such fairness and impartiality;
none has granted such freedom in its columns to its opponents; none has
so scrupulously and uniformly presented all sides of every question discussed in its pages; none has so readily and exhaustively published,
without note or comment, what its enemies have said to its disparagement, and the vilification of its editor; none has vindicated primitive
Christianity, in its spirit and purpose—"the higher law," in its supremacy
over nations and governments as well as individual conscience—the
Golden Rule, in its binding obligation upon all classes—the Declaration of
Independence, with its self-evident truths—the rights of human nature,
without distinction of race, complexion or sex—more earnestly or more
uncompromisingly; none has exerted a higher moral or more broadly
reformatory influence upon those who have given it a careful perusal;
and none has gone beyond it in asserting the Fatherhood of God and
the brotherhood of man. All this may be claimed for it without egotism
or presumption. It has ever been "a terror to evil-doers, and a praise to
them that do well." It has excited the fierce hostility of all that is vile
and demoniacal in the land, and won the affection and regard of the
purest and noblest of the age. To me it has been unspeakably cheering, and the richest compensation for whatever of peril, suffering and
defamation I have been called to encounter, that one uniform testimony has been borne, by those who have had, its weekly perusal, as to
the elevating and quickening influence of the *Liberator* upon their character and lives; and the deep grief they are expressing in view of its

discontinuance is overwhelmingly affecting to my feelings. Many of these date their subscription from the commencement of the paper, and they have allowed nothing in its columns to pass without a rigid scrutiny. They speak, therefore, experimentally, and "testify of that which they have seen and do know." Let them be assured that my regret in the separation which is to take place between us, in consequence of the discontinuance of the *Liberator,* is at least as poignant as their own; and let them feel, as I do, comforted by the thought that it relates only to the weekly method of communicating with each other, and not to the principles we have espoused in the past, or the hopes and aims we cherish as to the future.

Although the *Liberator* was designed to be, and has ever been, mainly devoted to the abolition of slavery, yet it has been instrumental in aiding the cause of reform in many of its most important aspects.

I have never consulted either the subscription list of the paper or public sentiment in printing, or omitting to print, any article touching any matter whatever. Personally, I have never asked any one to become a subscriber, nor any one to contribute to its support, nor presented its claims for a better circulation in any lecture or speech, or at any one of the multitudinous anti-slavery gatherings in the land. Had I done so, no doubt its subscription list might have been much enlarged.

In this connection, I must be permitted to express my surprise that I am gravely informed, in various quarters, that this is no time to retire from public labor; that though the chains of the captive have been broken, he is yet to be vindicated in regard to the full possession of equal civil and political rights; that the freedmen in every part of the South are subjected to many insults and outrages; that the old slaveholding spirit is showing itself in every available form; that there is imminent danger that, in the hurry of reconstruction and readmission to the Union, the late rebel States will be left free to work any amount of mischief; that there is manifestly a severe struggle yet to come with the Southern "powers of darkness," which will require the utmost vigilance and the most determined efforts on the part of the friends of impartial liberty—&c., &c., &c. Surely, it is not meant by all this that I am therefore bound to continue the publication of the *Liberator;* for that is a matter for me to determine, and no one else. As I commenced its publication without asking leave of any one, so I claim to be competent to decide when it may fitly close its career.

Again—it cannot be meant, by this presentation of the existing state of things at the South, either to impeach my intelligence, or to impute to me a lack of interest in behalf of that race, for the liberation and elevation of which I have labored so many years. If, when they had no friends, and no hope of earthly redemption, I did not hesitate to make their cause my own, is it to be supposed that, with their yokes broken, and their friends and advocates multiplied indefinitely, I can be any the less disposed to stand by them to the last—to insist on the full measure of justice and equity being meted out of them—to retain in my breast a lively and permanent interest in all that relates to their present condition and future welfare?

I shall sound no trumpet and make no parade as to what I shall do for the future. After having gone through with such a struggle as has never been paralleled in duration in the life of any reformer, and for nearly forty years been the target at which all poisonous and deadly missiles have been hurled, and having seen our great national iniquity blotted out, and freedom "proclaimed throughout all the land to all the inhabitants thereof," and a thousand presses and pulpits supporting the claims of the colored population to fair treatment where not one could be found to do this in the early days of the anti-slavery conflict, I might—it seems to me—be permitted to take a little repose in my advanced years, if I desired to do so. But, as yet, I have neither asked nor wished to be relieved of any burdens or labors connected with the good old cause. I see a mighty work of enlightenment and regeneration yet to be accomplished at the South, and many cruel wrongs done to the freedmen which are yet to be redressed; and I neither counsel others to turn away from the field of conflict, under the delusion that no more remains to be done, nor contemplate such a course in my own case.

The object for which the *Liberator* was commenced—the extermination of chattel slavery—having been gloriously consummated, it seems to me specially appropriate to let its existence cover the historic period of the great struggle; leaving what remains to be done to complete the work of emancipation to other instrumentalities, (of which I hope to avail myself,) under new auspices, with more abundant means, and with millions instead of hundreds for allies.

Most happy am I to be no longer in conflict with the mass of my fellow-countrymen on the subject of slavery. For no man of any refinement or sensibility can be indifferent to the approbation of his fellow-men, if it be rightly earned. But to obtain it by going with the multitude to do evil—by pandering to despotic power or a corrupt public sentiment—is self-degradation and personal dishonor:

> For more true joy Marcellus exiled feels,
> Than Caesar with a senate at his heels.

Better to be always in a minority of one with God—branded as madman, incendiary, fanatic, heretic, infidel—frowned upon by "the powers that be," and mobbed by the populace—or consigned ignominiously to the gallows, like him whose "soul is marching on," though his "body lies mouldering in the grave," or burnt to ashes at the stake like Wickliffe,[1] or nailed to the cross like him who "gave himself for the world,"—in defence of the RIGHT, than like Herod, having the shouts of a multitude, crying, "It is the voice of a god, and not of a man!"

Farewell, tried and faithful patrons! Farewell, generous benefactors, without whose voluntary but essential pecuniary contributions the *Liberator* must have long since been discontinued! Farewell, noble men and women who have wrought so long and so successfully, under God, to break every yoke! Hail, ye ransomed millions! Hail, year of jubilee! With a grateful heart and a fresh baptism of the soul, my last invocation shall be—

> Spirit of Freedom! on—
>   Oh! pause not in thy flight
> Till every clime is won
>   To worship in thy light:
> Speed on thy glorious way,
>   And wake the sleeping lands!
> Millions are watching for the ray,
>   And lift to thee their hands.
> Still 'Onward!' be thy cry—
>   Thy banner on the blast;
> And, like a tempest, as thou rushest by,
>   Despots shall shrink aghast.
> On! till thy name is known
>   Throughout the peopled earth;
> On! till thou reign'st alone,
>   Man's heritage by birth;
> On! till from every vale, and where the mountains rise,
> The beacon lights of Liberty shall kindle to the skies!

Wm. Lloyd Garrison

Boston, December 22, 1865

---

[1]Protestant dissenter. See Document 28, note 1.

Garrison at thirty

My father was of medium height, and he became bald while still a young man. The remnant of his hair was like fine silk and quite black, turning gray only late in life. His eyes were large and full, of a hazel color, hidden somewhat by glasses, but giving an expression of great benevolence to his countenance, and his nose was strong and well shaped.

The mouth with its firm deep lines was the feature that indicated the dauntless courage and iron will of the man who stood almost alone when he began the agitation which ended in the emancipation of the slaves. It gave to his face its intense earnestness of purpose; yet it was wonderfully mobile and the slightest movement of the lips gave him the kindest and sunniest of expressions.

Garrison at seventy-four

It was easy to note the changes of his ever-varying countenance on his smoothly shaven face. His complexion in youth was singularly white, his cheeks "like roses in the snow," as one of his old friends told me. He had, as long as he lived, a fine color in spite of the fact that he was compelled to keep very irregular hours because of his labors in the printing office and his lecturing experiences. He held himself erect and walked with a firm brisk step, all his movements indicating alertness and vigor of mind and body.
—Fanny Garrison Villard, *Garrison on Non-Resistance* (1924)

A Garrison Chronology
(1805–1879)

1805

December 10 or 11:   Born in Newburyport, Massachusetts, son of Abijah (b. 1773) and Fanny Garrison (b. 1776). Newburyport was a seaport town, population 5,000.

1808

Father abandons family; mother works as a domestic.

1812

Mother and eldest child, James, move to Lynn, Massachusetts; younger children, William and Elizabeth, remain in Newburyport.

1814

Begins several years as apprentice to a shoemaker, a cabinetmaker, and a printer.

1815

October: Family moves to Baltimore, Maryland; population 50,000.

1816

Fall: William returns to Newburyport; separated from mother for seven years.

December 16:   American Colonization Society formed; first election of officers, January 1, 1817.

1818

October 18:   Apprentice in office of Federalist paper, the Newburyport *Herald;* reads articles and books on politics and literature.

1820

Missouri Compromise: Missouri admitted as slave state, Maine as free state; slavery to be excluded in Louisiana Purchase territory north of latitude 36°30'.

1823

September 3: Mother's death in Baltimore.

1826

March: Purchases newspaper, the *Essex Courant,* renames it *Newburyport Free Press.*

1827

Works as a compositor in Boston, population 50,000.

1828

January 4–July 4: Editor of the *National Philanthropist* (Boston).

March 17: Meets Benjamin Lundy (1789–1839), editor of *The Genius of Universal Emancipation.*

Edits *Journal of the Times,* in Bennington, Vermont; first issue published on October 3.

British abolitionists unite in single society for emancipation of slavery in the empire.

1829

April: Returns to Boston, accepts post as coeditor of *The Genius of Universal Emancipation.*

July 4: Delivers address at Park Street Church in Boston on behalf of colonization society—first antislavery speech.

August: Sails for Baltimore to join Lundy.

September 2: First issue of new *Genius* published (first editorial states, "The slaves are entitled to immediate and complete emancipation").

David Walker (1785–1830), publishes *Appeal to the Colored Citizens of the World* (2nd and 3rd eds., 1829, 1830).

1830

January: Sued in Baltimore for November 13, 1829, article libeling Francis Todd, Newburyport merchant and slave trader; tried on March 1 and jailed on April 7 for forty-nine days.

March 5: Ends partnership with Lundy.

Meets Arthur (1786–1865) and Lewis (1788–1873) Tappan, merchants and reform-minded Christians in New York City.

August–September: Lectures in Philadelphia and meets antislavery Quakers James (1788–1868) and Lucretia (1793–1880) Mott.

1831

January 1: Publishes first issue of *The Liberator* (1831–1865); 400 copies circulated in Boston; partnership with Isaac Knapp (1804–1843).

August: Nat Turner's slave insurrection in Southampton, Virginia; sixty whites killed.

November 13: Meeting in Boston to plan for antislavery society.

Georgia legislature offers $5,000 reward for Garrison's capture.

1832

January: First anniversary of *The Liberator,* only fifty white subscribers, largely supported by free blacks in North.

January 6: Small band of abolitionists (including Garrison) meet in Boston's African Baptist Church, form New England Anti-Slavery Society.

1833

May 2: Sails for Liverpool for five-month visit; arrives May 22. Meets British abolitionists, including Charles Stuart (1783–1865) and George Thompson (1804–1878). (Returns September 29.)

July 13: Two-hour lecture in Exeter Hall attacking slavery and the American Colonization Society.

August 29: Great Britain ends slavery in British West Indies.

December: American Anti-Slavery Society formed in Philadelphia.

Garrison publishes "Declaration of Sentiments" for American Anti-Slavery Society.

1834

July and October: Riots against blacks in New York and Philadelphia.

September 4: Marries Helen Benson (b. 1811) of Brooklyn, Connecticut; her father, George Benson (1752–1836) was president of New England Anti-Slavery Society.

September 20: George Thompson, agent of London Anti-Slavery Society, begins antislavery tour in New York City.

1835

July: Most Southern states bar all abolitionist writings.

August: Fifteen hundred Bostonians meet in Faneuil Hall to protest abolitionist agitation.

October 21: Attacked by Boston mob.

December: Dissolves partnership with Isaac Knapp.

1836

January: Abolitionists petition Congress to end slavery in the District of Columbia.

Five hundred abolitionist societies active in the North.

1837

Battles clergy and champions nonresistance and women's rights.

Wins support of British abolitionist Elizabeth Pease (1807–1897) and of Wendell Phillips (1811–1884) and Edmund Quincy (1808–1877) in Boston.

Congress adopts Gag Rule to prohibit antislavery petitions.

Garrison publishes "Declaration of Sentiments Adopted by the American Peace Convention."

1838

May: Pennsylvania Hall in Philadelphia burned during Anti-Slavery Convention of American Women.

September 18: Helps form New England Non-Resistance Society in Boston.

1839

February 23: Largest meeting yet of Massachusetts Anti-Slavery Society, successor (as of 1835) to New England Anti-Slavery Society.

August: Slaves revolt aboard Spanish slave ship *Amistad;* granted freedom by U.S. Supreme Court in March 1841 and allowed to return to Africa.

1840

April–May: Liberty Party (based on antislavery principles) formed in Albany, New York; nominates James Birney for president.

May: Schism in American Anti-Slavery Society at convention in New York City, caused by differences over women's rights and political action. Anti-Garrisonian group, American and Foreign Anti-Slavery Society, formed.

May 22: Travels to England; arrives June 16. (Returns August 17.)

June: Attends worldwide antislavery convention in London, which is split over admission of women delegates.

1841

July: Fights against steamship and railway segregation in Massachusetts.
August: Becomes acquainted with Frederick Douglass (1818–1895) at anti-slavery gatherings in New Bedford and Nantucket.
November: Slaves revolt aboard U.S. ship *Creole* and escape to Nassau.

1842

March: *Prigg vs. Pennsylvania*—Supreme Court upholds the right of slaveholders to seize fugitive slaves in free states.
July–November: Lectures in Massachusetts, Maine, New Hampshire, New York.
Promotes "disunion" (adopted as policy by American Anti-Slavery Society in January 1843) and attacks U.S. Constitution.

1844

December: U.S. House rescinds Gag Rule of 1836 prohibiting discussion of antislavery petitions.
Denounces the Constitution and political action.
American Anti-Slavery Society adopts motto "No Union with Slaveholders."

1845

December: Texas admitted as slave state.
Frederick Douglass publishes his *Narrative*.

1846

May: Mexican War begins (1846–1848).
July 16:   Leaves for England. (Returns November 17.)
August: Abraham Lincoln (1809–1865) elected to Congress from Illinois.
Wilmot Proviso introduced to prohibit slavery in territories acquired from Mexico.
August 4:   Attends World Temperance Convention in London.
Lecture tour with Frederick Douglass in England and Scotland.

1847

August 2–October 28:   Undertakes speaking tour with Frederick Douglass in Ohio, Pennsylvania, and New York; becomes seriously ill in Cleveland, Ohio.
The North Star, edited by Douglass and Martin R. Delany (1812–1885), begins publication (until 1851).

1850

May: American Anti-Slavery Society meeting in New York City disrupted by mob.

Opposes Compromise of 1850, with its Fugitive Slave Law requiring persons in free states to aid in the recapture of escaped slaves.

1851

April: Boston abolitionists attempt rescue of fugitive slave Thomas Sims.

June: *Uncle Tom's Cabin* by Harriet Beecher Stowe (1811–1896) begins serialization in *The National Era*.

Charles Sumner (1811–1874) elected to U.S. Senate from Massachusetts.

Frederick Douglass' Paper (formerly *The North Star*) begins publication (until 1860).

1852

Harriet Beecher Stowe publishes *Uncle Tom's Cabin*.

1854

May–June: Kansas-Nebraska Act repeals Missouri Compromise of 1820 and opens western territories to slavery; antislavery forces in Boston attempt rescue of fugitive slave Anthony Burns.

July 4: Burns copy of U.S. Constitution in Framingham, Massachusetts.

1855

April: Massachusetts outlaws segregation based on color and religion in schools.

Proslavery and antislavery groups engage in armed conflicts in Kansas.

Frederick Douglass publishes *My Bondage and My Freedom*.

1856

May: Radical abolitionist John Brown (1800–1859) fights proslavery groups in Kansas territory.

May 21: Congressman Preston Brooks (1819–1857) of South Carolina assaults Charles Sumner in the U.S. Senate for his "Crime against Kansas" speech of May 19.

Republican Party, opposed to slavery extension, nominates John C. Fremont (1813–1890) for president; he carries eleven of the sixteen Northern states but loses to Democratic candidate James Buchanan (1791–1868).

1857

January: Meets John Brown.

January 15: Massachusetts Disunion Convention ("no union with slaveholders") in Worcester, Massachusetts.

March: Dred Scott decision in Supreme Court declares that neither slaves nor free blacks can be citizens.

1858

Stephen A. Douglas (1813–1861) debates and defeats Abraham Lincoln for U.S. Senate seat from Illinois.

1859

October: John Brown's raid on Harpers Ferry, Virginia; Brown executed in December.

1860

November: Lincoln elected president with 39 percent of popular vote.

December: South Carolina secedes from Union.

1861

February: Formation of the Confederate States of America, with Jefferson Davis (1808–1889) elected president.

March: Lincoln inaugurated.

April: South Carolina attacks and seizes Fort Sumter; Lincoln declares that Southern states have committed "insurrection"; Virginia secedes.

July: Declares support for Northern cause.

December: New motto for *The Liberator:* "Proclaim Liberty throughout All the Land, to All the Inhabitants of the Land."

1862

Urges Lincoln to emancipate the slaves of rebels and emancipate with compensation the slaves of loyal citizens.

1863

January 1: Lincoln's Emancipation Proclamation declares freedom for slaves in states in rebellion against U.S. government. Does not apply to slaves in areas already under control of Union armies or to border states of Delaware, Kentucky, Maryland, and Missouri.

1864

Supports Lincoln's reelection; attends Republican convention in Baltimore; meets Lincoln at White House reception on June 9.

Republican convention supports constitutional amendment to abolish slavery.

1865

February: Congress passes Thirteenth Amendment, abolishing slavery (ratified December).

April: Travels with George Thompson and Henry Ward Beecher (1813–1887) to Fort Sumter and Charleston, South Carolina.

April 9:   Confederate General Robert E. Lee's surrender to Union General Ulysses S. Grant at Appomattox Courthouse, Virginia, ends Civil War.

May 10:   Resigns as president of American Anti-Slavery Society.

October–November: Lectures in Midwest.

December 29:   Last issue of *The Liberator.*

1866

January 25:   Withdraws from Massachusetts Anti-Slavery Society.

1867

May 8–November 6:   Travels to England and to France as delegate to Paris Anti-Slavery Conference (meets August 26–27).

June 29:   Public breakfast in Garrison's honor held at St. James Hall, London; speakers include statesman and orator John Bright (1811–1889) and philosopher and economist John Stuart Mill (1806–1873).

Supports Radical Republican plans for reconstruction of the South.

1868

March 10:   Receives National Testimonial (cash gift of $33,000) from friends and distinguished citizens.

Begins writing for the New York *Independent* (until 1875).

Fourteenth Amendment declares that blacks are citizens.

1869

Supports free trade and civil service reform.

Favors prohibition, supports woman suffrage, criticizes U.S. treatment of Indians and Chinese, advocates open immigration, attacks racial prejudice.

1870

April 9:   Formal dissolution of the American Anti-Slavery Society at mass meeting in New York City.

Fifteenth Amendment grants black men the right to vote.

1876

January 25:   Wife, Helen, dies.

1877

May 23–September 4:   Final trip to England; last meeting with George Thompson.

1879

May 24:   Dies in New York City.

May 28:   Funeral services held in First Religious Society church in Roxbury, Massachusetts; buried at sunset in Forest Hills cemetery.

Questions for Consideration

1. What was at the center of Garrison's opposition to slavery?
2. Did Garrison have a specific strategy for bringing slavery to an end?
3. What might account for Garrison's inability or unwillingness to take up the cause of workers and labor unions and organizations?
4. Was Garrison wholly opposed to slave resistance and rebellion? to violent means?
5. Was Garrison mistaken in linking abolition to other reform movements?
6. What connections did Garrison see between abolition and women's rights?
7. Why did many persons object to the kind of language with which Garrison made his antislavery arguments? How did he respond to these objections?
8. What were the reasons for Garrison's refusal to vote and to join political parties?
9. Describe Garrison's response to and criticism of Harriet Beecher Stowe's *Uncle Tom's Cabin*? How might Stowe have answered Garrison?
10. What was Garrison's relationship to African Americans? Was he truly comfortable with the prospect of their freedom and equality?
11. What did Garrison mean by "disunion"?
12. Did Garrison's rhetoric and antislavery agitation contribute to *causing* the war?
13. Did the nonresistant Garrison contradict himself when he supported Abraham Lincoln and the Northern side during the Civil War?
14. Examine Garrison's commentary on important statesmen and figures of the period: John C. Calhoun, Daniel Webster, Nat Turner, Frederick Douglass, John Brown, Abraham Lincoln. How does he assess their strengths and limitations?

15. How would you evaluate Garrison's style and strategy as a reformer, particularly in view of his hostility toward the Constitution and the Union?

Selected Bibliography

The best source is the thirty-five volumes of *The Liberator,* available on microfilm.

Wendell Phillips and Francis Jackson Garrison's *William Lloyd Garrison, 1805–1879: The Story of His Life Told by His Children* (Boston: Houghton Mifflin, 1885–89), published in four large volumes, is packed with primary materials.
The major work of modern Garrison scholarship is *The Letters of William Lloyd Garrison,* edited by Walter M. Merrill and Louis Ruchames, 6 vols. (Cambridge: Harvard University Press, 1971–1981). These volumes are richly and meticulously edited.

Also see the following by William Lloyd Garrison:

Thoughts on African Colonization. Boston, 1832.
Sonnets and Other Poems. Boston, 1843.
Selections from the Writings and Speeches of William Lloyd Garrison. Boston, 1852.
Helen Eliza Garrison: A Memorial. Cambridge, Mass., 1876.
Words of Garrison: A Centennial Selection. Compiled by his sons Francis Jackson and Wendell Phillips Garrison. Boston, 1905.
There are copies of addresses, essays, and pamphlets in the Garrison collection and in other collections at Harvard University and at the Boston Public Library.

BIOGRAPHICAL STUDIES

Merrill, Walter M. *Against Wind and Tide: A Biography of William Lloyd Garrison.* Cambridge: Harvard University Press, 1963.
Nye, Russel B. *William Lloyd Garrison and the Humanitarian Reformers.* Boston: Little, Brown, 1955.
Stewart, James Brewer. *William Lloyd Garrison and the Challenge of Emancipation.* Arlington Heights, Ill.: Harlan Davidson, 1992.

Thomas, John L. *The Liberator: William Lloyd Garrison, A Biography*. Boston: Little, Brown, 1963.

STUDIES OF ABOLITIONISM AND ANTI-SLAVERY

Aptheker, Herbert. *Abolitionism: A Revolutionary Movement*. Boston: Twayne, 1989.

Dillon, Merton. *The Abolitionists: The Growth of a Dissenting Minority*. De Kalb: Northern Illinois University Press, 1974.

Dumond, Dwight Lowell. *Antislavery: The Crusade for Freedom in America*. Ann Arbor: University of Michigan Press, 1961.

Filler, Louis. *The Crusade against Slavery, 1830–1860*. New York: Harper and Row, 1960.

Finkelman, Paul, ed. *Antislavery*. Articles on American Slavery, vol. 14. New York: Garland, 1989.

Friedman, Lawrence J. *Gregarious Saints: Self and Community in American Abolitionism, 1830–1870*. New York: Cambridge University Press, 1982.

Kraditor, Aileen S. *Means and Ends in American Abolitionism: Garrison and His Critics on Strategy and Tactics, 1834–1850*. New York: Vintage, 1969.

McKivigan, John R. *The War against Proslavery Religion: Abolitionism and the Northern Churches, 1830–1865*. Ithaca: Cornell University Press, 1984.

Perry, Lewis. *Radical Abolitionism: Anarchy and the Government of God in Antislavery Thought*. Ithaca: Cornell University Press, 1973.

Quarles, Benjamin. *Black Abolitionists*. New York: Oxford University Press, 1969.

Stewart, James Brewer. *Holy Warriors: The Abolitionists and American Slavery*. New York: Hill and Wang, 1976.

Walters, Ronald G. *The Antislavery Appeal: American Abolitionism after 1830*. Baltimore: Johns Hopkins University Press, 1976.

Wyatt-Brown, Bertram. *Lewis Tappan and the Evangelical War Against Slavery*. New York: Atheneum, 1971.

Index

Abbott, Lyman, 43–44
Abolitionist movement. *See also* Anti-slavery movement
antislavery societies and work of, 13–14
call for end of racial prejudice as part of, 115–18
Civil War and, 52, 56, 168–70
Christian principles in, 29, 55, 101–05
criticisms of harsh language describing slavery used by, 37, 41–42, 45, 72
"disunion" espoused by Garrison for, 30–31, 37–38, 112–15, 141–44
exclusion of women from meetings in, 14–15
Garrison's early involvement in, 4, 9
Garrison's pledge of support to slaves in, 109–11
government call for suppression of mailings and papers supporting, 5–6, 80
human face of slavery portrayed in literature of, 25
immediatism and, 11–12
language used by Garrison in, 37–45, 72
language used by opponents to describe, 38–39
lectures by Douglass and Garrison in, 46–47, 48, 118–20
link between women's rights and, 27–28
mission of *The Liberator* in, 7
moral appeal against slavery in, 15, 21, 28–30, 57
newspaper coverage of, 151–52
nonresistance used in, 104–05

period after American Revolution and, 22
public attitudes toward, 3
reform movement and, 144–46
state laws and support for, 22, 65–67
support for colonization as reaction to, 11, 12
violent measures used in, 18–20, 56
voting and, 106
Walker's *Appeal* pamphlet and, 76–77
Adams, John Quincy, 42
Africa
blacks' plans for emigration to, 50
colonization and emigration to, 9, 10
Agriculture, and economic argument for slavery, 23–24, 43–44
Alcott, A. Bronson, 40, 56
American and Foreign Anti-Slavery Society, 14, 127
American Anti-Slavery Society, 46, 47, 171
addresses by Garrison before, 20, 30, 31
antislavery movement and, 13, 134–35, 139–40
formation of, 12, 13, 50
Garrison's Declaration of Sentiments on aims of, 50–51, 90–94
Garrison's resignation from, 54–55
petitions against slavery from, 42
American Colonization Society, 61
founding of, 9
Garrison on, 10–11
support for, 10
American Peace Society, 38
American Revolution
justification for use of violent resistance traced to, 18, 19

199

American Revolution (*cont.*)
status of slavery during period of, 21–23
Anderson, Robert, 53
Antislavery movement. *See also* Abolitionist movement
antislavery societies and work of, 13–14
Christian principles in, 29, 55, 101–05
colonization and, 10, 11
"disunion" espoused by Garrison for, 30–31, 37–38, 112–15, 141–44
exclusion of women from meetings in, 14–15
Garrison on progress of, 94–96, 160–61
Garrison's identity with, 7–8
Garrison's view of compromise in, 29–30
government call for suppression of mailings and papers supporting, 5–6, 80
growth of, as reform movement, 13
human face of slavery portrayed in literature of, 25
immediatism and, 11–12
language used by Garrison in, 37–45, 72
lectures by Douglass and Garrison for, 46–47, 48, 118–20
link between women's rights and, 27–28
mission of *The Liberator* in, 7, 37–38
moral appeal against slavery in, 15, 21, 28–30, 57
newspaper coverage of, 151–52
political measures and work of, 14, 15–17, 27, 28, 56
Antislavery societies. *See* American and Foreign Anti-Slavery Society; American Anti-Slavery Society; Bristol Anti-Slavery Society; Massachusetts Anti-Slavery Society; New England Anti-Slavery Society
Attucks, Crispus, 3, 149, 150

Bailey, Ebenezer, 2
Bailey, Gamaliel, 27
Bancroft, George, 37
Beecher, Henry Ward, 44, 53, 55
Bennett, James Gordon, 8–9, 136, 152
Benson, George W., 7

Birney, James, 39
antislavery movement and, 13, 14, 23, 29, 127
colonization movement and, 10
Blacks
colonization movement and, 9–12
freed slaves and settlement of, 23, 27
Garrison's commitment to a biracial society and, 12–13, 50–51
plans for emigration to Africa of, 50
racism in North and, 49–50, 52
slavery as form of control of, 26–27
as soldiers in the Union army, 3, 168, 169–70
Bolles, J. A., 97
Booth, John Wilkes, 54
Boston, mob pursuit of Garrison in, 1–3, 54
Bourne, George, 11
Bristol Anti-Slavery Society, Garrison's speech before, 46, 107
Brooks, Preston S., 146
Brown, John
Garrison on, 56, 153–55, 156
Harpers Ferry raid of, 19, 36, 153
Buchanan, James, 36
Burns, Anthony, 18, 35–36, 158
Bushnell, Horace, 40
Butler, Andrew P., 146
Butler, Benjamin, 176
Buxton, Thomas Fowell, 8, 9

Calhoun, John C., 34, 39
on abolition petitions in Congress, 42
Garrison on, 53, 121–26
Campbell, John A., 34–35
Channing, William Ellery, 33–34, 39
Child, Lydia Maria
colonization movement and, 11
on Garrison's views, 28, 56
on the slave trade, 22
Christianity and Christian principles
antislavery movement and, 3, 29, 55, 64, 101–05
language used by Garrison related to, 37
women's rights and, 140–41
Civil War
abolition of slavery and, 52, 56, 168–70
black troops in, 3
Garrison on, 36, 54, 164–70
number of wounded and dead in, 20